From Post-Industrial to Post-Modern Society

New Theories of the Contemporary World

Krishan Kumar

BLACKWELL
Oxford UK & Cambridge USA

First published 1995
Reprinted 1996

Blackwell Publishers Ltd
108 Cowley Road
Oxford OX4 1JF, UK

Blackwell Publishers Inc.
238 Main Street
Cambridge, Massachusetts 02142
USA

British Library Cataloguing in Publication Data

A CIP catalogue record for this book is available from the British Library.

Library of Congress Cataloging-in-Publication Data

Kumar, Krishan.
    From post-industrial to post-modern society : new theories of the
contemporary world / Krishan Kumar.
        p.   cm.
    Includes bibliographical references (p.   ) and index.
    ISBN 0–631–18558–5. — ISBN 0–631–18559–3 (pbk.)
    1. Postmodernism—Social aspects.   I. Title.
HM73.K83   1995
303.4'01—dc20   95–34497
                                                                                              CIP

Copy-edited and typeset in 10½ on 12 Palatino
by Grahame & Grahame Editorial, Brighton
Printed in Great Britain by T.J. Press Ltd, Padstow, Cornwall
This book is printed on acid-free paper

From Post-Industrial to Post-Modern Society

ty-
g

ㅋ|ㅋ.

B

To Katya

Contents

Preface

Over the past quarter of a century there have been persistent claims that Western societies have entered a new era of their history. While still being undoubtedly industrial, they have undergone, it is suggested, such far-reaching changes that they can no longer be considered under the old names and by means of the old theories. Western societies are now in various ways 'post-industrial': 'post-Fordist, 'post-modern', even 'post-historical'.

Some years ago, in *Prophecy and Progress* (1978), I considered the claims of the earlier varieties of post-industrial theory. These were associated particularly with such figures as Daniel Bell and Alain Touraine, together with a significant section of East European opinion. Their theories concentrated largely on the move to a service economy and a 'knowledge society', and the social and political changes that could be expected to follow from this.

Those theories are still with us, but they have been joined by others with a more ambitious scope. In these newer theories we encounter claims that go beyond economics and politics to encompass western, and indeed world, civilization in their entirety. In the information and communication revolution, in the transformation of work and organization in the global economy, and in the crisis of political ideologies and cultural beliefs, these theories see the signs of a turning point in the evolution of modern societies.

In this book I consider three of these newer varieties of post-industrial theory: the idea of the information society, and the theories of post-Fordism and post-modernity. Though they all share common features, which I note, initially I examine them separately.

Chapter 2 deals with the information society. This is essentially a restatement, by Daniel Bell and others, of the original post-industrial idea advanced by them in the 1970s. As such it can be discussed more briefly than the more recent theories.

Chapter 3 considers the theory of post-Fordism. Though economic changes lie at its core, in the hands of several of its proponents it is broadened to include wide-ranging political and cultural changes. In this it overlaps to a good extent with some central aspects of post-modern theory. These broader changes are dealt with more fully under that heading.

About half the book – chapters 4 and 5 – is concerned with the theory of post-modernity. This is not simply because it is the most comprehensive – and provocative – of the theories, overlapping not just post-Fordism but also the idea of the information society. It also forces us to consider what we might mean by modernity, whose principles, it alleges, are no longer operative or valid. What is this modernity that is being superseded?

Chapter 6 looks back and critically interrogates, separately and together, the theories expounded in the earlier chapters. It notes their coincidence with the fin-de-siècle mood, and considers how this may affect their character. It also speculates on the effects of some very contemporary changes in the world, especially the break-up of communism in Eastern Europe. How do these affect the standing of our theories? Do they, as some assert, decisively negate them? Or do they rather increase their plausibility? Academic theories sometimes seem to float loftily above mere mundane matters. What concerns them are largely their own coherence. It is a welcome feature of all our three theories that they eschew this lifeless purity. They are rough in their form – 'thick' might be the fashionable description – and many-layered. While this does not satisfy the requirements of strict 'testability', it means that they engage with the real life of the societies in which they appear. The experience of those societies, the discernible changes and continuities within them, are therefore directly relevant to their validity.

The main purpose of this book is to give as full and clear an account of these new theories as possible. But I should not have been satisfied merely to expound. Nor should I have spent so much time on them if I had thought they were simply wrong. It is extraordinary how much energy is expended, in the critical literature on these theories, in showing them to be hopelessly crass, if not infantile. This seems a rather wearisome and pointless exercise, academic in the worst sense of that word. The persistence of these theories, despite this critical battering, is some indication that they speak to our contemporary condition. I have tried to see how this might be so, and how they can help us to understand that condition. Theories of society have a plurality of uses. They are not simply a series of testable propositions. Often their main value lies in directing our attention to developments that have so far escaped our proper notice. If, in the process, they overstate their case, they are only doing what all interesting theories do, and should do.

A note, finally, about the bibliography. It is very long, in what is a relatively short work. Partly this reflects the fact that in this book I have combined a discussion of three theories that are usually treated separately. Each has its own extensive literature. But there is another reason. Theoretical discussion in sociology is increasingly becoming a 'battle of the books'. The critical literature has grown voluminously, and theoretical debates are conducted largely with reference to this literature. This has long been the case in literary criticism, where the book or poem under discussion quite soon gets lost amidst the critical commentary. The practice now seems to be spreading to social theory. This book of course continues that process. The justification has to be that it contributes something to the debates, if only by way of clarification. But I can't help feeling that it also in some way testifies to the post-modern belief that the whole world is text.

A number of people have been very generous with material and helpful advice: Pat Ainley, Ash Amin, Phil Brown, Tim Clark, Rosemary Crompton, John Jervis, Kevin Robins, Dick Walker, Frank Webster. I am very grateful to them, and absolve them of all responsibility for anything said here. I also learned much from my involvement in the Acton Society's research project on the 'Third Italy' in the 1980s; Edward Goodman and Julia Bamford were the leading lights in this. At Blackwell Publishers, Simon Prosser has as always been the most sympathetic and supportive of editors. I hope he feels the waiting has been justified. I should also like to thank the University of Kent for two periods of study leave during which much of this book was written. For those of us who work in social theory this kind of support is particularly important; institutions such as Kent, which maintain a generous policy of study leave, deserve our gratitude.

Krishan Kumar
Canterbury, Kent

From Post-Industrial to
Post-Modern Society

1

Introduction: The Revival of Post-Industrial Theory

Labels, like rumours, can take on a life of their own. The labels of intellectual discourse are no exception. Once sufficiently established, they can govern reality, at least scholarly reality. They inspire conferences, books, television programmes. They can create a whole climate of critical inquiry which, especially in these days of academic entrepreneurship and the multinational scholarly enterprise, feeds on itself. 'The lonely crowd', 'the affluent society', 'the technological society', 'the hidden persuaders', 'the power elite': these are all well-known examples of labels which in recent decades have generated much activity of this sort.

This is not to say that all this intellectual activity is simply self-indulgent. Genuine hypotheses can often be formed out of it; it gives rise to reflections which can be illuminating even and especially in disagreement. But an element of self-regarding publicity inevitably surrounds its utterances. We need to guard ourselves against that in assessing their worth.

During the 1960s and early 1970s, several prominent sociologists elaborated a view of contemporary society that they labelled the theory of post-industrial society. The best-known proponent of this was the Harvard sociologist Daniel Bell, especially as expressed in his book, *The Coming of Post-Industrial Society* (1973). Bell himself, in international conferences and in semi-popular journals such as *The Public Interest*, was an active and able propagator of his views. But the theory of post-industrialism gained even wider currency through some vivid popularizations, notably in such books as

Peter Drucker's *The Age of Discontinuity* (1969) and Alvin Toffler's *Future Shock* (1970). In such works the educated public of the west was asked to prepare itself for the possibly uncomfortable transition to a new society, one as different from industrial society as that had been from agrarian society.

The post-industrial idea has been intensively debated. Its short-comings, as well as the stimulating questions it raises, have been widely noted (see, for example, Gershuny 1978; Kumar 1978). Partly as a result of that, partly as the result of the changed climate of feeling in the western world following the 1973 oil shock, one had the distinct impression that 'post-industrialism' had had its day. The debates of the later 1970s all seemed to be about 'the limits to growth', about containing – not exploiting – the dynamic potential of industrialism. They were about the revival of distributional conflicts as industrial societies ceased to be able to make pay-offs from increased growth (see, for example, Hirsch 1979). A mood of crisis replaced the optimism of the 1960s. Right-wing parties capitalized on this mood, preaching a return to 'Victorian' values and practices of self-help and *laissez-faire*. They called for the abandonment of central planning and state intervention, the most obvious features of the post-1945 settlement and a key premise of the post-industrial idea.

Whatever the future of industrial societies, then, they still seemed to be preoccupied by the same difficulties and dilemmas that had beset them for the past hundred years.[1] In the history of industrialism it was the post-war era of continuous growth that now looked like the exceptional episode, the happy accident. Its ending had restored some of the classic conflicts and debates of industrialism (see, for example, Stretton 1976). The past had reasserted itself. At a time when 'deindustrialization' and economic decline became issues to grapple with, visions of a post-industrial society were bound to appear fanciful, if not irresponsible.

Malcolm Bradbury has called the 1970s 'the decade that never was'. But the 1980s of course came out of the 1970s (just as the 1960s came out of the 1950s). We can now see that during that decade various new forms of post-industrial theory were in the making. On the whole, these forms lack the confident optimism of the 1960s varieties. They do not look forward to the 'super-industrial' society so euphorically anticipated by Alvin Toffler. As the product of left- as much as right-wing thinking, they foresee great stresses and conflicts ahead. But they are as insistent as earlier post-industrial theorists that industrial societies have crossed a divide. Classic industrialism, the kind of society analysed by Marx, Weber and Durkheim, the kind of society inhabited by most westerners for the past century and a half, is no more.

The greatest continuity with earlier post-industrial theory is shown in the view of contemporary society as 'the information society'. Daniel Bell is here again the most prominent exponent. His post-industrial idea had already singled out 'theoretical knowledge' as the most important feature – the source of value, the source of growth – of the future society. In his later writing he has come to identify this more firmly with the development of the new information technology and its potential application to every sector of society. The new society is now defined, and named, by its novel methods of acquiring, processing and distributing information. Bell is as confident now as in his earlier analysis that this amounts to a revolutionary transformation of modern society.

The concept of the information society fits in well with the liberal, progressivist tradition of western thought. It maintains the Enlightenment faith in rationality and progress. Its current exponents belong generally to the centre of the ideological spectrum. To the extent that knowledge and its growth are equated with greater efficacy and greater freedom, this view, despite its pronouncement of a radical shift in societal arrangements, continues the line of thought inaugurated by Saint-Simon, Comte and the positivists.

More unexpected is the view of the new society that has emerged from the left side of the ideological spectrum. Marxists had been amongst the most vigorous denouncers of the original post-industrial idea, as the clearest demonstration of late bourgeois ideology (see, for example, Ross 1974). Now some of them have come up with their own version of post-industrial theory. It has most commonly been expressed under the banner of 'post-Fordism'. As mostly Marxists of a kind, they still generally hold to some concept of capitalist development as the engine of change. But so struck are they by the differences between the old and the new forms of capitalism that they feel forced to speak of our times as 'new times', or as the era of 'the second industrial divide'. For many of them Marx, as the supreme theorist of capitalism, remains a relevant thinker. But the changes in society in the latter part of the twentieth century are regarded as so momentous, and constitute so sharp a break with earlier capitalist patterns and practices, that it is clear to these writers that severe revisions will need to be made to Marxist theory if it is to remain serviceable.

A third strand of post-industrial theory has a less familiar provenance. This is the theory of 'post-modern' society. Post-modernism is the most comprehensive of recent theories. It includes in its generous embrace all forms of change, cultural, political and economic. None is seen as the privileged 'carrier' of the movement to post-modernity. What others see as the evidence for 'post-Fordism' or 'the information society' it smoothly subsumes as components of its own ambitious conceptualization of current developments. As eclectic – and elusive – in its ideological make-up as the eclecticism it sees as the principal feature of the contemporary world, post-modernism is the most difficult of contemporary theories to assess. Its terms can lead one into a bewildering circle of self-referentiality. Nevertheless its evident appeal to theorists from all parts of the ideological spectrum gives it a compelling claim on our attention.

Moreover, whether or not the larger claims of the theory carry conviction, it is clear that post-modernism has struck a chord among much of the educated population of the western world. It appears, that is, to speak to their condition – or at least their subjective experience of it.[2] That sociologists have often in the past regarded such feelings as trivial by comparison with the more determining structures of society is only the more reason for attending to such matters of sentiment now. Can post-modernity be a myth if many people believe, or can be persuaded, that they are living in such a condition?

This leads to some final remarks by way of introduction. Most of this book is concerned with expounding and assessing the three theories just mentioned. I am conscious that this may itself be regarded as contributing to the self-reinforcing discourse referred to at the beginning. I hope, however, to show the real value of conducting such an inquiry – to show, that is, how much recent theories can tell us about our times and ourselves. They do this, it is true, as much by the critical opposition they provoke as by any insights of their own. But the latter is as important as the former. Much of the literature on post-industrial theory is excessively negative – not necessarily wrong in its criticism, but unwilling to see the value of this kind of thinking, and blind to the very real perceptions of contemporary populations to which it is at least partly a response. Marxist critics in particular seem peculiarly and perversely insensitive to the dialectic of intellectual inquiry, and its well-known potential for gains in knowledge.

There is a further point. Whatever our judgements as to the adequacy of the new theories, it seems important to ask also why such theories, in their various forms, have repeatedly arisen in the past twenty-five years. Why is there such a widespread feeling, in the west at least, that a new epoch or new phase of development is under way?[3] Why even talk of 'the end of history' – which taken literally (and when not referring to the nuclear holocaust) is clearly absurd, but which has found a meaningful echo in the minds of many sober commentators on the contemporary world?[4] There appears something genuinely at work here, something in the experience of contemporary modern societies that persistently provokes not just 'the sense of an ending' but also one of new beginnings. The millennial year 2000 will no doubt stimulate many more views of this kind. Before that next wave is upon us, and without indulging in apocalyptics, it seems sensible to examine some of the possible reasons for the continual resuscitation of post-industrial theory.

2

The Information Society

The computer promises by technology a Pentecostal condition of universal understanding and unity . . . Our current translation of our entire lives into the spiritual form of information seems to make of the entire globe, and of the human family, a single consciousness.

Marshall McLuhan (1967: 90)

The computer . . . can be asked by us to 'think the unthinkable' and the previously unthought. It makes possible a flood of new theories, ideas, ideologies, artistic insights, technical advances, economic and political innovations that were, in the most literal sense, unthinkable and unimaginable before now. In this way it accelerates historical change and fuels the thrust toward Third Wave social diversity.

Alvin Toffler (1981: 177)

People who have no clear idea what they mean by information or why they should want so much of it are nonetheless prepared to believe that we live in an Information Age, which makes every computer around us what the relics of the True Cross were in the Age of Faith: emblems of salvation.

Theodore Roszak (1988: 10)

The Computer and the Coming of Information

Information, as a concept, comes into the world trailing clouds of glory. It is nothing less, its most eminent popularizer Norbert Wiener has said, than the main part of life's counter-offensive against the entropic impulse that will eventually cause the universe to run down. 'In control and communication' – the heart of information – 'we are always fighting nature's tendency to degrade the organized and to destroy the meaningful; the tendency . . . for entropy to increase.' Information is a requirement of our survival. It permits the necessary exchanges between us and our environment.

'To live effectively is to live with adequate information. Thus, communication and control belong to the essence of man's inner life, even as they belong to his life in society' (Wiener 1968: 19).

Wiener, the inventor of 'cybernetics', the 'theory of messages', was writing in the late 1940s and early 1950s. The timing is significant. The grand claim for information sprang from certain revolutionary developments in these years in the technology of control and communication – 'information technology', or IT, as it came to be called. The birth of information, not merely as a concept but also as an ideology, is inextricably linked to the development of the computer. This was an accomplishment of the war years and the immediate post-war period.

The timing as well as the tempo of growth indicate the computer's close relationship to the evolving military requirements of the west, principally as interpreted by the United States. Such key components of the computer as miniaturized electrical circuits were developed by the Americans for specific military uses during the Second World War – in this case proximity fuses for bombs. The electronic digital computer itself was created primarily for ballistics calculations and atomic bomb analysis. The civilian research centres where most of these developments took place, such as the Bell Laboratories of AT&T, were heavily funded by the wartime American government and supervised by such government agencies as Vannevar Bush's Office of Scientific Research and Development. As the American trade magazine *Electronics* put it in 1980, electronics 'has held an integral place in national defense since World War Two' (Noble 1986: 8, 47–56).

Just as America's world-wide military role provided both the motive and the opportunity for the development of more and more sophisticated systems of information technology, so too did the world-wide expansion of the American corporation in the years following the Second World War. 'The American corporation was faced with a "command and control" problem similar to that confronting its military counterpart . . . Like the Pentagon, it was increasingly diversified and internationalized' (Weizenbaum 1976: 27). The multinational corporation lives by communication. It is what gives it its identity as an enterprise spanning the world. Computers and satellites are as essential to its operation as the workers and plant that produce its goods and services.

Origins do not determine destinations. The atom was split as a direct result of military planning but nuclear energy has a multitude of uses. Similarly the military origins of the information revolution do not limit its effects in a vast range of

non-military spheres. But origins tell us something about moti-
vating force and shaping influences. The emergence, in the 1950s,
of a military-industrial-scientific complex is not the whole story of
the information society. But it is a central part of that story.[1]

The Third Industrial Revolution

In his 1952 novel, *Player Piano*, Kurt Vonnegut painted a satiric,
anti-utopian portrait of a society that had undergone the Third
Industrial Revolution. 'The First Industrial Revolution devalued
muscle work . . . the second one devalued routine mental work.'
The Third Industrial Revolution was in the process of devaluing
human thinking – 'the real brainwork' (Vonnegut 1969: 19–20).
A giant computer EPICAC controlled and co-ordinated all the
economic and political operations of society. All but a small handful of engineers and managers found their skills and knowledge
redundant. To keep them busy they were employed on useless
tasks in the Reconstruction and Reclamation Corps.

Vonnegut's EPICAC echoed the real-life computer ENIAC, the
world's first electronic digital computer, which was developed
during the war by J. P. Eckert and J. W. Mauchly for the American
Army. ENIAC was forty feet long and twenty feet high; it ran on
eighteen thousand vacuum tubes and fifteen hundred relays. As
developments in microelectronics accelerated, and ENIAC's tasks
could be performed on a microcomputer the size of a postage
stamp, talk of a third industrial revolution became commonplace.
If the first two revolutions were energy revolutions – based on
steam power and electricity – the third revolution, it was generally
agreed, was an information revolution (see, for example, Bell
1987: 11). Such a revolution had been gestating for more than
a century. Its earlier expressions were the electric telegraph, the
telephone, the gramophone, film, radio and television. But it was
the computer that marked its culmination. For, as it was put by
one of America's most distinguished computer scientists, Herbert
Simon, 'the computer is unique in its capacity for manipulating
and transforming information and hence in carrying out, automatically and without human intervention, functions that had
previously been performable only by the human brain' (Simon,
1980: 420; see also King 1982: 14).

It is the computer, too, as the 'central symbol' and 'analytical
engine' of change that Daniel Bell puts at the heart of his account
of the coming of the Information Society. Here he owes a debt to

an earlier commentator, Zbignieuw Brzezinski, who rejecting the term 'post-industrial' as empty of content proposed instead 'the technetronic society'. It was in Brzezinski's view the new technology of electronic communications that was ushering in the new age (Brzezinski 1971: 11). 'The technetronic society' did not catch on (it was perhaps too much of a mouthful); but the idea behind it ultimately did. As early as *The Coming of Post-Industrial Society* Bell had stated that 'the post-industrial society is an information society, as industrial society is a goods-producing society' (Bell 1973: 467; see also Ferkiss, 1979: 65).[2]

But the basic idea of the post-industrial society was the movement to a service society and the rapid growth of professional and technical employment (Kumar 1978: 185–240). The idea of information itself remained relatively undeveloped. Now, fortified perhaps by the rush of new technical developments in computers and communications, Bell is more confident. Information now names the post-industrial society. It is what produces and sustains it.

> My basic premise has been that knowledge and information are becoming the strategic resource and transforming agent of the post-industrial society . . . just as the combination of energy, resources and machine technology were the transforming agencies of industrial society. (Bell 1980a: 531, 545; see also Bell 1980b)

John Naisbitt's popular account in *Megatrends* snappily summarizes this: 'Computer technology is to the information age what mechanization was to the industrial revolution' (Naisbitt 1984: 22).

It has been one of the notable features of the idea of the information society that, just as with the idea of post-industrial society, its exposition and explication in the scholarly literature and at academic conferences have been accompanied by extensive popularization in the mass media and through journalistic best-sellers. Alvin Toffler, who popularized the post-industrial idea in *Future Shock*, has had an even greater success with his popularization of the idea of the information society in *The Third Wave* (1981). Almost equally successful has been John Naisbitt's bite-size rendering of the idea in *Megatrends* (1984). These popular works make helpfully explicit what are often understated or over-qualified positions in the writings of more cautiously-minded academics. In what follows I shall use Daniel Bell for the main statement of the thesis of the information society; Toffler, Naisbitt and other popularizers can supply, where necessary, the clarifying chorus.

The computer by itself would transform many of the operations of industrial society. But what has brought the Information Society into being, argues Bell, is the explosive convergence of the computer with telecommunications (a marriage some have blessed with the unlovely name 'compunications'). This has broken down the long-standing distinction between the processing of knowledge and its communication (Bell 1980a: 513). Marshall McLuhan had looked to television to bring into being the 'global village'; far more effective in linking the world has been the communications satellite. 'The real importance of Sputnik is not that it began the space age, but that it introduced the era of global satellite communications' (Naisbitt 1984: 2). The combination of satellites, television, telephone, fibre optic cable and microelectronic computers has meshed the world together into a unified knowledge grid. It has 'collapsed the information float. Now, for the first time, we are a truly global economy, because for the first time we have on the planet instantaneously shared information' (Naisbitt 1984: 57; see also Naisbitt and Aburdene 1990: 14).

The increase in knowledge is qualitative, not just quantitative. The old mass media transmitted standardized messages to uniform mass audiences. The new media of communication allow 'narrowcasting' as well as broadcasting. Linked to the computer, cable and satellite permit the segmentation and splitting of both senders and receivers into discrete and discontinuous units. Information can be processed, selected and retrieved to suit the most specialized, the most individualized requirements. 'The Third Wave thus begins a new era – the age of the de-massified media. A new info-sphere is emerging alongside the new techno-sphere' (Toffler 1981: 165; cf. Bell 1980a: 529).

The new info-sphere operates in a global context. No need to move; the information can be brought to your home or local office. A world-wide electronic network of libraries, archives and data banks comes into being, accessible in principle to anyone, anywhere, at any time. 'All the books in the Library of Congress can be stored in a computer no larger than a home refrigerator' (Sussman 1989: 61). The information technology revolution compresses space and time into a new 'world *oikoumene*' orientated towards the future. Past societies, says Bell, were primarily space-bound or time-bound. They were held together by territorially-based political and bureaucratic authorities and/or by history and tradition. Industrialism confirmed space in the nation state while replacing the rhythms and tempo of nature with the pacing of the machine. The clock and the railway timetable are the symbols of the industrial age. They express time in hours, minutes, seconds. The computer, the symbol of the information age, thinks in nano-seconds, in thousandths of microseconds. Its conjunction with the new communications technology thus brings in a radically new space–time framework for modern society.

> What the changes in transportation and communication – the infra-structures of society – have meant in recent years has been the eclipse of distance and the foreshortening of time, almost to the fusion of the two. Space has been enlarged to the entire globe, and is tied together, almost, in 'real time'. The sense of time, religiously and culturally, which had been oriented to continuity and the past, now, sociologically, becomes geared to the future. (Bell 1980b: 62; cf. Williams 1982: 230–1; Meyrowitz 1986: 328; Lash and Urry 1994)

As with his earlier exposition of the post-industrial idea, Bell is meticulous in giving statistical flesh to the structural bones of the information society. Knowledge does not simply govern, to an unprecedented extent, technical innovation and economic growth; it is itself fast becoming the principal activity of the economy and the principal determinant of occupational change.

In his earlier account Bell had relied for his assessment of the 'knowledge factor' in the economy on the celebrated calculations of Fritz Machlup (1962). Latterly he has come to rely on the more sophisticated and widely reported calculations by Marc Porat (1977) of the extent of the US 'information economy'. Bell combines Porat's calculations, centred on the year 1967, of the 'primary information sector' (industries which directly produce marketable information goods and services) with his calculations of the 'secondary information sector' (information activities in the 'technostructure' of both public and private organizations, which contribute indirectly – through planning, marketing, etc. – to output, but which are not formally counted as information services in the national accounts). Together these suggest that the information economy in the United States amounts to about 46 per cent of GNP and more than 50 per cent of all wages and salaries earned, that is, more than half of the national income. 'It is in that sense that we have become an information economy' (Bell 1980a: 521; see also Stonier 1983: 24).[3]

This remarkable degree of information activity – and Bell assumes it to have grown considerably since 1967 – is matched by the rapid growth of information workers in the occupational structure. Separating out an 'information sector' from the more general tertiary category of services, Bell shows that by the

mid-1970s information workers in the United States had come to
constitute the largest group of workers – almost 47 per cent – in
the civilian work-force (industrial workers accounted for a further
28 per cent, service workers for 22 per cent and agricultural workers
for 3 per cent). Using what he calls a more 'inclusive definition'
Bell claims that already 'by 1975 the information workers had
surpassed the non-information groups as a whole' (Bell, 1980a:
523–4).

Naisbitt goes even further. Basing himself on David Birch's
study of occupational change in the 1970s, he estimates that by
the early 1980s more than 65 per cent of the US work-force were
in the information economy (Naisbitt 1984: 4). Such a claim is
substantiated by similar figures from other industrial countries
– for example the estimate for Britain that 'information occupations . . . amount to 65 per cent of the working population' (Barron
and Curnow 1979: 19).[4]

'We now mass-produce information the way we used to
mass-produce cars . . . this knowledge is the driving force of the
economy' (Naisbitt 1984: 7). The information society, according
to its proponents, brings about change at the most fundamental
level of society. It initiates a new mode of production. It changes
the very source of wealth-creation and the governing factors
in production. Labour and capital, the central variables of the
industrial society, are replaced by information and knowledge
as the central variables. The labour theory of value, as classically
formulated by a succession of thinkers from Locke and Smith to
Ricardo and Marx, must give way to a 'knowledge theory of value'.
Now 'knowledge, not labour, is the source of value' (Bell 1980a:
506). 'The micro processor,' says Hazel Henderson, 'has finally
repealed the labour theory of value' (Henderson 1978: 77). Stonier
argues that 'information has upstaged land, labour and capital
as the most important input into modern production systems'
(Stonier 1983: 8). And Yoneji Masuda, the leading Japanese
exponent of the information society concept, proclaims that in the
new society 'the information utility . . . consisting of information
networks and data banks', the core organization for the production
of information, 'will replace the factory as the societal symbol'. It
will have 'the fundamental character of an infrastructure, and
knowledge capital will predominate over material capital in the
structure of the economy' (Masuda 1985: 621, 626; see also Masuda
1981; Stehr and Böhme 1986; Castells 1989: 7–21).

It is clear from this statement, as well as from the whole cast of
the accounts given by the information society theorists, that what

Masuda calls 'the past developmental pattern of human society' is used as 'an historical analogical model for future society' (Masuda 1985: 620). This is in fact no more than the familiar evolutionary typology to be found in sociology since the eighteenth century. Current changes are seen according to a model derived from (assumed) past changes, and future developments are projected following the logic of the model. So just as industrial society replaced agrarian society, the information society is replacing industrial society, more or less in the same revolutionary way. Bell, using a three-fold evolutionary schema based on the movement from 'pre-industrial extractive' to 'industrial-fabrication' to 'post-industrial-information' activities, produces an elaborate and systematic comparison of all three types of society. The three are seen as distinct but equivalent modes of production, analysable according to the same principles of structure and function (Bell 1980a: 504–5; see also Stonier 1983: 23; Jones 1982: 11).

Bell, more cautious than most of his disciples, does not 'read off' from his predominantly economic model all the features of cultural and political life in the information society. As before, and with something of the same vexing stubbornness, he insists on the principle of 'the disjunction of realms'. Economy, polity and culture are distinct realms which 'respond to different norms, have different rhythms of change, and are regulated by different, even contrary, axial principles' (Bell 1976: 10; see also Turner 1989). Others, perhaps wisely, are less inhibited. If the coming of the information society is, as all claim, as revolutionary a change as the coming of industrial society, then one would surely expect profound changes to occur throughout society, and not simply – as Bell would have it – in the 'techno-economic structure'.

Such is the view of the majority of information society advocates. Toffler, for instance, connects as a systematic pattern changes in the 'info-sphere' with changes in the 'techno-sphere', the 'socio-sphere', the 'power-sphere', the 'bio-sphere' and the 'psycho-sphere' (Toffler 1981: 5). Moreover it is clear that for most of these thinkers the new information society, for all its stresses and problems, is to be welcomed and celebrated not simply as a new mode of production but as a whole way of life. Toffler speaks of 'the death of industrialism and the rise of a new civilization.' He seeks to counter the 'chic pessimism that is so prevalent today.' The emergent civilization of the Third Wave can be made 'more sane, sensible, and sustainable, more decent and more democratic than any we have ever known' (Toffler 1981: 2–3). Naisbitt likewise sees enormous potential for a fresh wave of initiative, individualism and democracy. He looks forward to a complete restructuring of institutions, based on the computer. Information is 'the great equalizer'.

> We are beginning to abandon the hierarchies that worked well in the centralized, industrial era. In their place, we are substituting the network model of organization and communication, which has its roots in the natural, egalitarian, and spontaneous formation of groups among like-minded people. Networks restructure the power and communication flow within an organization from vertical to horizontal . . . The computer will smash the pyramid: we created the hierarchical, pyramidal, managerial system because we needed it to keep track of people and things people did; with the computer to keep track, we can restructure our institutions horizontally. (Naisbitt 1984: 281–2; see also 211–29)

In the hands of Tom Stonier and Yoneji Masuda the information society takes on positively utopian dimensions. The information society, says Stonier, eliminates 'the primary social need for war, the need to expand resources to match growing populations'. It does this through 'technological ingenuity and relative population stability'. This miraculous sleight-of-hand is not further explained. The information society also enhances democracy, as it diffuses information throughout society, making for a more alert and educated public. Information is 'the new coin of power'. Unlike money or land in former times, it is widely distributed. 'No dictator can survive for any length of time in communicative society as the flows of information can no longer be controlled from the centre'. Orwell's *Nineteen Eighty-Four* was wrong: television, and *a fortiori* the newer media, liberate, they do not enslave. A 'consensus democracy' is coming into being (Stonier 1983: 202–3; see also Meyrowitz 1986: 321–3; Sussman 1989: 62–3).

For Stonier the post-industrial information society is not only peaceful and democratic, it is also an era of plenty. It is an era in which everyone will live a life of learning and leisure.

> . . . everyone an aristocrat, everyone a philosopher. A massively expanded education system to provide not only training and information on how to make a living, but also on how to live. In late industrial society we stopped worrying about food. In late communicative society we will stop worrying about all material resources. And just as the industrial economy eliminated slavery, famine and pestilence, so will the post-industrial economy eliminate authoritarianism, war and strife. For the first time in history, the rate at which we solve problems will exceed the rate at which they appear. (Stonier, 1983: 214; see also King 1982: 27)

It is in Masuda that the information society takes on an almost mystical cast. Masuda offers a vision of 'computopia', the information society of the twenty-first century. It will be a 'universal society of plenty'. Individuals, largely freed by automation from the need to labour, will form themselves into voluntary communities for the fulfilment of diverse ends. 'The future information society . . . will become a classless society, free of overruling power, the core of society being voluntary communities.' Computer-communications technology will make it possible to do without centralized politics and administration. Instead there will be participatory democracy and local 'citizen management systems' (Masuda 1985: 625–32). Finally, at its highest level, computopia aims at a new, quasi-religious, symbiotic union of man with nature, in a 'synergistic system'. Ten thousand years ago men created the first material civilization. Thus began a never-ending struggle with nature which has turned into the threat of nature's destruction. We are now on the threshold of a new civilization whose principle of operation is entirely different.

> We are moving towards the twenty-first century with the very great goal of building a Computopia on earth, the historical monument of which will be only several chips one inch square in a small box. But that box will store many historical records, including the record of how 4 billion world citizens overcame the energy crisis and the population explosion, achieved the abolition of nuclear weapons and complete disarmament, conquered illiteracy, and created a rich symbiosis of god and man, without the compulsion of power or law, but by the voluntary cooperation of the citizens . . . Accordingly the civilization to be built . . . will not be a material civilization symbolized by huge constructions, but will be virtually *an invisible civilization*. Precisely, it should be called an 'information civilization' . . . (Masuda 1985: 633–4)[5]

Old and New: Work in the Information Society

It would be perverse and foolhardy to deny the reality of much of what the information society theorists assert. The common experiences of daily life alone are enough to confirm that. Automatic tellers in banks, automatic billing at supermarket check-outs, the virtual disappearance of cheques along with cash in most monetary transactions, word processors and fax machines, direct on-line hotel and airline bookings, direct broadcasting by satellite from any part of the world: all these are facts of everyday life for most sections of the population in the advanced industrial countries.

The linking of information world-wide for scholars and specialists is also fast becoming a reality. The catalogues of the major libraries and archives can be scanned from a multitude of points by means of a computer terminal. Much of the material deposited in these libraries can also be read locally on microfilm or microfiche. The principal stock markets of the world are electronically linked, allowing for instantaneous adjustment of stock prices in response to minute-by-minute information conveyed by the computer screens. Round-the-clock trading becomes for the first time a possibility and increasingly the practice.

The information revolution has most clearly invaded our homes (Miles 1988a). Television is still the most obvious symbol of this, enhanced now by the additional facility of the video cassette recorder and the variety provided by cable and satellite. But 'telebanking', 'teleshopping' and 'teleworking' are also now making considerable inroads into our lives (see, for example; Hakim 1988). 'Tele-education' may turn out to be an even more significant development. At the younger ages collective institutionalized provision would still seem to be desirable, for social as much as educational reasons. But the Open University in Britain already provides a model for home-based higher education. The potential for expansion into something like a World University of the Air is evident.

The 'home-centred society' and the 'electronic cottage' (Toffler 1981: 194–207) are somewhat exaggerated descriptions of what is happening or likely to happen on a very large scale. But even critics of the information society concept, such as Colin Gill, acknowledge the very real impact of the new technology on home-based activities.

> It is probable that within two or three decades . . . personal computers linked to a television at home will become the central means for providing access to a wide range of services. Through this equipment, people will be able to order consumer goods after they have ascertained their bank balance on the screen, and they will be able to scan through a wide range of electronic mail, including newspapers and periodicals to which the household subscribes. They will also have immediate access to a wide range of databanks of knowledge, and the possibilities for education and undertaking training in particular skills will be considerable. Leisure-related activities may well be pursued in the form of sophisticated computer-based games involving friends and relatives at a great distance . . . (Gill 1985: 6; cf. King 1982: 7; Williams 1982: 268; Barry Jones 1982: 71)

I shall return later to the 'home-centred society'. Here I mention it, along with other developments, simply to note the extent to which critics of Bell, Masuda, Stonier and others accept the reality of an information revolution, and the need to incorporate it in their analyses. Information technology, says Gill, is not just another technology, it is 'a revolutionary technology', comparable in its impact to revolutionary technologies of the past. 'Our way of life is going to be radically altered, for better or worse, just as it has been in the past by such technological advances as the steam engine, electricity, the internal combustion engine and air travel' (Gill 1985: 2).

Tessa Morris-Suzuki, while arguing that the concept of the information society was an ideological weapon forged in response to the industrial crisis of the late 1960s in Japan, nevertheless insists that information activities have become critical in the current phase of capitalism. Monopoly capitalism, she argues, is now to a good extent 'information capitalism', 'the private appropriation of social knowledge'. With the spread of automation, the extraction of surplus value (profit) now turns on 'the perpetual innovation economy' whose key resource is knowledge. This is reflected in a distinct 'softening of the economy' in capitalist countries. In Japan, for instance, in 1970 more than half of all industries could be classified as 'hard', in the sense that material goods made up 80 per cent or more of the total value of inputs. By 1980, only 27 per cent of industries could be so classified; this indicates the growing share of corporate capital expended on non-material inputs such as software, data services, planning, and research and development (Morris-Suzuki 1984: 116; see also Morris-Suzuki 1986, 1988; Castells 1989: 28–32).

Still, the acceptance of the growing importance of information technology, even an information revolution, is one thing; the acceptance of the idea of a new industrial revolution, a new kind of society, a new age, is quite another. Here the criticism has been voluminous, sharp and largely persuasive. It has also been, to a somewhat wearisome degree, familiar. This is not surprising. Since the concept of the information society has evolved smoothly out of the earlier idea of a post-industrial society, since the two share many of the same analytical features, and since they are propagated in both cases by much the same people, we should expect that the objections to the thesis of the information society would substantially repeat those levelled against the earlier idea of the post-industrial society.

Such is the case. The information society theorists can be attacked, firstly, for their short-sighted historical perspective. As with the post-industrial theorists, they attribute to the present developments which are the culmination of trends deep in the past. What seem to them novel and current can be shown to have been in the making for the past hundred years. James Beniger, for instance, accepts the correctness of the designation of present-day society as the information society. But his detailed historical study shows this to be merely the current manifestation of a much more profound change in the character of industrial societies that took place over a century ago. This change he labels 'the Control Revolution'.

The Industrial Revolution, Beniger argues, so speeded up 'the material processing system' of society that it precipitated a crisis of control. Information-processing systems and communication technologies lagged behind those of energy generation and use. The application first of steam power and later of electricity forced innovations in communication and control in every sphere of society. Fast-moving steam trains had, for urgent reasons of safety, to be carefully monitored and controlled. The speeding up of commercial distribution as a result of steam trains and steam boats imposed wide-ranging changes in wholesale and retail organization. The pace of material through-put in factories called forth the moving assembly line (Fordism) and the 'scientific management' of labour (Taylorism). Overarching all these, and modelled as often as not on the centralized, systematized railway system that was the pioneering response to the control crisis, was the growth of a formal Weberian bureaucracy in business and governmental organizations. By 1939 at the latest, Beniger convincingly shows, the structural elements of the Information Society – including the basic principles of the computer – were all firmly in place. Post-war developments were largely extensions and applications of the control techniques – the Control Revolution – that were elaborated by an immensely creative group of scientists, technologists and marketing specialists in the period from the 1880s to the 1930s.

> The Information Society has not resulted from recent changes . . . but rather from increases in the speed of material processing and of flows through the material economy that began more than a century ago. Similarly, microprocessing and computing technology, contrary to currently fashionable opinion, do not represent a new force only recently unleashed on an unprepared society but merely the most recent installment in the continuing development of the Control Revolution. This explains why so many of the components of computer control have been anticipated, both by visionaries like Charles Babbage and by practical innovators like Daniel McCallum, since the first signs of

a control crisis in the early nineteenth century. (Beniger 1985: 435; see also Rosenbrock et al. 1985: 640)

A similar charge of historical shortsightedness is made by those, such as Kevin Robins and Frank Webster (1987, 1989), who see the information society as essentially the further application of Taylorism. Taylorism, the principles of 'scientific management' advocated by Frederick Winslow Taylor in the early years of this century, is actually best thought of as a powerful system of work organization capable of more or less indefinite application in a variety of industrial contexts. This means that what Taylorism connotes – the radically refined division of labour, the rigid separation of conception and execution, the standardization and splitting of tasks into the simplest possible form – might well continue apace even though many of Taylor's practical recommendations have fallen into disfavour (Littler 1978).

In response to the earlier thesis of the post-industrial 'service society', Harry Braverman (1974) had already shown that much service work is as 'Taylorized' as work in manufacturing industries. The office, it turned out, could be industrialized as readily as the workshop; much white-collar work was subjected to the same routinization, fragmentation and de-skilling as blue-collar work. Braverman concluded that the belief in the spread of some new principle of work, some new ethic of professionalism, as services grew in industrial economies, was misguided.

Braverman can help us understand the further expansion of scientific management in the information society. It is important to remember that Taylorism was not intended to apply simply to the lower levels of the work-force. It contained the explicit principle of 'functional management' that implied that standardization and simplification were to be features of managerial as well as manual work. Moreover, when Taylor enjoined that 'all possible brain work should be removed from the shop and centred in the planning or laying-out department' he explicitly included the brain work of managers as well as of humbler employees. Knowledge – the skill and judgement of all workers, at whatever level – was to be gathered from every part of the organization and concentrated exclusively in the planning department. The 'science' of scientific management was not to be the possession of the generality of managers but only of a specialized core concerned with overall planning. The de-skilling of most middle level managers, their loss, along with other workers, of overall comprehension and control of their work, was not some later refinement but central to the original principles of Taylorism (Littler 1978: 190–2). This goes some way to explaining the striking fact that the greatest resistance to Taylorism in the factories came not from the mass of shopfloor workers or their unions but from middle management and supervisors (Littler 1982: 190; Lash and Urry 1987: 170–1).

In practice Taylorism up to the mid-century was confined largely to manufacturing industry and to manual workers. Computerization has made possible its extension to spheres of activity and bodies of workers previously untouched. The suppliers of microelectronic office equipment have made this an explicit part of their sales pitch. Addressing a conference of business executives Franco de Benedetti, managing director of Olivetti, referred to electronic data-processing as a new 'organizational technology' which, 'like the organization of labour, has a dual function as a productive force and a control tool for capital'.

> The Taylorization of the first factories . . . enabled the labour force to be controlled and was the necessary prerequisite to the subsequent mechanisation and automation of the productive processes . . . Information technology is basically a technology of co-ordination and control of the labour force, the white collar workers, which Taylorian organization does not cover. (de Benedetti 1979)

'Taylorian organization' can of course be adapted not just to routine white-collar work but to the work of many professionals and skilled technicians, new and old. The computer has been hailed by many as an instrument of liberation. It will automate the tedious and tiring work and free workers to engage in more interesting and creative tasks (see, for example, Hyman 1980). This remains, currently at least, a hope or a promise rather than widespread practice. For many information workers, the application of the new technology has continued the 'dynamic of de-skilling' (Littler 1978: 189) intrinsic to Taylorian principles, complemented as these were by the tighter technical control made possible by the moving assembly line of the Fordist factory. Here was first made clear the extent to which control could be not only a system of managerial prerogatives, a bureaucratic pattern, but also a technical fact built into the very structure of the machine (Edwards 1979: 111–29).

Clerical work was once largely a man's job, involving considerable degrees of skill and levels of discretion. There was a 'craft' as well as a quasi-managerial element involved. The advent of office machinery in the form of adding machines and the Hollerith punched-card processor began the process of de-skilling, symbolized by the 'feminization' of the clerical work-force (women were 21 per cent of clerks in England in 1911 and 70 per cent by 1966). The office worker, once a craft worker, became increasingly a simple machine operator and form-filler.

The widespread application of the computer and other forms of electronic data-processing (EDP) in the office has continued this process. Clerical workers have become, as they often put it, 'slaves to the computer', mere machine feeders with virtually no comprehension of the overall purpose of their work or control of its pace. Little knowledge or training are required to carry out the routine tasks involved in preparing data for the computer or punching them onto disk or tape. It is the machine that is smart, not the worker. A vast gulf opens between the largely unskilled, largely female mass clerical work-force and the small elite of qualified managers and computer professionals, most of whom are male.

> Clerical deskilling, therefore, involves both the process of fragmentation, simplification, and standardization of work tasks and the diminution of the clerical worker's role as an 'intermediary' between management and the mass of routine workers . . . The particular characteristics of the computer as office technology is its capacity to store and process information which was once the domain and possession of the clerk, and to impose internal controls on these operations . . . which would once have depended on the experience and acquired knowledge of the individual worker. The clerk can no longer entertain the possibility of a 'total view' of the work process, nor exercise responsibility and discretion based on experience and delegated direct from management or employer . . . Functions of capital are relocated in the higher supervisory and managerial strata, or, progressively, in the work of those who plan, control and co-ordinate the use of the computer. (Crompton and Reid 1983: 175–6)[6]

But why expect managers, professionals and technical workers to be themselves immune to Taylorism and technical control? Scientific management was, as we have seen, intended to apply to all levels and types of workers. And the very people who designed and operated the new technology were, as many recognized, thereby putting themselves at risk. Vonnegut's *Player Piano* (1952) long ago vividly illustrated the predicament of highly-skilled engineers who, having taught the computer their skills, put themselves out of a job.

In manufacturing, computer numerically controlled (CNC) machines are already replacing 'some of the most highly-skilled and satisfying work on the shop floor, such as jig boring, milling, universal turning and highly skilled workshop practices' (Barker

1981: 7; see also Noble 1979, 1986: 231–64; Evans 1982: 162–4). In the printing trade, previously skilled typesetters and compositors may have hung on to their high wages but for many their work has been reduced by computerized typesetting to the skill level of a typist (Weber and Robins 1986: 139). Architects and industrial designers have had their work 'simplified' – that is, de-skilled – by Computer Aided Design (CAD) (Cooley 1981), while many other professionals – in medicine and education, for instance – are having their work monitored and their expertise challenged by 'Expert' systems of artificial intelligence (Boden 1980; Forester 1987: 45–9; Cooley 1982; Rosenbrock et al. 1985: 640–1). Some students of the new technology indeed argue that automation, in the office at least, is leading to a re-skilling (accompanied by redundancy of routine workers) of lower level occupations; it is the professionals who are the main victims of de-skilling (Baran 1988: 697).

Most notably of all, the continuing development of computers has Taylorized the computer professionals themselves. Computer work has followed the familiar pattern of the separation and splitting of tasks, leading to increasingly routinized work for the mass of workers and highly specialized work for a small group of designers and researchers. First systems analysts were separated from programmers, marking a significant distinction between those who conceived and those who executed software programmes. Later programmers were themselves distinguished from a more routine class of operators, who were concerned largely with the repetitive task of coding. The development of computer languages – Cobol, Fortran, etc. – and 'structured programming' have further polarized software production along skill lines. All the creativity goes into the design and preparation of programme 'packages' – such as those for payroll calculations – which are then capable of simple implementation by programmers. The de-skilling of computer programmers in particular, taken with the general de-skilling of white-collar work in automated offices, has led Morris-Suzuki to single out 'the semi-skilled computer worker' as the typical worker of the future (Morris-Suzuki 1988: 124). Webster and Robins agree: 'Many computer workers possess but an aura of skill: their daily work is little more than specialized clerical labor' (Webster and Robins 1986: 146). The 'feminization' of computer work, at the lower levels of programmers and operators, is a further, familiar, indication of fragmentation and de-skilling (Kraft 1987; Webster and Robins 1986: 177).

The Knowledge Worker

Knowledge, according to information society theorists, is progressively supposed to affect work in two ways. One is the upgrading of the knowledge content of existing work, in the sense that the new technology adds rather than subtracts from the skill of workers. The other is the creation and expansion of new work in the knowledge sector, such that information workers come to predominate in the economy. Moreover it is assumed that it is the more skilled, more knowledgeable information workers who will come to constitute the core of the information economy. We have seen that for many existing workers the new information technology spells a decrease, not an increase, in knowledge and control.[7] But perhaps this is the wrong way to view things. Are these workers not rather being displaced altogether? Is the future not more likely to be one where low-level routine jobs are automated out of existence and new, more creative, ones take their place?

The impact of information technology on employment was one of the most hotly debated issues of the 1980s. Would the new technology increase or decimate jobs? And where would the effects be most felt? Optimists were naturally to be found a-plenty in the information technology industry and its governmental off-shoots, such as the Department of Trade and Industry in Britain (for example, Baker 1982). Pessimists tended to be among academics and trade unionists, abetted by some financial journalists. But the most celebrated scare was raised in an official report by two civil servants presented in 1977 to the French President, Valéry Giscard d'Estaing. In *L'Informatisation de la Société* (first volume in English as *The Computerization of Society*: Nora and Minc 1980), Simon Nora and Alain Minc predicted a wholesale devastation of the world of work as a consequence of *télématique* (telematics), the 'synergistic' marriage of computers and telecommunications. They drew attention in particular to the service sector, where they expected telematics to produce such prodigious gains in productivity as to eliminate whole groups of workers in banks, insurance companies, government departments, telecommunications, and the tertiary departments of manufacturing (Nora and Minc 1980: 34–7).

Nora and Minc refused to offer precise figures for the loss of jobs, but others were less inhibited. For Britain, Iann Barron and Ray Curnow suggested that the impact of information technology would be to produce an unemployment rate of 10–15 per cent by

the end of the 1980s (Barron and Curnow 1979: 201); Clive Jenkins
and Barrie Sherman predicted a rate of 20 per cent in a progressive
'collapse of work' (Jenkins and Sherman 1979: 115; see also Merritt
1982: 74; Hines and Searle 1979; King 1982: 32; Friedrichs 1982:
200).

In the event, the more scary predictions have proved – so
far, at least – unfounded. Information technology has displaced
some workers – not only or always office workers – but has
also created new jobs in several areas (Webster and Robins 1986:
90–127; Morris-Suzuki 1988: 87–105; Lyon 1988: 66–72; Freeman
and Soete 1987; Castells 1989: 173–88). Redeployment has been
more common so far than widespread redundancy, either because
increased productivity has lowered costs and so led to increased
demand, or because firms have retrained displaced workers to
offer an expanded range of services. Volkswagen is a good example
of the first case, Barclays Bank of the second (Leadbeater and Lloyd
1987: 85, 95).

But the main problem in assessing the impact of information
technology on employment is that we are at too early a stage
in the process. It is impossible yet to generalize about the long
term. Optimists are as plausible as pessimists. It can be argued
that the new technology will, or at least could, in the long run
provide another of those 'gales of creative destruction' that Joseph
Schumpeter believed periodically renewed capitalism. The constellation of information technology industries – computers, electronic
components, telecommunications – could, like cars and domestic
electrical goods in the first half of the century, be the springboard
for a period of renewed economic expansion and job creation
(Perez 1985; Miles and Gershuny 1986; Freeman 1987). Equally,
though, it is easy to see the force of the argument that new jobs
created by information technology are an initial, once-and-for-all
time, bonanza, the product of the massive reorganization forced on
companies as they absorb the impact of the new technology. Once
the initial shock has been absorbed, the capacity for information
technology to displace workers will be felt with a vengeance
(Webster and Robins 1986: 127). There is also a third, more radical,
position that combines 'pessimism' with optimism. That is, it
accepts that information technology will drastically diminish paid
employment. But it welcomes this, seeing in it not so much a threat
as an opportunity to redirect time and energy to more fulfilling
activities outside the formal economy of paid work (Gorz 1982,
1989; King 1982: 33–5; Barry Jones 1982).

The debate about the *quantity* of jobs lost or gained through the applications of information technology is not, however, the main concern of the information society theorists. They generally assume a numerical gain, as their figures for the steady growth of 'information workers' suggest. But more important is the quality of the new work-force. Information society theorists look forward to the rise of a new service class of knowledge workers, men and women whose work is characterized by high levels of technical skill and theoretical knowledge, and which correspondingly demands long periods of education and training. In support of this they point to the fact that scientific, technical and professional workers have been the fastest growing occupational groups in all industrial societies in the last fifty years. Similarly, they argue, it is the 'knowledge factories', the universities and research institutes, that have now become the powerhouses of modern society, replacing the goods-producing factory of the industrial era (Drucker 1969: 52; Bell 1980a: 501; Simon 1980: 429; Stonier 1983: 43–4).

We have already had reason to doubt, on general grounds, that the work-force is increasing in skill and autonomy. In so far as Taylorism remains the master principle, information technology has a greater potential for proletarianization than for professionalization. This process can be quite effectively disguised by occupational statistics that suggest a more educated and better trained work-force. The growth of credentialism – that is, demanding higher qualifications for the same jobs – and the familiar process of the inflation of job labels and occupational self-advertisement, can all give a quite misleading impression of the growth of a more 'knowledgeable' society (Kumar 1978: 211–19).

The more detailed picture of recent occupational changes confirms this impression of a statistical sleight-of-hand designed to promote the idea of an increasingly professionalized society. Bell, for instance, singles out workers in health, education and social welfare, along with scientific and technical workers in information technology, as the key professionals of the information society. These, the workers in 'human services' and in 'professional services', are the mainstay of the new service class (Bell 1980a: 501). Over the century, the censuses do indeed record a striking rise in the number of professional, administrative and managerial employees. From constituting no more than 5–10 per cent of the work-force at the beginning of the century, they now in all western societies make up between 20–25 per cent of workers (Goldthorpe 1982: 172).

But many of these workers are professionals only in name

– plumbers as 'heating engineers', shop-keepers as 'managers', etc. Moreover the variety and heterogeneity of workers in the information sector make any general claim of increased skill·and knowledge highly contentious (Miles and Gershuny 1986: 23). The same point can be made about the variety existing between different societies. For instance, while most professionals and managers are graduates in Germany, Japan and the United States, in Britain only 30 per cent of professionals and 12 per cent of managers are graduates (*Social Trends* 1990: 62).

More problematic for information society theory is the expectation of the continued growth and expansion of the class of knowledge workers. The assumption of the continued growth of service workers in general has already been challenged on theoretical as well as empirical grounds. There is no natural or inevitable 'march through the sectors', from agriculture to manufacturing to services, as economies develop (Gershuny 1978; Singelmann 1978). It has been shown, for instance, that 'self-service' provisioning, using service goods such as washing machines and television sets, has already displaced some service workers and may displace more in the future (Gershuny and Miles 1983). The same uncertainty surrounds the future growth of knowledge workers. In the last two decades there has already been a sharp decline in the growth of professionals in the human services; and the growth of information workers generally – including those in the computer and telecommunications industry – has slackened and tailed off in most industrial countries (Jones 1982: 19; Guy 1987: 175; Kraft 1987: 101). An area that has been particularly hard hit – mainly as the result of computerization – is the area of middle management. The future organization, it has been suggested, may have an hour-glass shape: a few executives and research and development specialists on the top, and many clerks and operatives on the bottom. 'The middle, which used to be filled with managers, is replaced by a communications channel' (Kraft 1987: 107; Perez 1985: 455; Baran 1988: 697). A similar pattern is predicted specifically for manufacturing organizations, as microelectronics continue their advance: a relatively few highly skilled designers, planners and technicians at the top, and unskilled machine operators and maintenance men at the bottom. What will have gone is the body of skilled machinists and middle-level technical staff (Evans 1982: 168–70).

Most of the growth in jobs in the last two decades has indeed come from a quite different quarter: not from the knowledge sector, but from the lower levels of the tertiary economy, where the extent of skill and knowledge is not notably high. For instance, between 1973 and 1980 almost 13 million new jobs were created in the United States. Most of these were in the private sector, and most – over 70 per cent – in services and the retail trade. The typical new workers were in 'eating and drinking' establishments, including fast-food restaurants; in 'health services', mainly nurses and ancillary staff in private hospitals and private nursing homes; and in 'business services', mainly routine information workers concerned with data processing, copying and mailing. Many of the new workers were women, many of them part-time or temporary. Pay levels were low, job security and career prospects virtually nil. This pattern continued during the 1980s – in Britain as much as the United States.[8] In Japan too, the growth of information workers has been skewed in the direction of lower level jobs concerned with 'information transfer' rather than the more skilled jobs concerned with 'information production'. In 1982, 'information transfer' workers accounted for 20 per cent of the Japanese work-force, but 'information production' workers only 13 per cent (Morris-Suzuki 1988: 131).

Politics and Markets

It is clear from this account of developments in the information economy that there is a distinct politics, as well as a political economy, of the information society. The growth of knowledge work, for instance, has evidently been directly affected by recent governmental policies. Knowledge workers in the public sector – especially those in human services – have declined while those in the private sector – especially those in business services – have increased. But state involvement in the information economy also operates at a far deeper structural level. Governments have taken a leading role in promoting and disseminating the idea of an information society – including vigorous attempts to encourage a 'computer culture' in schools and universities (Roszak 1978; Robins and Webster 1989). In Britain, not notably in the forefront of the information technology revolution, more than half of all research and development (R&D) in information technology (IT) is funded by the government; the government is responsible, as customer, for more than half of the total market in electronics; and it absorbs more than a third of all computer capacity (Webster and Robins 1986: 273).

Moreover, whatever their free-market propensities, it has been

clear that governments have not been willing to give up a co-
ordinating and directing role in the development of information
technology. British Telecom may be privatized, for instance, but
it preserves its privileged role in the telecommunications network
and its break-up – urged by free marketeers – is successfully
resisted on the grounds that this would be against the national
interest of maintaining internationally-competitive British companies in the IT field. In France, the IT industry is predominantly in
the hands of the state, and in Japan, whose example inspired the
French effort, the state-owned telecommunications monopoly NTT
(Nippon Telegraph and Telephone) is 'the lynchpin of Japanese IT
strategy'. Government direction of IT has been especially energetic
in these countries, spearheading what amounts almost to a call
to national mobilization for entry into the information society
(Morris-Suzuki 1988: 25–41; Webster and Robins 1986: 258–73).

But it is in the military connection that we can perhaps most
intimately see the link between government and the information
society. From the very first development of the semiconductor
industry at the Bell Laboratories in New Jersey in the 1940s,
to the Star Wars and 'Strategic Computing' projects of the US
Department of Defense in the 1980s, it has been obvious that
military (defence, space, etc.) requirements have in nearly all
societies been the main engine of growth of the IT industries (Japan
and Germany are partial, and perhaps temporary, exceptions).
Military R&D, on one estimate, is responsible for 40 per cent of
total world expenditure on research, and absorbs the activities of
40 per cent of the world's research scientists and engineers. Since
it is microelectronics that has revolutionized military technology
– especially in missile and intelligence systems – in the past
twenty years, it is not surprising to find that a large part of
this vast military expenditure on R&D is devoted to work in
information technology (Barnaby 1982: 243–4; see also Lyon 1988:
26–30).

In the United States, over half of government-financed R&D is
military R&D (Roszak 1988: 40). The same is true of Britain, where
the Ministry of Defence's spending on R&D amounts to a half of
all government expenditure on R&D, and a quarter of all R&D
spending in the nation. For Britain it is the electronics industry that
is at the heart of the military-IT complex. Electronics companies get
46 per cent of all government aid to industry, and the government
funds 60 per cent of the total R&D budget in electronics; 95 per
cent of all government-financed R&D in electronics originates from
one department, the Ministry of Defence. The whole of the British

electronics industry is in fact heavily dependent on the military. As the National Economic Development Office stated in 1983: ' The UK electronics industry's biggest single customer is the Ministry of Defence.' The Ministry of Defence purchases more than 20 per cent of the total output of the British electronics industry (a further 30 per cent is purchased by other government departments) (Soete 1987: 207; Webster and Robins 1986: 273–6; Robins and Webster 1988: 29–30).

Political and military actors, though they have their own motivations and interests, do not operate in a social vacuum. That social space is forcibly occupied, to a good extent, by large private multinational corporations that have their own pressing need for the most comprehensive development of information technology. The growth in the scale and complexity of organizations, their bursting of their national boundaries, have necessitated a degree of coordination and communication that has itself been a major force in the expansion of information technology. Westinghouse Corporation, the large American energy company, which also has extensive interests in cable and robotics, made its own IT requirements clear in its 1982 Annual Report:

> An integrated world-wide strategic planning process was put in place, linking products and country planning efforts. A global communications center is being established to provide timely and detailed information for every part of the world. This centralization of planning and intelligence will give Westinghouse a competitive edge in the world-wide deployment of its resources. (Webster 1986: 396; see also Newman and Newman 1985: 505)

The big commercial organizations, like government departments, have developed an appetite for IT which other companies, old and new, have hurried to satisfy. In the process a powerful new group of IT multinationals has risen to prominence. These then not only further the growth of IT by their own organizational needs but are active in generating and pressing new services on other giants. These others, also partly out of their own necessities and partly to get a share of the rich pickings, begin to move in on the act. A spiral develops whose main effect is the continuous creating of IT goods, services and workers (Webster and Robins 1986: 219–56; Douglas and Guback 1984: 234–5; Traber 1986: 3).

The names of the IT multinationals have become household: IBM in computers, AT&T and IT&T in telecommunications, Xerox and Olivetti in office equipment, Philips and Siemens in electronics. But the original bases in particular products and services are fast becoming irrelevant. All these companies, and the many others that are in or trying to enter the field, aim to become 'integrated information' concerns. The goal, substantially achieved in several cases, is to exploit economies of scale and mutual dependencies so as to offer the complete IT package: computers, telecommunications, electronic goods and components, cable, satellite and broadcast systems, TV and video goods and programming services, film and photography. The bulk of IT has so far been developed for the state or business user. This is where expansion has been easiest and the profits greatest. But the home has also already been firmly targeted, along with leisure and entertainment. From the point of view of information technology, distinctions between office and home, work and leisure, are largely unimportant. Indeed IT is in the business of making them unimportant.

Information technology is in fact making most of the standard industrial classifications meaningless. Hallowed divisions between 'secondary' and 'tertiary' activities become increasingly unreal. The electronics industry, the heart of the IT revolution, now integrates manufacturing and service activities so completely that it is impossible to tell where one ends and the other begins – for example, computer manufacture and computer services (Patel and Soete 1987: 123). Robots, computer-aided design and computer-aided manufacturing clearly encourage manufacturers to get into IT themselves; and companies such as the giant motor manufacturer GM have been doing just that.

Oil companies, such as Exxon and British Petroleum, have felt a particularly urgent need to diversify and to incorporate substantial IT activities. And companies such as RCA, which have traditionally been in the field of entertainment, have been restructuring to turn themselves into all-purpose IT companies. They are taking on everything from TV manufacture and television networks to cable equipment and programming, video and satellite manufacture, private telephone systems, and computers and data communications. It is only a symbol of the total interpenetration of all spheres of IT activity that in the midst of all this restructuring RCA should be taken over (in 1985) by one of the other IT giants, General Electric.

Information technology is clearly big business. It is at the heart of corporate capital in the late twentieth century. Corporate capital is both its main instigator and principal user. It has been estimated that about 90 per cent of all data flow via satellite systems is intra-corporate, and about 50 per cent of all trans-border data

flow takes place within the communications networks of individual transnational corporations (Jussawalla 1985: 299–300). Herbert
Schiller has argued that this is more or less the whole story of the
so-called information technology revolution, and the real content
of the information society:

> The new information technologies were developed *in*, *by* and *for* highly
> advanced capitalist economies – that of the USA in particular. It is to
> be expected, therefore, that these technologies are now being employed
> single-mindedly to serve market objectives. Control of the labour force,
> higher productivity, capture of world markets, and continued capital
> accumulation are the propelling influences under which the new
> information technologies are developed. (Schiller 1985: 37)

Taken with the military and political motives noted earlier,
the clearly capitalist character of much IT activity has led to a
widespread questioning of the whole theoretical underpinning of
the idea of an information society. There is no new age, no new
revolution comparable to the Industrial Revolution of the nineteenth century (Nowotny 1982: 101; Rosenbrock et al. 1985: 641).
The information society is a myth developed to serve the interests
of those who initiate and manage the 'information revolution':
'the most powerful sectors of society, its central administrative
elites, the military establishment and global industrial corporations' (Hamelink 1986: 13). It is no more than the latest ideology
of the capitalist state. 'Capitalism is still the name of the game'
(Arriaga 1985: 294). 'If there is a revolution, then it is certainly
around the hub of capitalism' (Douglas and Guback 1984: 236).
'Capitalist industrialism has not been transcended, but simply
extended, deepened and perfected' (Walker 1985: 72; see also
Slack 1984: 250; Robins and Webster 1987: 114; Lyon 1988: 155;
Morris-Suzuki 1988: 84; Roszak 1988: 204).

Bell, Masuda, Stonier and other enthusiasts portray the information society as a hopeful and progressive development. It is
leading to a future of greater prosperity, leisure and satisfaction
for all. But so far at least it is a society designed, as of old, by and
for the few: the rich and powerful classes, nations and regions of
the world. 'The information revolution has not yet arrived and is
nowhere yet in sight, except in the offices of stockbrokers, bankers,
spy masters, meteorologists and the headquarters of transnational
companies' (Traber 1986: 2). Its objectives and effects are strictly
defined by the traditional goals of the political and economic elites:
to increase the power of the state, both as against its own citizens
and against other states; and to boost the productivity and profits

of capitalist enterprises, largely by creating an integrated global market.

Ideology and the Information Society

The main burden of the critique of the information society idea is that the development and diffusion of information technology have introduced no fundamentally new principle or direction in society. The remarkable speed of IT's diffusion is admitted; so too its potentiality for bringing about radical change in social arrangements (for example, Gill 1985: 181). But the new technology is being applied within a political and economic framework that confirms and accentuates existing patterns, rather than giving rise to new ones. Work and leisure are further industrialized, further subjected to Fordist and Taylorist strategies of mechanization, routinization and rationalization. Existing social inequalities are maintained and magnified. A new 'information gap' opens up between the producers and users of the new technology and those – ordinary citizens, semi-skilled operators, Third World countries – who are its (their) passive clients, customers and consumers (Rada 1982). Information abounds, but there is little concern with embodying it in a framework of knowledge, let alone cultivating wisdom in its use (Slack 1984: 254; Marien 1985: 657).[9] Knowledge and information, once amongst the most public and freely available resources in society, now become privatized, commodified, appropriated for sale and profit (Morris-Suzuki 1986).

The theme of this criticism of the information society is one of fundamental continuity. The instruments and techniques may change, but the overriding goals and purposes of capitalist industrial societies remain the same as before. One of the most far-reaching critiques has gone so far as to see the whole information society idea as simply the latest expression of a long-standing tradition of thought and practice that they call 'social Taylorism'. Taylorism, argue Frank Webster and Kevin Robins, was not just a doctrine of factory management but 'a new social philosophy, a new principle of social revolution, and a new imaginary institution in society' (Webster and Robins 1989: 333).

Taylorism became the hub of a new technocratic ideology that did not stop at the factory or office but moved out to the world at large. Having conquered production it now turned its sights on consumption. 'Ultimately what was required was the Scientific

Management of need, desire and fantasy, and their reconstruction in terms of the commodity form' (Webster and Robins 1989: 334). Scientific management in the 1930s and 1940s achieved new forms and techniques in the rise of mass advertising, systematic market research, and the whole science of making and manipulating consumer taste. Television, cable and satellite were later added to its armoury, as the market became increasingly global and in need of ever more careful management. Nor was the political sphere – the consumer as citizen – excluded from social Taylorism. Mass democracies too needed to be carefully monitored and managed. Surveillance, propaganda and public opinion measurement became standard tools in the government and administration of complex societies. The open public sphere of former liberal polities, the space made available for public discussion and debate, increasingly gave way to the administered sphere, dominated by technical expertise and narrow concepts of instrumental rationality.

The whole development of the twentieth-century state and society can therefore be regarded as the application of the principles of scientific management. Information, knowledge and science – including social science – are self-evidently the central requirements of this process. They provide the means necessary to co-ordinate and control the increasingly complex operations of the economy and the polity. Thus it can be argued that 'it was the exponents of Scientific Management, in its broadest sense, who unleashed an Information Revolution'. Particularly important were the 'consumption engineers' who took the lead in regulating business transactions and consumer behaviour. 'It was these advocates of big business who first turned to the "rational" and "scientific" exploitation of information in the wider society, and it is their descendents – the multinational advertisers, market researchers, opinion pollers, data brokers, and so on – who are the heart of information politics in the eighties' (Webster and Robins 1989: 336; see also Robins and Webster 1987: 104–14; Webster and Robins 1986: 309–19, 328–43).

'Taylorism' or 'scientific management' is evidently having to do a lot of work in this analysis; as, in an analogous way, is capitalism in the broader critique of which it is a part. This is not to object to the presentation of the 'dark underside of the information revolution' (Webster and Robins 1989: 330), nor to deny the fundamental truth of these accounts. The information society has not evolved in some neutral, value-free way. Information technology, like all technology, has been selected and shaped in conformity with certain determinate social and political interests. These interests may not always be able to control all its effects. Television, for instance, can disturb as much as it can soothe. Word processors can be as handy for the publishing activities of small oppositional groups as for the rationalizing strategies of office managers. But the bulk of information technology is complex and expensive. It requires massive capital investment and large teams of researchers. Only the most powerful interests in society – governments and large private corporations – have the resources to promote it. 'The automated office, the robotic factory and the electronic battle-field' account for over 80 per cent of the IT business (Webster and Robins 1986: 282). Not surprisingly, these interests have developed IT largely to serve their needs, as they perceive them. Power and profit, as in the past, dominate these calculations.

This is not however the whole story of the information society. To call the information society an ideology, and to relate that ideology to the contemporary needs of capitalism, is to begin, not to end the analysis. Capitalism has had many ideologies over the past two hundred years – *laissez-faire*, managerialism, welfarism, even, arguably, varieties of fascism and communism. Each has had its own kind of relation to capitalist society; each has contained its own distinctive contradictions. What kind of ideology is the ideology of the information society, and what are its particular contradictions? Ideologies, as many people have pointed out, are not just ideas in the head, but real practices, as real as any other social practices. They are lived realities. They constrain our thinking about ourselves and our world, and thus have practical consequences. 'The information society' may be a partial and one-sided way of expressing the contemporary social reality, but for many people in the industrial world it is now an inescapable part of that reality. To describe this as 'false consciousness' misses the point. As Jennifer Slack says:

> [T]he discourse of the information revolution appeals powerfully to common sense, regardless of class, race, gender, or ethnicity. It is not a mere tool used by the capitalists in order to dupe us; it is embraced and promoted – often even by its detractors. It is, at the very least, the world within which we are surviving . . . There is a real information revolution going on, and it is the revolution that is being promoted in the media, in public relations, in advertising, and in ourselves. I see no sense in denying that . . . (Slack 1984: 249–50).

We shall come back to this later. The precise significance of the information revolution, its meaning as both ideology and reality, will be easier to assess when we have considered the other varieties of post-industrial theory. It is possible that all these theories are feeding off the same or similar developments in modern societies. As partial glimpses of those developments, they may, when put together, better enable us to see the fuller picture.

3

Fordism and Post-Fordism

Vast changes in the techno-sphere and the info-sphere have converged to change the way we make goods. We are moving rapidly beyond traditional mass production to a sophisticated mix of mass and de-massified products. The ultimate goal of this effort is now apparent: completely customized goods, made with wholistic, continuous-flow processes, increasingly under the direct control of the consumer.

Alvin Toffler (1981: 185–6)

We can see in this country a culture of post-Fordist capitalism emerging. Consumption has a new place. As for production the keyword is flexibility – of plant and machinery, as of products and labour. Emphasis shifts from scale to scope, and from cost to quality. Organisations are geared to respond to rather than regulate markets. They are seen as frameworks for learning as much as instruments of control. Their hierarchies are flatter and their structures more open. The guerrilla force takes over from the standing army.

Robin Murray (1989a: 47)

Post-Fordism is not a reality, not even a coherent vision of the future, but mainly an expression of hope that future capitalist development will be the salvation of social democracy.

Simon Clarke (1990: 75)

Technological Determinism and Social Choice

The different theories of post-industrialism – the information society, post-Fordism, post-modernism – overlap one another. The differences are more than those of emphasis, certainly; but certain themes and figures recur. Information technology, for instance, which more or less defines the information society idea, is also central to the analysis of the other two theories. Globalization is another common denominator. Decentralization and diversity feature prominently in all accounts of the new era.

What distinguishes these accounts is therefore not so much the particular development they single out as the frameworks they use to examine them. Information society theorists tend to adopt an optimistic, evolutionary approach that puts all the emphasis on major new clusters of technological innovations. The information revolution is the latest, and by so much the most progressive, step in the sequence of changes that have transformed human society since earliest times (history is 'a succession of rolling waves of change': Toffler 1981: 13). Like the agricultural and industrial revolutions before it, its basis is in new techniques and new types of energy, new forms and forces of production (both Bell and Toffler are ex-Marxists and seem reluctant to throw off all the habits of a misspent youth). The new technology determines, in a more or less regular way everywhere, new forms of life. Work, play, education, family relationships and structures of feeling gradually adapt or succumb to the pressures and opportunities of the new technical forces.

If the theory of the information society emphasizes the forces of production, post-Fordist theory emphasizes the relations of production. Technology loses its neutral or inherently progressive character and is put instead within a matrix of social relations that determines its use and application. This does not, it must be stressed, necessarily entail a gloomy view of current developments. Post-Fordists tend to be left-wing radicals of various sorts; but this can lead them to view the new state of things with optimism as much as disquiet.

The contrasting attitudes to recent changes in Italy illustrate this very well. Italy is also a good example because it was developments there that first gave rise to post-Fordist theory. The Italian case can therefore usefully provide us with the elements of post-Fordist analysis.

The Third Italy

During the 1970s and 1980s, Italian and other observers began to document and discuss a phenomenon that they came to call *la Terza Italia*, the Third Italy. The Third Italy was distinguished from, on the one hand, the First Italy of large-scale mass production, concentrated in the industrial triangle of Turin, Milan and Genoa; and, on the other hand, the Second Italy of the *mezzogiorno*, the economically undeveloped South. The Third Italy was, by contrast, a dynamic area of small firms and workshops in the central and north-eastern regions of the country: Tuscany, Umbria, the Marche, Emilia-Romagna, Veneto, Friuli, Trentino-Alto Adige.

In these regions, small workshops and factories employing usually no more than 5–50 workers, and often less than 10, had come to constitute the core of thriving 'industrial districts'. Each region specialized in a range of loosely related products. Tuscany specialized in textiles and ceramics; Emilia-Romagna produced knitwear, ceramic tiles, automatic machines and farm machinery; in the Marche, shoes were the main product; Veneto also produced shoes as well as ceramics and plastic furniture.

The main features of production in the Third Italy were what one of its leading students has called 'productive decentralization and social integration' (Brusco 1982). This is another way of stating the principles of the industrial district, as classically expounded by Alfred Marshall in his account of the industrial districts of nineteenth-century Birmingham and Sheffield (Bellandi 1989b; Beccatini 1990). But it would be wrong if this reference to the past were to make us think of the Italian industrial districts as somehow traditional and old-fashioned. There were indeed artisanal and even, in agriculture, co-operative traditions in this area. But most of the workshops and factories were brand new. They were 'high-technology cottage industries' employing the latest numerically controlled tools. Their products were sophisticated and design-conscious, enabling them to penetrate international as well as national markets. Their workers were as well-paid as workers in the large plants in the north; unemployment rates in the area were generally lower than elsewhere in Italy. Transport, housing, education and social security benefits were all of a markedly high standard, thus providing an additional 'social wage'.

Social relations within the firm, between firms, and between the firms and their surrounding community, were certainly on the pattern of the classic industrial district. Most workers were highly skilled, and there was little sense of distinction between them and their supervisors. It was easy to move from being an artisan to being an entrepreneur. The aim of designing new products, and of exploiting gaps in the market, meant that there was constant collaboration between entrepreneurs, designers, engineers, and workers. Taken with the small size of enterprises, this made for a flexible division of labour and flattened hierarchies within the firm. Conception and execution, separated in the Taylorist and Fordist practices of the large firms, were here to a good extent reunited.

The collaborative, collective character of relations within the firm was reproduced in its relation with other firms. As with industrial districts elsewhere, a 'monocultural' area emerged. Firms had a low degree of vertical integration and depended on each other for a wide range of specialized activities. A dense system of subcontracting lay at the heart of the local economy. The 'extraordinarily rich and complex relationship' (Brusco 1989: 261) between clients (producers of finished goods) and subcontractors (producers and designers of parts and services) kindled innovation and enhanced adaptability. Clients, it was often said, arrived to ask not that a product be made but that a problem be solved (Sabel 1984: 223; Brusco 1986: 188).

Collaboration went further. Firms passed on orders to each other and shared in the costs of expensive equipment. They pooled their resources to set up local associations of specialists for the collective provision of marketing, accounting and technical services. Ash Amin has stressed how different all this is from the traditional pattern of small firms and traditional systems of subcontracting:

> We are not talking about independent small firms in the traditional sense, nor about subcontractors for large firms, but about the development of an industrial system (almost a corporation) composed of inter-linked but independently owned production units . . . The model's economic power lies in its approximating, as it were, to a corporation with its labour divided between many spontaneous centres of production, whose relationship with each other is nevertheless competitive – a corporation without a roof. The single elements of the system flourish as a result of their interdependence . . . (Amin 1989: 118–19)

There is lastly the role of the local community as a whole, in its social and political aspects. The financial and political institutions of the region did not just respond positively to the individual or collective approaches of firms, for loans and other forms of support; banks and city and regional political authorities themselves took an active part in promoting and sustaining the small- firm economy in their area. In the regions of the Third Italy, 'localist' traditions had grown up, fostered by Socialist and Communist subcultures in the central regions and Catholic subcultures in the north-east. The political parties and other institutions of the subculture had created a climate of mutual support and reciprocity among employers and workers – a 'social compromise' – and had undertaken to mitigate the social costs of the economic flexibility and rapid readjustments of the small-firm economy. They had constructed industrial estates at low rents, promoted professional training, arranged low interest loans, negotiated favourable tax arrangements with central government, and established an infrastructure of social services to support workers and their families (Triglia 1989; 1990).

These initiatives of the political subcultures of the Third Italy were well rewarded. Modena and Reggio, for instance, which ranked respectively the 17th and 12th richest provinces in Italy in 1970, were by 1979 the 2nd and 4th richest (Brusco 1982: 168). The success of the regions as a whole was reflected in the fact that by 1977 they contributed nearly 28 per cent of Italy's manufacturing exports, compared with 20 per cent in 1968 (Amin 1989: 114). Similarly, the Third Italy was responsible for the fastest growth rate in employment in the country between 1971 and 1981 (Sforzi 1990: 106).[1]

The Third Italy is not, it is clear, the product of some spontaneous, undirected development. Values, purposes and politics have played a significant part in its growth. But whose values and purposes? Some critics claim to have discerned a less happy and more sinister intent behind the prosperous and harmonious appearance. The Third Italy, they argue, is largely the result of a flight from the power of organized labour and an attempt to regain control of the labour force. It is no coincidence, they say, that small firm development took off in the early 1970s. Employers in the large plants of the North reacted to the massive strikes and labour disturbances of the late 1960s by decentralizing production and resorting to subcontracting on a large scale. In particular they sought to head off the threat posed by the 1970 *Statuto dei Lavoratori* and the other labour legislation of the early 1970s, the most tangible gain of the workers following the *autunno caldo*, the 'hot autumn', of 1969.

The statutes of these years gave workers almost cast-iron security of employment and allowed unions to establish factory councils with considerable powers. Small firms – less than twenty members – were however exempted from the principal provisions of the acts. They were also given fiscal concessions, such as exemption from VAT, and were exempted from social security payments. Large employers, therefore, in alliance with skilled craftsmen who felt their position threatened by unskilled, largely migrant, labour, busied themselves in setting up or encouraging small firms which could handle much of the business of production without the restrictions set by the labour legislation and without having to take on the unions. They resorted to labour in the 'black economy' to restore the flexibility of employment that had been lost in the larger firms.

Many of the small firms, which as subcontractors depended heavily on the large northern firms, were established in the north-central and north-eastern regions. On this argument, therefore, the Third Italy is not primarily a phenomenon of independent small firms, organically linked to the local community, but a creation of large-scale capitalism faced with its most serious post-war challenge from organized labour. Further evidence for this view, it is suggested, is provided by the powerful re-emergence of the large firms in the Italian economy of the later 1980s, as economic conditions changed and industrial militancy waned (Bellandi 1989a: 51; Rey 1989: 92).[2]

This is a picture accepted in part even by those who champion the Third Italy as a hopeful development, perhaps even a portent of the future shape of things (for example, Brusco 1989: 259; Sabel 1989: 24). But generally they insist on the largely autonomous development of the Third Italy. Although some small firms were started by large firms seeking to evade statutory protection of workers, they soon broke their dependence and diversified both their customers and their activities (Sabel 1984: 222–3; Amin 1989: 116). In any case, most small firms were not the result of decentralization policies and their ties with large firms were largely non-existent (Bamford 1987: 3; Triglia 1989: 177). Moreover, though informal, casual labour played some part in the first stage of development, in the second stage the Third Italy was firmly based on a system of regular formal employment – an indication of its strength and stability (Mingione 1991: 320–1). Finally, small firms were holding their own in the 1980s in competition with the large firms (Brusco 1986: 195; 1989: 263).

The Third Italy, for its apologists, is not simply an economic phenomenon. It is also a social, cultural and political phenomenon of the first importance. It points towards the possibility, for almost the first time in the history of industrialism, of the reunification of mental and manual labour, and of work and the community. 'If', says Charles Sabel of the skilled workers in the small firms,

> you had thought so long about Rousseau's artisan clockmakers at Neuchâtel or Marx's idea of labor as joyful, self-creative association that you had begun to doubt their possibility, then you might, watching these craftsmen at work, forgive yourself the sudden conviction that something more utopian than the present factory system is practical after all. (Sabel 1984: 220)

'The high-technology industrial district,' says Edward Goodman, 'is an innovation of great importance in the realm of ideas which carries with it few of the moral objections to capitalism and few of the political objections to communism.' The Italian experience confirms the continuing relevance of the industrial district. It concerns moreover 'not only a small-firm economy' but 'a polity as well'.

> With their familial relationships, their generational build up of skills, their asymptotic dependence upon both competition and cooperation, their obvious sense of community and camaraderie, the industrial manufacturing districts of Italy are important cultural entities . . . The Italian small-firm economy offers at least one approach to the liberal dream of free and creative work as an essential part of liberty. (Goodman 1989: 20, 26, 29; see also Sabel and Zeitlin 1985: 152; Piore 1990)

The industrial district, it is clear, belongs on this account not just to the past but, adapted to new technology and new market conditions, the future of industrialism. Dualism, the co-existence of economic organizations with different principles of work and different relations to the community, is not an aberrant or outmoded feature of industrialism but one intrinsic to its very development. The Fordist pattern of mass production, where unskilled labour is put to work on single purpose machines to produce standard goods, is only one part of the story of industrialism. Alongside mass production there has always co-existed craft production, where skilled labour works on multi-purpose or universal machines to make specialized products, in limited quantities, for a variety of customers (Berger and Piore 1980; Samuel 1977; Brusco 1982: 179–80).

Historically, mass production has come to overwhelm craft production, in the sense of setting the pace and determining the purposes of production. But this was not because of some technological imperative or for reasons of economic efficiency. The dominance of mass production in the twentieth century was the result of social choices and political decisions (including those prompted by world war). That being so, social choice and political will can bring about a revitalization of small firms and industrial districts, especially in the conditions of the late twentieth century. This could mean a recovery of skill in work and, as in the past, a stronger tie between economic life and valued social purposes (Sabel and Zeitlin 1985).

The Italian example is therefore conceivably the harbinger of new times, a new kind of future for industrial societies. This is not, it must again be stressed, necessarily something that all welcome. For some it is a matter of the greatest apprehension. The critics of the Third Italy see in it a warning of the onset of a new, harsher phase of capitalism. But many of them accept that, taken with other examples from other parts of the industrial world, the Italian case is a revealing symptom of a possible movement to a new phase of industrial history. The industrial societies are becoming 'post-Fordist'. We have so far, in concentrating on the Italian example, considered post-Fordist features only implicitly. We need now to look at the theory in its most general form.

Flexible Specialization: The Second Industrial Divide?

Sebastiano Brusco notes, as an observable cause of the movement towards productive decentralization in Italy, 'the emergence since the mid-1960s of a significant demand for more varied and customized goods, produced in short series . . . ' (Brusco 1982: 171). This points to one of the most important sources of post-Fordist production everywhere (Piore and Sabel 1984: 183–93). Fordism was unparalleled in its ability to deliver standardized goods cheaply and on a mass scale. This was all right so long as there were sufficient groups in the population still awaiting their turn to enjoy the fruits of mass production. But what when these new groups of mass consumers were exhausted? What when demand significantly changes? What when the dictates of fashion, new styles of life, ceaseless technological innovation all call out for rapid turnover and swift changes of production? What when the mass market fragments into a diversity of consumer groups, each pursuing different things, each restlessly and rapidly discarding current patterns of consumption in search of new ones? And what, too, if this suits the requirements of contemporary capitalist firms, seeking to find ever new ways of exploiting and expanding markets? A novel pattern – novel at least in its scale – of production and consumption emerges, the pattern of 'flexible specialization'.

Flexible specialization depends on the new information technology (thus highlighting the interpenetration and overlap of current theories of social change). Numerically controlled machine tools allow for the economic production of small batches of goods – capital as well as consumer – directed to specialized sections of the market. The new tools make possible speedy changes of output, in response to new opportunities and new needs. New products do not require new tools, nor the expensive and lengthy readjustment or reassembly of old ones. Numerically controlled tools are non-specialized universal machines. New designs and new products are the result of relatively simple changes in the computer controlled programmes that direct the tools.

Flexible technology gives rise to flexible specialization. New ideas can be quickly turned into new products, newer ideas into newer products. Production is customized, geared to highly specific wants and needs in a constant state of flux. And since, as Adam Smith insisted, the division of labour is limited by the extent of the market, the segmentation of markets and their rapidly shifting patterns can lead to a lowering of the division of labour in enterprises. Customized, short-run production neither requires the large-scale plant and technology necessary to achieve economies of scale (which can be justified only by production in long series), nor can it depend on the unskilled or semi-skilled detail worker common in the industrial establishments of the Fordist kind. Flexible specialization calls for skill and flexibility in the worker as much as in the machines. It is this that has led some observers to hail the new developments as heralding a renaissance of craft production (Piore and Sabel 1984: 258–80; Sabel 1989: 32–3). Flexible specialization clearly works to the benefit of small firms, at least to the extent of offsetting the competitive advantages of economies of scale traditionally enjoyed by large firms. The rise of flexible specialization as a significant, not merely peripheral or 'interstitial', phenomenon in contemporary industrial economies is undoubtedly partly responsible for the strong revival of small firms, as widely observed and documented (for example, Lash and Urry 1987: 104, 115, 133, 148).

But there is no reason why large firms should not also benefit from flexible specialization, and there is considerable evidence that they are embracing it with conspicuous success. Economies of scale are replaced by 'economies of scope' – that is, the use by large plants of flexible manufacturing technologies to produce for several relatively small or segmented markets (Perez 1985: 449). Accompanied by the judicious use of subcontracting this can allow large firms to flourish in the new environment (Pollert 1988b: 61; Sabel 1989: 31–40).

A good example is Benetton, the highly successful Italian clothing company. Benetton is a family firm with 2,500 national and international outlets (all of them franchised). Specially designed electronic cash registers in these outlets constantly transmit on-line full data about sales – type of article, colour, size, etc. This information is centrally received and forms the basis for decisions about design and production. Benetton's own main production facilities – employing about 1,500 workers – are complemented by a network of over 200 subcontractors. These are small firms of 30–50 workers each, employing in all about 10,000 workers. These firms provide – at some cost to themselves – additional flexibility of volume. It is said that through this integrated system of flexible production Benetton has reduced the response time to market changes to ten days (Perez 1985: 454; Wood 1989b: 24–5; Murray 1989b: 57). Certainly Benetton is internationally famed for its capacity to catch fashion on the wing, to gear its production precisely to the changing styles of different subcultures and age groups.

The giant American computer firm IBM provides another good example of how, in a different way, the large firm can adapt to the era of flexible specialization. In the 1960s IBM tried, with its IBM 360, to produce the complete standardized computer – 'the Model T of the computer industry'. It was meant to be a machine for everyone and everything, a system complete in itself, a single product that would integrate the whole market and open the way to the economies of mass production. But by being a totally self-contained system, incorporating exclusively its own hardware and software, the 360 made it difficult to attach or substitute foreign components, which increasingly came to offer greater flexibility, efficiency or cheapness. Demand for the single, integrated computer system fell; the mass market disintegrated. IBM's strategy for the 1980s, the era of the microcomputer, reflected this experience. Instead of supplying a self-contained system, IBM designed and marketed its microcomputer so that all other producers could attach their hardware and software to it.

> IBM thus became not the manufacturer of a single integrated device but rather the organizing center of a community of computer companies, which collectively supplies the consumer with parts to build a customized system. In this way it no longer attempts to define the final product . . . Instead, IBM makes its mark by being the infrastructure of the home-computer industry, rather than the industry itself. (Piore and Sabel 1984: 204)

This is clearly highly reminiscent of classic accounts of the industrial district. IBM has been instrumental in creating a 'mono-culture' for the computer industry, though not so much now on a local as on a global plane. Self-limitation is the key to its success (it

holds a healthy 20 per cent share of the market). It has abandoned
the effort to monopolize the market, to saturate it with its products,
and to achieve total vertical and horizontal integration. It has let
go, in other words, the ways of classic mass production. Rather
it has seen itself as a part – a pivotal part – of a federation
of companies, each contributing specialist products and services
which can be combined in a variety of ways to suit the specific
needs of customers.

We can see, in fact, the beginnings of the erosion of the distinction between small firms in an industrial district and large
firms operating in an environment that puts the premium on
'disintegration' and 'disorganization'. Large firms now look to a
future in which they will increasingly appear as confederations of
small firms, rather than as large-scale, centralized, hierarchically-
coordinated organizations of the Taylorist kind. Such is the vision
of a leading British industrialist, Sir Adrian Cadbury:

> We will want, in future, to break these organizations down into their
> separate business units and to give those units freedom to compete
> in their particular markets. Large companies will become more like
> federations of small enterprises – not because 'small is beautiful' but
> because big is expensive and inflexible . . . I would expect tomorrow's
> companies . . . to concentrate on the core activities of their business,
> relying for everything else on specialised suppliers who would compete
> for their custom. (Quoted in Lash and Urry 1987: 106)

It is not, therefore, just in the survival or revitalization of small
firms that post-Fordist developments can be discerned. At all
levels of the economy similar tendencies are appearing. Small
firms in many cases led the way, but big firms, at least in some
countries, were not slow to catch on. In Italy, the 'First Italy' of
large plants has learnt from the 'Third Italy' of high-technology
cottage industries and has been making a successful come-back.
In Germany it is the large firms that have taken the initiative
towards reviving craft production, mainly through a system of
internal decentralization. So too in the United States the (much
slower) move towards flexible specialization has often occurred
within the larger rather than the smaller companies. Steel and
chemicals have been especially prominent here. The director of
Polaroid's speciality chemicals division describes his plant as a
set of 'giant test tubes, arranged as in a huge laboratory to let you
make whatever you want' (quoted in Piore and Sabel, 1984: 212).

In the new environment, the most successful economies tend to
be those in which large and small firms do not see each other as

rivals but as partners. In Germany and Japan the large firms have for long existed in co-partnership with a network of small firms that have maintained older traditions of craft production. Large firms in these countries have often encouraged and supported the small firm sector. In Japan it is the large firms that have been the main producers of numerically controlled general-purpose equipment that is easily programmed and suited to the thousands of small and medium-sized shops that do much of the batch production in metal-working. That many of these large firms themselves depend upon small subcontractors in the making of the general-purpose machines only shows how wrong it would be to regard post-Fordism as merely a partial or peripheral phenomenon, affecting only minor or dependent sectors of the economy (Piore and Sabel 1984: 217–20).

For all thinkers, flexible specialization has been at the heart of the theory of post-Fordism. It combines the capability of the new technology with the idea of a fundamental shift in the nature of the market in late twentieth-century industrial society. For some, it points to the way out of the global economic crisis of the 1970s and 1980s. In their much-discussed book, *The Second Industrial Divide*, Michael Piore and Charles Sabel argue that 'we are living through a second industrial divide' in our time, a transition comparable to the first industrial divide that saw the rise of mass production in the later nineteenth century (Piore and Sabel 1984: 5, 251–80). The way ahead is not certain – alternative strategies are possible – but they see some real hope in the current revival of craft production. Craft production, the suppressed alternative to mass production and for long a minor current in its stream, is once more showing itself to be a real possibility. Its return in more propitious circumstances could mean not just economic but social and political gains.

The computer, Piore and Sabel claim, 'is a machine that meets Marx's definition of an artisan tool: it is an instrument that responds to and extends the productive capacities of the user'. Put to the purposes of flexible specialization, it 'restores human control over the production process' (Piore and Sabel 1984: 261). The advent of flexible specialization thus means greater involvement and enhanced work satisfaction for the bulk of workers. Flexible specialization puts a premium on craft skills, and it also depends on collaboration between all grades of workers in the enterprise. Moreover, as in the industrial districts of the Third Italy, it can also bring about a closer integration between economic production and the general life of the local community.

Deliberately searching for the brightest prospect, Piore and Sabel speculate on the revival of a 'yeoman democracy' in the west, a form of 'collective individualism' that they see as the 'political analogue' of the 'co-operative competition' that characterized craft production in the nineteenth century. 'In the end, then, if we are right, the future refers to the past' (Piore and Sabel 1984: 306).

Other thinkers, while accepting the reality of flexible specialization, are less sanguine about its impact. For Scott Lash and John Urry, the crisis of mass production is central to what they call 'the end of organized capitalism'. Capitalism, they argue, achieved an 'organized' state in most western societies in the period from the 1870s to the Second World War. Organized capitalism – which follows 'liberal capitalism' – consisted of some familiar features of industrial society: the concentration, centralization and regulation of economic enterprises within the framework of the nation state; mass production along Fordist and Taylorist lines; a corporatist pattern of industrial relations; geographical and spatial concentration of people and production in industrial towns; cultural modernism.

'Disorganized capitalism', a still continuing process whose onset varied in different countries but which essentially started in the 1960s, reverses or modifies many of these central features. The development of an integrated world market has led to a de-cartelization and de-concentration of capital, as seen from the perspective of the nation state. Flexible specialization and flexible forms of work organization increasingly displace mass production. The mass industrial working class contracts and fragments, leading to a decline of class politics and the dissolution of the national corporatist system of industrial relations. A distinctive service class, originally an effect of organized capitalism, in its later development becomes a source of new values and new social movements that increasingly disorganize capitalism. Industrial de-concentration is accompanied by spatial de-concentration, as people and work move out of the older industrial cities and regions and as production is decentralized and dispersed globally ('de-industrialization'), much of it to the Third World. Pluralism and fragmentation increase in all spheres of society. The culture of post-modernism replaces that of modernism (Lash and Urry 1987: 3–7, 300–13; see also Offe 1985; Lash and Urry 1994).

'Disorganized capitalism' evidently takes in rather more than the flexible specialization that is the main plank of Piore and Sabel's theory. Moreover, despite its name it is not meant to suggest a system in a state of dissolution, or even necessarily of disorder. Disorganized capitalism, unfortunate as the choice of term might be, is simply counterposed to organized capitalism; it is a new phase of capitalism, a systematic process of restructuring in the face of new circumstances (Lash and Urry, 1987: 8). It is unstable, but that has been the condition of capitalism for most of its existence. We might even say, with Marx, that that has been capitalism's very principle (Berman 1983; Kumar 1988b). The chief novelty, according to Lash and Urry, is the demise – forever? – of the (putative) working-class project to reshape history.

> It once appeared that a whole set of economic, spatial and social developments in organized capitalism were propelling the working class forwards: it was on the side of history, it represented the 'modern'; it was interconnected with the forces which would reorganize society so as to realize some at least of this class's potential causal powers . . . What our claim amounts to is that such a possibility has in a number of specific western societies disappeared. Time cannot be set in reverse, the moment has passed. The power of a mass industrial working class to shape society in its own image are [*sic.*] for the foreseeable future profoundly weakened. (Lash and Urry 1987: 310–11; see also Murray 1988)

Unlike André Gorz, however, Lash and Urry do not wish to say 'goodbye to the working class' (Gorz 1982). They can envisage a future in which different sections of the working class will make common cause with sections of the service class in the new social movements, many of which will be locality-based or will express 'radical-democratic' rather than class-struggle ideologies. Much of the impetus to the new movements will come from post-modern culture which, although it has its negative and reactionary side, is also 'antihierarchical and consistent with principles of radical democracy'. It has the potentiality not simply to disintegrate older modes of individual and collective identity but also to reconstitute new ones. Above all, disorganized capitalism expresses capitalism's inherent instability and restlessness in a more extreme form than ever before, and so points to qualitative changes of culture and politics in the future.

> The world of a 'disorganized capitalism' is one in which the 'fixed, fast-frozen relations' of organized capitalist relations have been swept away. Societies are being transformed from above, from below, and from within. All that is solid about organized capitalism, class, industry, cities, collectivity, nation-state, even the world, melts into air. (Lash and Urry 1987: 312–13)

'New Times'

Before we decide what reality this flight of rhetoric might reflect, we should consider one further general view of current changes. Post-Fordist theories – following in the footsteps of Antonio Gramsci's influential treatment of Fordism in the *Prison Notebooks* – usually have a left-wing provenance. They are attempts by radical theorists to come to terms with what are seen as fundamental and far-reaching changes in the nature of contemporary capitalism. Many thinkers remain hopeful that, despite what these changes might suggest about capitalism's capacity to renew itself, there may still be some scope for the realization of socialist aims, as historically conceived. But a basic ambivalence remains. Post-Fordist capitalism is still, after all, capitalism. It is driven as insistently as ever before by the motor of the accumulation process. The restructuring implicit in post-Fordism is intended to strengthen, not weaken, capitalism. There may be some unexpected bonuses for radicals – the revival of craft skills, a service class not necessarily wedded to capitalism and willing to challenge it at certain points – but these clearly have to be assessed in the context of a global economic system whose outstanding feature is dominance by transnational corporations of unprecedented wealth and power.

This ambivalence is most acutely to be felt in the variety of post-Fordist theory presented by British Marxists under the banner of 'New Times'. First stated in a series of articles in the journal *Marxism Today*, the perspective was later substantially adopted by the executive committee of the British Communist Party and published by them as *The Manifesto for New Times* (June 1989). Subsequently many of the original articles, accompanied by extracts from the *Manifesto* and together with critical responses, were brought together in a book, *New Times* (Hall and Jacques 1989a).

Gramsci, in his 'Americanism and Fordism' (c.1931), had defined Fordism in the broadest possible terms. Fordism had introduced a new epoch in capitalist civilization. It marked the passage to a 'planned economy'. But it was not just production that was planned, it was also the person. Fordism did not stop at the factory gates but invaded the home and the most private and intimate spheres of the worker's life.[3] The aim was the creation of 'a new type of worker and of man'. Fordism meant the assembly line, but it also mean Prohibition and 'puritanism', the attempt to regulate the sexual and familial life of the worker along with his work life. 'The new methods of work,' said Gramsci, 'are inseparable from a specific mode of living and of thinking and feeling' (Gramsci 1971: 302).

Post-Fordists of the 'New Times' school have been similarly wide-ranging in their accounts of the new times. As with other post-Fordists, they single out flexible specialization as the force that is 'orchestrating and driving on the evolution of the new world.' But in the spirit of Gramsci they argue that 'diversity, differentiation and fragmentation' – the hallmarks of post-Fordism – are replacing 'homogeneity, standardization and the economies and organizations of scale' in more than simply the economic sphere.

> Just as Fordism represented, not simply a form of economic organisation but a whole culture . . . so post-Fordism is also shorthand for a much wider and deeper social and cultural development . . . The transition, then, is epochal – not in the sense of the classic transition from feudalism to capitalism, but as fundamental and far-reaching as, say, the transition in the closing stages of the 19th century from the 'entrepreneurial' to the advanced or organised stage within capitalism. (Hall and Jacques 1989b: 12)

As these quotations suggest, the New Times theorists agree with much of the analysis that we have already considered in the works of Piore and Sabel and Lash and Urry (whose writings they freely draw upon). For the New Times thinkers, too, the Italian experience has a special significance. Likewise they also stress the importance of the new information technology. What distinguishes the New Times approach – reflecting perhaps the more decidedly Marxist orientation of this group – is the breadth of its analysis and the more schematic nature of its presentation. It binds, within its opposition of Fordism and post-Fordism, elements of politics and culture together with changes in work and organization, and in production and consumption. In Marxist terms, its concern is as much with the reproduction of the social relations of production as with the system of production itself. This means it has drawn attention to changes in education and socialization, to a new role for the state, to the restructuring of the mass media in the information industries, and to new forms and patterns of consumption and consumer behaviour.

Various attempts have been made to express schematically the differences between Fordism and post-Fordism, in all their various dimensions (see, for example, Harvey 1989: 174–9; Rustin 1989: 56–7). Put simply, the changes are generally said to be as follows.

In the *economy*: the rise of a global market and of global corporations, and the decline of national enterprises and the nation state as the effective units of production and regulation; flexible specialization and the dispersal and decentralization of production, replacing mass marketing and mass production; flatter hierarchies and an emphasis on communication rather than command in organizations; vertical and horizontal disintegration, and an increase in subcontracting, franchising, internal marketing within firms, and the hiving-off of functions; rise in the number of flexi-time, part-time, temporary, self-employed and home workers.

In *politics and industrial relations*: the fragmentation of social classes, the decline of national class-based political parties and class voting, and the rise of social movements and 'networks' based on region, race or gender or on single-issue politics (for example, the anti-nuclear movement); 'peripheral', sub- and supra-national movements; the decline of mass unions and centralized wage bargaining and the rise of localized, plant-based bargaining; a labour force divided into core and periphery; the end of the class compromise of corporatism; the break-up of standardized, collectivist welfare provision, and the rise of consumer choice and private provision in welfare.

In *culture and ideology*: the rise and promotion of individualist modes of thought and behaviour; a culture of entrepreneurialism; the end of universalism and standardization in education, and the rise of modularity and pupil- and parent-choice; fragmentation and pluralism in values and life-styles; post-modernist eclecticism, and populist approaches to culture; privatization in domestic life and leisure pursuits.

New Times theorists admit that post-Fordist changes have benefited the Right more than the Left; or, at least, that the Right has been quicker to capitalize on the changes than the Left. Reaganism and Thatcherism have been the principal beneficiaries of post-Fordist developments. Left-wing thinkers and parties have been slow to throw off the heritage of theories and policies conceived within the framework of national, organized capitalism. The Keynes–Beveridge managerial/welfare state has been for them the premise of all their thinking about the future; they have found themselves floundering when the ideas and institutions that underpinned that system have crumbled. 'The shadow of Fordism haunts us even in the terms in which we oppose it' (Murray 1989a: 42). 'We do not yet . . . speak the language of the future' (*Manifesto for New Times* 1989: 4).

Especially acute is the crisis for socialists in eastern Europe, as societies there throw off their own kind of Fordist heritage. 'Soviet-type planning,' Robin Murray reminds us, 'is the apogee of Fordism. Lenin embraced Taylor and the stopwatch. Soviet industrialisation was centred on the construction of giant plants, the majority of them based on western mass-production technology' (Murray 1989a: 41). Now that system is being destroyed by its very fidelity to Fordism. 'Its statist and inflexible social, economic and political forms have been undermined, not only in competition with the west, but by its own species of Fordism – an obsession with quantity, the centralised plan, the masses, the suppression of variety, and the suffocating grip of centralism and authoritarianism' (Hall and Jacques 1989b: 16).

Nevertheless New Times theorists have accepted the challenge of post-Fordism – even if largely in the Carlylean spirit of 'you'd better'. They refuse to give way to pessimism in the face of the failure of certain historical outcomes as classically predicted by Marxism. The world has changed, but that is what any good Marxist should have expected. Capitalism remains in place, is indeed, in its global phase, more deeply entrenched than ever before; but in both east and west new opportunities for challenging it are opening up. A marked feature of the New Times, say Hall and Jacques, is 'the proliferation of the sites of antagonism and resistance, and the appearance of new subjects, new social movements, new collective identities – an enlarged sphere for the operation of politics, and new constituencies for change' (Hall and Jacques 1989b: 17). The *Manifesto* gives, as examples from Britain, the Green movement, 'local campaigns' on such matters as health services, transport, and food hygiene, and 'anti-inequality campaigns' over the poll tax and in defence of child benefit (*Manifesto for New Times*, 1989: 27). Others have championed social movements structured around the 'collective identities' of gender, sexuality and race, or strategies designed to foster a culture of 'socialist individualism' around the concept of citizenship (Brunt 1989; Leadbeater 1989; Weeks 1989).

According to many New Times theorists, globalization itself – the source of so many of the changes leading to post-Fordism – should be seen as an opportunity as much as a threat. Globalization lifts politics and culture above the parochial level of the nation state, and suggests new connections and interdependencies between all the peoples of the world. It makes possible alliances between First, Second and Third World movements to an extent impossible in earlier phases of capitalism. And it is not just the relationship between peoples of the world that New Times presses us to renegotiate. New Times also demands 'a new conception of the relationship between the human race and the planet earth. Globalisation suggests interdependence and cooperation on a new scale and in new forms, not simply competition based on narrow national and economic interests. New Times, in short, is about making a new world' (Hall and Jacques 1989b: 20; see also *Manifesto for New Times* 1989: 27–8).

New Times, Old Story?

It would be easy to condemn post-Fordism, especially in its New Times form, as a 'Thatcherism (or Reaganism) of the Left'. It has been accused of promoting 'designer socialism', of being, indeed, 'the socialism of designers', a vision of the future as it looks to the new service class based in the media, the universities and the information technology industries (Rustin 1989: 63). The language it uses, the language of individualism, choice and diversity, can be said to pay excessive homage to the vocabulary of the New Right. When a New Times theorist speaks of 'consuming as a source of power and pleasure', and of 'the hyper-eroticisation of a visit to the shops' (Mort 1989: 161–2), it is difficult not to feel that even where the language is used ironically there has been a considerable shift towards the perspective of the Left's traditional antagonists.[4] 'For socialists,' as Michael Rustin says, 'there has to be more to life than shopping . . . ' (Rustin 1989: 68).[5]

More serious is the accusation that not only have some sections of the Left conceded too much to the New Right, they have failed to see that the principal elements of what they embrace are precisely the source of the current strength of the Right and the basis of its repeated electoral success. 'Thatcherism,' says Rustin, 'may be understood as a strategy of post-Fordism initiated from the perspective of the right. That is to say, a determined attempt to use the advantages of new technology, mobility of capital and labour, the centrality of consumption, and more decentralized forms of organization, to strengthen capital and to attack the corporate structures of labour' (Rustin 1989: 75).

Other critics have observed that one of the key components of post-Fordist analysis, the break up of mass production and of the mass homogeneous working class formed around it, provides the central building block of New Right strategy. The New Right has seized the opportunity of a divided work-force to make inroads into the working class, the old heartland of the Left.

> The post-Fordist division of the work-force between a skill-flexible core and a time-flexible periphery, which is now replacing the old manual/non-manual distinction, underlies a shift from the post-war vision of a one-nation mass consumption system to a two-nations model based on the affluent flexible worker plus a social security state. Whereas the Labour Party, *qua* social democratic, could gain from the Fordist system with its Keynesian welfare state politics, it is the Conservative Party which is pioneering the transition to post-Fordism and identifying itself with the class interests of workers at its core. (Jessop et al. 1987: 109–10)

This is, as it were, the complaint of the old Left against the New. There is, however, another variety of contemporary left-wing thinking which, like the New Times group, accepts that there is a crisis of Fordism but sees its resolution in different terms. The so-called 'Regulation School' of French theorists do not see, not yet at any rate , a passage into a potentially hopeful post-Fordist society. What others characterize as post-Fordist they rather regard as 'neo-Fordist' strategies designed to enable capitalism to over-come its current crisis.

The Regulationists – chief among whom are Michel Aglietta, Robert Boyer and Alain Lipietz – see the history of capitalism as marked by successive 'modes of development' in which a particular 'regime of accumulation' is guided by a particular 'mode of regulation'. That is to say, at any given time the capitalist's efforts to extract surplus-value at an increasing rate is dependent on the particular constellation of class forces – especially in the work-place – and the institutional arrangements governing relations between firms and between capital and labour. In the nineteenth century, effective craft control on the shop floor and largely unregulated competition between a multitude of firms made for a regime of accumulation that was marked by 'extensive' growth: a form of growth largely dependent not on technical innovation or increases in productivity but on large reserves of cheap labour and simple geographical expansion of the system.

With the advent of scientific management (Taylorism) and the automated factory (Fordism) in the 1920s – and 'Fordism is nothing more than Taylorism plus mechanization' – a new regime of accumulation and a new mode of regulation supervened. The regime of accumulation was now characterized by 'intensive' growth: that is, growth came predominantly through investment in fixed capital embodying technical advance. This created the potential both for regular increases in productivity and for mass consumption. The new mode of regulation was slower to develop – it needed the slump and social upheaval of the 1930s to speed it on – but it was more or less established throughout the industrial world following the Second World War. As opposed to the competitive mode of the nineteenth century, it can be called the monopoly mode (similar to the 'organized capitalism' of Scott and Urry). Its basis was the scientific management of organizations, oligopolistic price arrangements between firms, and the determination of wages and levels of consumption through a complex system of employer-labour and governmental institutions (Keynesian fiscal policies buttressed by the welfare state).

It is this Taylorist–Fordist mode of development – responsible for the great postwar boom and prevalent until the late 1960s – that is now, according to the Regulationists, in crisis. It has exhausted its potential for growth. This is shown especially in declining productivity, as Taylorist–Fordist intensifications of the labour process bring diminishing returns, partly through increased worker alienation and resistance. Since the late 1960s there has been a sharp fall in the rate of profit throughout the capitalist world.

The Regulationists' own solution to the crisis, as they interpret it, is a return, in a more explicit and thoroughgoing way, to the 'class compromise' (or 'social contract') of the post-war era that made possible the period of sustained growth. In present conditions this would involve, they accept, nothing less than an anti-Taylorist, post-Fordist revolution. Workers would be made formal participants in decision-making; their commitment to the system would be sought by enriched forms of work and guarantees of job security and welfare benefits. This would break the current blockage on increased productivity, and both capital and labour would benefit from a faster growing economy.

Instead, according to the Regulationists, what has happened is the attempt by capital to resolve the crisis by establishing a system of 'global Fordism'. This has taken the form of a series of 'neo-Fordist' strategies. Production has been decentralized, not simply nationally but internationally, by removing it to the cheap-wage regions of the world – the newly industrializing countries of East Asia and South America, and certain parts of southern Europe. The central control and research functions meanwhile remain in the metropolises of the advanced industrial countries. Flexible specialization and devolved management have also been employed as part of a strategy to lessen the burdens of firms and to bypass or break strong labour organizations. So 'post-Fordist' elements in the First World co-exist alongside classic Fordism and 'peripheral Fordism' in the Third World. Actually there are not three worlds (especially after the collapse of state socialism in eastern Europe); there are only segments of a global capitalist system trying to maintain its dynamism in a period of crisis.[6]

The Regulation theorists have their own shortcomings – among other things, an overestimation of the 'Taylorist–Fordist watershed' in capitalist development – but in their account of the contemporary world there is much that is convincing. Above all they allow us to consider many allegedly post-Fordist developments in a new light. Unlike many of the old Left they do not dismiss the changes as merely superficial variations on an old theme. Something new *is* afoot, even if it does not bear the interpretation of many of the more optimistic adherents of the post-Fordist idea. The new features demand a framework of understanding that is cast on the widest possible (world) plane, not narrowly focused on the advanced industrial nations. In that light much that appears post-Fordist can be shown to carry the stamp of a system of production that remains substantially Fordist, even though it is under considerable strain – and, according to the Regulationists, in its global form ultimately burdened by the same contradictions that afflicted classic Fordism.

The Regulationist critique chimes in well with the general charge made against post-Fordist theory: namely, that it mistakes effects for causes, that what it sees as the primary facts are derivative or dependent products of less visible processes. Post-Fordism has for instance made much of the rise or revival of localism and particularism, the cultivation of identity through attachment to place and to local cultures and traditions. It not merely picks out but celebrates the ethnic revival, the rise of 'peripheral nationalisms', the struggles to conserve local ways and local histories.

But to what extent are localism and pluralism autonomous phenomena, the self-willed responses of individuals to mass production and mass centralized politics? To what extent are they rather the consequences and outcomes of far-reaching changes in the strategies of transnational corporations seeking to make the most effective mix of economies of scale and scope? The cultivation of local differences, the celebration of ethnicity, and the stimulation of consumer preference for a variety of exotic, 'authentic' cultural objects and experiences, make good sense to 'flexible transnationalists' in search of new market niches to exploit

(Robins 1989; Harvey 1989: 141–97). The global standardization of *Dallas* and McDonald's can co-exist quite happily with the artificial diversity of Disneyland and the manufactured localism of the heritage industry. All are of course big business, among the biggest and fastest growing today. Again, this is not the whole story, as we shall see when we consider the phenomenon again under the heading of post-modernism. But at the very least it forces us to acknowledge in 'localism' and 'diversity' a motive and a force not very different from those that have propelled capitalism for most of its history.

This is part of a familiar argument – we have met it already with the idea of the information society – and it may be as well to list here some of the detailed criticisms that have been made of the post-Fordist theorists. There is, firstly, the importance attached to the Third Italy in post-Fordist accounts. The Third Italy, many writers allege, is historically and culturally unique. Its pattern of industrial districts makes it untypical not just in the case of Italy but in the industrial world as a whole. The same is true of the other examples of industrial districts that feature so prominently in the post-Fordist literature: Route 128 and Silicon Valley in the United States, the Cambridge–Reading–Bristol complex in Britain, Oyonnax in France, Baden-Württemberg in Germany, and several regions in Japan, such as the industrial district of Sakaki (Sabel 1989: 22–31). These are not only very different from each other but represent distinct economic tendencies – from the persistence of pre-industrial craft traditions (for example, Baden-Württemberg) to the rise of new high-technology complexes (for example, Silicon Valley) and the practice of sub-contracting (for example, Japan). Industrial districts have always been a part – but only a part – of industrial production. Their survival or re-emergence in several places does not, as such, make them the harbingers of a new world. The post-Fordists, on this view, have taken a motley crop of isolated examples from across the world and bundled them together into a composite but highly misleading picture of a general world-wide phenomenon (Murray 1987: 92–3; Sayer 1989: 672; Clarke 1990: 80; Amin and Robins 1990: 195–207; Amin 1991: 136–7).

Then there is 'flexible specialization' and the 'flexible firm', the heart of the post-Fordist analysis of economic change. This envisages the division of the work-force into a 'core' of multi-skilled craft-type workers, permitting 'functional flexibility' of tasks and products, and a 'periphery' of casually-employed, relatively unskilled workers, permitting 'numerical flexibility' in the labour market. This, say the critics, is not happening on any great scale, and certainly not in anything like the terms suggested by the post-Fordists. It is not in fact occurring very much in 'leading edge' manufacturing firms – those highlighted by post-Fordist theorists – but, in so far as it is happening, rather in service industries and in public sector employment. Moreover it affects not so much men – the focus of the post-Fordist Proudhonian vision of the resurgence of the independent craft worker – as women, together with other traditionally weak groups such as ethnic minorities, migrant workers, and young people. In other words, the rise of flexibility, to the extent that it is a reality, is not the sign of some new principle of work and organization but a continuation of traditional patterns of labour market segmentation by gender, race and age. These have been adapted to sectoral changes in the economy – the move from manufacturing to services – and intensified by government policies, such as those designed to deal with youth unemployment. Thus for instance women workers, who were the mainstay of the mass production industries of the 1930s – men were always a minority in the mass assembly-line system of production – became the insecurely-employed and low-skilled ('numerically flexible') service workers of the 1970s and 1980s (Pollert 1988a, 1988b, 1991b; Hakim 1988: 610; Jensen 1989; Walby 1989; Lovering 1990; Hyman 1991).

The most fundamental charge against the post-Fordists is that they have mythologized Fordism itself. They have merged Taylorism and Fordism, identified both with mass production, and assumed the dominance of this unified formation in the industrial systems of the advanced economies in the first half of the twentieth century. Now, post-Fordists argue, mass production industries have run up against a wall; Taylorist methods of work organization have met with increasing resistance from workers; and new kinds of industries, based on the principles of flexibility and local production, are emerging to challenge the old mass centralized forms. A new system is coming into being, sufficiently different in kind from the old to warrant the name 'post-Fordist'. Its birth-pangs are evident not only in the industrial system itself, narrowly defined, but in wide-ranging changes in politics, culture and social institutions.

But, respond the critics, this model collapses at virtually every important point. Taylorism is a different thing from Fordism; it was and is capable of application not just to mass production but to small- and medium-batch production. It can even be applied to the new forms of teamworking in supposedly 'post-Fordist' enterprises. Mass production, whatever its strategic importance in the economy, was never, nor could it be, the dominant form of industrial production. Small firms and 'craft production' – not of course necessarily the same thing – always persisted alongside mass production, as had been the case since the Industrial Revolution; they performed then as now not vestigial but indispensable functions. There is no revival or renaissance of these forms, merely continuation. The opposition, 'mass production versus flexible specialization', is false: even the car industry, supposedly the very type of mass production, employs both methods. The assembly-line itself, the very symbol of Fordism, was never present in more than a minority of plants in the advanced economies (Williams et al. 1987, 1992; Sayer 1989; Wood 1989b; Thompson 1989: 218–29; Clarke 1990a, 1990b).

The most serious criticism argues that the post-Fordists mistake the very nature of the Fordist revolution. They fail to see that what they call 'the crisis of Fordism' and its resolution into post-Fordist forms are in fact part of a continuing evolution – or rather, part of the 'permanent revolution' that is Fordism. Fordism cannot simply be equated with 'inflexibility', the assembly-line, and mass production. As Simon Clarke, following Gramsci, emphasizes, Fordism was not just a new technology; it was the systematic application of new techniques – social as well as scientific in the technical sense – to the organization of production in all its spheres, including the regulation of the relation between management and workers. In this sense it continued the basic drive of the Industrial Revolution: 'it marked the culmination of the penetration of capital into production, which means that Fordism is synonymous with capitalist production *as such*' (Clarke 1990a: 80).

Far from giving rise to 'inflexibility', the principles of Fordism have proved applicable in 'an extraordinarily wide range of technical contexts'. What Henry Ford actually introduced was *flexibility* in mass production, hence paving the way for constant technological dynamism and maximum adaptability of production methods. The fact that Ford himself was, in the 1930s, the victim of his own revolution did not prevent further conquests by Fordism under new leaders, for instance Albert Sloan of General Motors. And this has been the case ever since: Fordism has manifested itself in a number of technological and organizational guises. What has been hailed as 'neo-Fordist' or 'post-Fordist' is merely the latest, and is unlikely to be the last.

The Fordist sociological project is not a static one, but must develop
as it confronts obstacles to its resolution. This means that there cannot
be *one* Fordist project, but a range of them, some of which may prove
temporarily more successful than others, but none of which can ever
be fully realized. (Clarke 1990a: 81)[7]

Clarke remarks on the latest twist: 'Just as competitive pressures
from new, more highly developed and more flexible forms of
Fordism soon forced Ford to introduce Pinkerton's men and the
Service Department, so the flexible specialists and niche marketeers
are already coming under pressure from competitors who have
managed to reconcile economies of scope with economies of scale'
(1990a: 98). We have already noted that there is no intrinsic reason
why, faced with the challenge of new small companies exploiting
the new technology and changes in consumer taste, the older bigger
firms should not sooner or later also avail themselves of the new
opportunities. And that is precisely what has been happening.
Olivetti and Xerox are simply two of the best-known cases where
large companies have gone in for flexible specialization – involving
decentralized production and devolved managerial responsibility
– on a significant scale (Sabel 1989: 36).[8] In Britain, niche pioneers
such as Sock Shop and Tie Rack have collapsed spectacularly as
large clothing retailers such as Marks and Spencer have adapted
themselves to the market for more individualized and differentiated products (Pollert 1991b: 19). A similar story relates to the food
industry, where the large producers and retailers have pursued a
two-pronged strategy of the 'globalization of tastes' together with
the provision of specialized 'exotic' foods from all over the world.
McDonald's on the one hand; Safeways on the other (Smith 1991:
151–6).

The involvement of large firms in flexible specialization is not
in itself a riposte to the post-Fordists. Piore and Sabel, as we have
seen, have been happy to regard this development as, if anything,
strengthening their view of a general world-wide move towards
post-Fordism (Piore and Sabel 1984: 194–220; Sabel 1989). But
certainly it suggests, as Clarke indicates, a continuity of purpose
and outlook that casts doubt on the idea of a fundamentally
new departure, a 'second divide', in the evolution of industrial
societies. 'Fordism', it might seem, is still adequate to the task of
accounting for these developments in the large firms.

We can return, in this context, to the example of the giant
clothing firm, Benetton. Benetton has, for some post-Fordists,
been almost the banner company of post-Fordist practice (see, for

example, Murray 1989b). But it is an extremely ambiguous case. It undoubtedly prospered on the basis of flexible specialization, and in its origins has much of the Third Italy character about it. But it has now grown to such a size that it fits awkwardly – especially in the context of the Third Italy – into the model of interlinked small firms in an industrial district. In the 1980s Benetton became a huge multinational operation. It dominated its 'artisanal' subcontractors at home and its franchised retail outlets abroad. By 1990 it was said to open a new store somewhere in the world every day of the year. In a new move, it had also begun to open factories outside Italy, with different locations specializing in the production of one or more types of product. It did so for the familiar reason of taking advantage of cheaper labour costs outside Italy. Benetton hence came ever closer to the 'world car model' that is the very antithesis of the post-Fordist concept.[9] As Stephen Wood says, this raises many questions not just about Benetton but the whole theory reared on the opposition of mass production and flexible specialization.

> Ought we not to be emphasizing the similarities between the strat-
> egies of Benetton and the leading car companies: the globalization,
> increased automation, adaptation of just-in-time procedures and the
> intensified use of the computer for design, production and stock
> control? Benetton's development and dominance of a network of
> suppliers seems little different from that used by Japanese car firms,
> and its competitors have been considering ways of emulating it in the
> 1980s. Is the Benetton Economy . . . a world of flexible specialization
> or Japanese-led revitalized Fordism? (Wood 1989b: 25)

Which brings us neatly to Japan itself: like Benetton, a frequently-cited example of post-Fordist development and yet, also like Benetton, highly ambiguous. Sabel himself has called the Japanese model, with its decentralized production but centralized control, a case of 'flexible mass production'. He nevertheless believes that large Japanese corporations are 'adopting the organizational forms of the more decentralized large corporation' of the west. They are going in for 'quasi-disintegration', which will bring them closer to the post-Fordist model (1989: 38–9).

But for many commentators Japan, far from indicating the road to post-Fordism, is the most conspicuously successful example of the *alternative* to post-Fordism: a case perhaps of 'revitalized Fordism', but also perhaps of something quite different from any western system. For Andrew Sayer, Japan fits neither the model of Fordism nor of post-Fordism. He employs Ronald Dore's formula

of 'flexible rigidities' to describe an industrial system marked
by an exceptionally high degree of organization coupled with
an equally high degree of 'vertical disintegration' (58 per cent of
Japanese workers are in firms of less than 100 employees and 30
per cent in firms of only 1–4 employees). In Japan, vertical disintegration and mass production go hand in hand; sub-contractors
often do the same kind of routine, repetitive work associated with
mass production in the west. So, concludes Sayer:

> while the organizational forms of Japanese capital do have some things
> in common with flexible specialization, they also have characteristics
> which call into question not only the nature of 'flexibility', but also the
> central contrast between the alleged decline of mass production and rise
> of small-batch production, and the implicit association between vertical
> integration and mass production. (Sayer 1989: 691; see also Sayer and
> Walker 1992: 212–21)

'Whatever the conditions of mass production in the West it is
alive and well in Japan' (Sayer 1989: 666). Wood too notes that
'most of the products associated with the ascendancy of Japan in
world trade are classic mass-produced goods, such as cameras,
transistors, televisions and cars, and Japan more than any other
country has opened up the markets for such new mass products
as videos and cassette players' (1989b: 32). Moreover Japanese
management has, without abandoning its commitment to mass
production, been able to tackle many of the problems associated
with Taylorist work organization : by such well-known schemes of
worker involvement as quality circles, and by adopting generally
paternalistic attitudes not just towards their own workers but also
towards their regular suppliers. 'This has "turned on their head"
many of the features of Taylorism as conventionally practised,
but not necessarily the fundamental principles of Fordism' (Wood
1989b: 33).

Continuity and Change

It may seem, after all this, that there is not much left of the
theory of post-Fordism. *Plus ça change* – as the titles of so many
of the critical contributions proclaim. Fordism itself can be made
to disintegrate into a series of discrete innovations which do not
necessarily add up to a coherent, sweeping set of changes – a new
'regime of accumulation', a Fordist 'revolution'. And if there was
no Fordist revolution, the idea of a post-Fordist revolution must

appear equally suspect. There were changes in the 1920s – the introduction of the assembly line, the application of Taylorism in various branches of industry. Similarly there have been changes in the 1970s and 1980s – a move towards more customized production, a splintering of the labour force, a degree of disintegration of organization and decentralization of production. Both sets of changes are important; neither marks a fundamental break in the order of capitalist industrialism. All can be seen as expressions of the technological dynamism and the constant revolutionizing of production that were inherent in the Industrial Revolution from the outset. Where novel features have appeared these can mostly be attributed to the growing internationalization and globalization of production that, once more, have been implicit in capitalism from its very inception (Sklair 1991; see also Amin and Robins 1990: 207–13; Hyman 1991: 266).

The danger, as with the criticism of the idea of the information society, is to harp too much on the theme of continuity and to refuse to acknowledge that new things are afoot. At the very least we should protest again at the comprehensiveness of the category of 'capitalism' or even 'industrialism', and to insist that changes 'within the system' – when was there a change *of* the system? – should not be treated as trivial. In any case, changes within the system, if they continue, presumably modulate at some point into changes of the system. They may not at any one time be sufficiently widespread or obvious to give the appearance of a fundamental shift of principle, the rise of a new 'paradigm' in economic and social life.[10] We should imagine what commonsense observers might have made of the new cotton factories that appeared in the north of England early in the nineteenth century. In a world still predominantly agricultural and artisanal, it might have appeared absurd – to all but a handful of prophets such as Saint-Simon and Robert Owen – to see these as the harbingers of an industrial revolution that would transform not just England but the world.

It is too early to judge post-Fordist developments in those epochal terms. But another aspect of the parallel may be more immediately important. The Industrial Revolution, as became increasingly clear, was not just about changes in the economy but gradually affected every sphere of social life. The industrialization of production was ultimately followed by the industrialization of the mind.

Post-Fordism, whatever our assessment of its persuasiveness, similarly makes claims going well beyond the economic. The narrowness of the criticism that centres almost exclusively on 'flexible specialization' ignores this. It is one of the virtues of the 'New Times' group to have made bold extrapolations and imaginative leaps of thought from contemporary developments. Flexible specialization may be the heart of the changes taking place – or it may be itself the symptom of wider changes. In neither case can it be considered by itself. The change in working life for a considerable number of people – and few of the critics deny that this is affecting strategic groups of professionals and several other categories of service workers (see, for example, Lovering 1990) – chimes in with other changes in family life, leisure, culture and politics.

It may be that some post-Fordists interpret these changes too optimistically, as extensions of freedom and creativity. For their critics, to the extent that they are occurring they are bringing in new varieties of exploitation and unfreedom. We shall leave it to the final chapter to assess these claims. The important thing to stress here is the need to consider the changes together. It is unlikely, on past experience, that they are occurring independently of one another. Moreover, it is just as possible that changes in culture and politics are pushing on changes in the economy as the other way round – or, at least, that the causal connections are two-way.

It is one of the impressive – as well as problematic – features of the theory of post-modernity that it takes on the whole world of change. As well as its own characteristic contribution it touches on many of the kinds of changes that we have been considering in the last two chapters. In dealing with it therefore we can look again, from a different angle, at some of the questions that have arisen in connection with those changes.

4

Modernity and Post-Modernity (I): The Idea of the Modern

Apart from some earlier attempts, it has been reserved in the main for our epoch to vindicate, at least in theory, the human ownership of treasures formerly squandered on heaven; but what age will have the strength to validate this right in practice and make itself their possessor?

G. F. W. Hegel (1971: 159)

We who are born at the close of this wonderful age are at once too cultured and too critical, too intellectually subtle and too curious of exquisite pleasures, to accept any speculations about life in exchange for life itself.

Oscar Wilde (1975: 41)

We no longer believe . . . , like the Greeks, in happiness of life on earth; we no longer believe, like the Christians, in happiness in an otherworldy life; we no longer believe, like the optimistic philosophers of the last century, in a happy future for the human race.

Benedetto Croce (in Hughes 1958: 428)

The End of the Modern?

Like post-industrialism and post-Fordism, post-modernism is essentially a 'contrast concept'. It takes its meaning as much from what it excludes or claims to supersede as from what it includes or affirms in any positive sense. The primary, or at least initial, meaning of post-modernism must be that it is not modernism, not modernity. Modernity is over.

This need not mean, many post-modernists hurry to say, that we have gone *beyond* modernity, that we are living in an entirely new era. The 'post' of post-modernity is ambiguous. It can mean what comes after, the movement to a new state of things, however difficult it might be to characterize that state in these early days. Or it can be more like the post of *post-mortem*: obsequies performed over the dead body of modernity, a dissection of the corpse. The end of modernity is in this view the occasion for reflecting on the experience of modernity; post-modernity is that condition of reflectiveness. In this case there is no necessary sense of a new beginning, merely a somewhat melancholy sense of an ending.

We shall be looking at both, and other, varieties of post-modernist theory. What, however, they all evidently share is some conception of the modern. Whatever meaning they give to the term post-modernism must refer to some particular idea of modernity. To understand and interrogate the post-modern we have first to understand the meaning of the modern.

Ancient, Medieval and Modern

'Modernity' and 'modernism' are two terms that are sometimes used interchangeably, sometimes given distinct meanings. I shall follow the second course. 'Modernity' I take to be a comprehensive designation of all the changes – intellectual, social and political – that brought into being the modern world. 'Modernism' is a cultural movement that occurred in the west at the end of the nineteenth century and, to complicate matters further, was in some respects a critical reaction against modernity. The two terms, even in these distinct senses, are certainly connected, and it is not always possible to be completely consistent in keeping them separate (the same is even truer of the parallel terms 'post-modernity' and 'post-modernism'). That is partly because there is no general consensus on their meanings. But it seems useful to try to maintain the distinction.

To begin, as one should, with the word itself. *Modernus*, from *modo* ('recently', 'just now') was a late Latin coinage on the model of *hodiernus* (from *hodie*, 'today'). It was first used, as an antonym to *antiquus*, in the late fifth century AD. Later such terms as *modernitas* ('modern times') and *moderni* ('men of today') also became common, especially after the tenth century.

Modernity is therefore an invention of the Christian Middle Ages. This should, in principle, have established as forceful a contrast with the ancient world as it is possible to imagine. The ancient world was pagan, the modern world Christian. That is to say, the former had been shrouded in darkness, the latter transformed by the appearance of God among men in the form of his son, Jesus Christ. With Christ, the whole meaning of human history was changed – or rather, we should say, history was for the first time given a meaning.

Christianity recharged the notion of time and history. It overthrew the naturalistic conception of the ancient world, whereby time was seen in the mirror of the cyclical change of the seasons, or the ceaseless alternation of day and night, or the generational cycles of birth, death, and new birth. In such a perspective, human time was regular and repetitive. It partook of the cyclical character of all created matter. There was change but no novelty.

The impossibility of there being anything really new in the world was further emphasized in the cosmological speculations of those, such as Plato, who saw in the created universe merely the emblem of an essentially timeless and unchanging Eternal Being. God gave the universe time and motion, said Plato in the *Timaeus*; but he still created it according to the basic pattern of eternity, which has being but no becoming; neither 'was' nor 'shall be' but only 'is'. When God ordered the heavens 'he made in that which we call time an eternal moving image of the eternity which remains for ever at one'. Time was made 'as like as possible to eternity, which was its model'; it is the 'copy' of that model, and remains inseparably bound to it (Plato 1977: 51–2). This means that time forever mirrors an eternity which is itself outside time and which never changes. The consequences of this view are apparent in the writings of the ancient historians, for whom 'events are important chiefly for the light they throw on eternal and substantial entities of which they are mere accidents' (Collingwood 1961: 43; but see also Momigliano 1977: 179–204).

Christianity, making use of its Jewish messianic heritage, infused time with meaning and purpose by focusing on an event, unrepeatable and incomparable, which it endowed with unique significance: the coming of Christ. With Christ, something absolutely new had happened in the world. Time was now irrevocably divided into time 'before Christ' and time 'after Christ'. Past, present and future were linked in a meaningful sequence; Christ's appearance had revealed the secret of history concealed from the ancients. The events narrated in the Bible, from the creation to the Incarnation, and its promise and prophecy of a future consummation in the Second Coming and the Last Judgement, tells a story of sin and redemption which occurs in time. Moreover, it is human time, historical time. Humanity is lifted above all the other orders of creation and made the vehicle of the divine purpose. Human history has, and must have, a different principle from natural history. All creation is God's creation, and subject to his will. But he has freely chosen to send his son among men, and so injected into human history a value indescribably higher than any in the non-human world.

Christianity not only privileges human history; it privileges the future dimension of that history. It has an eschatological view of history. The whole of history is seen from the point of view of its final end or consummation; all else is preparation, or waiting. The connection between past, present and future is not simply chronological but more importantly teleological. It is the final redemption of humanity, through Christ's agency, that makes sense of the human story, with all its vicissitudes and apparent obscurities.

This view casts a peculiar perspective back on the past. The past, as a tract of time, gets its meaning only retrospectively, through its contribution to the future. The past is not neutral, but neither does it have any value in and for itself. History, said Augustine, unfolds itself in 'the shadow of the future'. The past can be subdivided into periods or epochs – extending the great periodization of 'before' and 'after' Christ – each with its own character and each with its own contribution to the swelling act of human redemption. Each is necessary; each must take place in the right sequence. Eschatological history uses its knowledge of the future to cast its light back on the past; it engages in 'prophecy in reverse, demonstrating the past as a meaningful "preparation" for the future' (Löwith 1949: 6; see also Collingwood 1961: 46–56; Manuel 1965: 10–23; Le Goff 1982: 29–42).

It has been worth dwelling a little on the contrast between pagan and Christian concepts of time because it reveals an interesting feature in the history of modernity. It must be evident how much of what we understand as modernity is contained in the Christian philosophy of history. Here we have time taken out of the natural sphere and thoroughly humanized (even though under divine guidance). It is portrayed as linear and irreversible, unlike the cycles and recurrences of ancient thought. Christianity tells a story with a beginning (the creation and the Fall), a middle (Christ's first coming), and an end (Christ's second coming) – and it insists on that necessary order of events. At the same time in its understanding of the story it reverses chronology and views the story backwards, from its end point. It is future-oriented. It fills the present with a sense of expectation, setting up a permanent tension between the present and the future. It views the past merely as prologue to a present on its way to fulfilling the promise of the future.

These are, as we shall see, some of the principal hall-marks of modernity. They should have led the medieval Christian world to construe its distance from the ancient world with all the force of the common contrast between 'ancient' and 'modern'. And yet although the Middle Ages invented *modernus* and *modernitas* they made remarkably little of them. So far as their attitude to their own time were concerned, their 'modernity' differed little from the time conceptions of the ancients. For more than a millennium, in fact, 'modernity' displayed towards both the present and the future an indifference, bordering on contempt, that is in startling contrast to the radical reorientation towards time implicit in the Christian philosophy of history. It was not until the end of the seventeenth century that this concept of history precipitated the idea of modernity as we understand it today – and then only by jettisoning the framework of religion that had made the conception possible in the first place.

There were certainly some people in the medieval world who were sufficiently affected by the new sense of time to regard their own times as radically different from all preceding time. The Christians of the first centuries after Christ lived in the belief that his Second Coming was imminent. Their own time was a time of preparation for that supreme event. For believers in the Apocalypse, the Second Coming would inaugurate Christ's millennial kingdom on earth. Later, the followers of the twelfth-century Calabrian monk Joachim of Fiore similarly prepared themselves for a new time, the impending 'Third Age' of the Holy Spirit. This too would be a millennial age, a period of love, peace and joy on earth. Wherever and whenever millenarianism flourished in the Middle Ages, in fact, believers were bound to feel that their own time was charged with a special significance, and to act accordingly.

But even in the case of the millenarians, their times were important mainly because they presaged the end of time. They were of value not for what they were in themselves, for what they created, but because they heralded the end of all earthy life (even if after the millennium). Now while there is a similar teleology in most ideas of modernity, the crucial difference is that modernity looks to a future consummation on earth. Its sense of time is secular. This is an obvious point, but it suggests why Christianity, even at its most radical, was unable to deliver up an unequivocal concept of modernity.

The Christian Middle Ages generally disparaged earthly time. In the orthodox view, as represented by Augustine, even millennial expectations were discouraged. Augustine argued that, with Christ's appearance, the millennium had already begun. There would not be a second millennium after Christ's Second Coming; rather that event would lead directly to the Last Judgement. Nor was 'the millennium' to be taken literally. For Augustine, Christ's coming had indeed initiated the sixth and last age of man, but it was for God, not man, to know exactly how long that age would last. As it is stated in Acts 1:7, 'It is not for you to know the times or the seasons which the Father hath put in his own power.' The Church was the custodian of the time of the last age; hence the only important history was the history of the Church. The task of Christians everywhere was to live piously within the Church, for as long as was necessary, and making due acknowledgement to the obligations of earthly life. Daily life was to be lived in a stoical spirit; its tribulations were to be borne as part of God's purpose. Eventually, in his own good time, God would fulfil the promise of redemption announced in the coming of Christ.

The effect of Augustine's teaching was a profound devaluation of secular as opposed to sacred time. Time belongs to the soul, said Augustine; it is a measure of spiritual development, and as such is indifferent to the normal periods of earthly time. There is the time of the Earthly City, and the time of the Heavenly City; between these two is an unbridgeable gap. Contrary to the view of some of the early Fathers, such as Origen and Eusebius, Augustine saw no progress in earthly affairs, nor for him did the concept have any meaning. In comparison with eternity, the 'time' of human existence is insignificant, its vicissitudes of no moral or philosophical importance. 'One day is with the Lord as a thousand years, and a thousand years as one day' (2 Peter 3:8). 'Earthly time is the shadow of eternity', said Honorius Augustodunensis. Earthly time is merely a series of variations on the ground-theme of the immutable and enduring time of the Scriptures. Times change, but the faith is unchanging. From this point of view, the customary earthly progression of past, present and future is illusory and irrelevant. So it was possible for Peter Lombard to declare that 'Christ will be born, is being born and has been born' (Gurevich 1985: 113–23; see also Löwith 1949: 160–90; Mommsen 1951; Manuel 1965: 25–35).

It is not difficult to see how, despite the radically different conception of time introduced by Christianity, this widely-held interpretation of the relation between sacred and secular time could lead to a view of earthly time not essentially different from that of the ancients. Time once more moved around the fixed point of eternity. It took all of its value and meaning – or lack of them – from that fact. The favourite medieval conceits – *memento mori* (remember you must die), *fortuna labilis* (the fickleness of fortune), *theatrum mundi* (the world as a stage) – all emphasized the illusoriness and transitoriness of human life, and the inability of human beings to control their own destiny. And just as the ancients were inclined to look back to a Golden Age, regarding their own times as suffering from the corruptions of old age, so medieval thinkers also came to see change as decay. *Mundus senescit* – 'the world grows old', was the frequently-repeated saying of a seventh-century Merovingian chronicler. 'Whatever changes, loses its value', ran a twelfth-century poem. Novelty was equated with triviality, and worse; it reflected precisely the superficiality of the earthly as compared with the divine order. For the Middle Ages, moved by the *contemptus mundi*,

> the terms *modernus*, *novus* and words derived from these were derogatory rather than temporal in meaning . . . To the medieval ear, the term *modernitas* tended to have an abusive, derogatory meaning; anything new, unhallowed by time and tradition, was viewed with suspicion . . . Value belonged exclusively to what was old . . . *Antiquitas* is synonymous with such concepts as *auctoritas* (authority), *gravitas* (dignity), *majestas* (greatness). In the medieval world, originality of thought counted for nothing, and plagiarism was not considered a sin. (Gurevich 1985: 124–5; see also Calinescu 1987: 19)

So medieval Christian thought made its rapprochement with the thought of classical antiquity. Contrary to what we might imagine, Christian thinkers of the Middle Ages did not – after a sharp early engagement – depreciate their pagan predecessors, as benighted creatures lacking the light of Christian revelation.[1] On the contrary, the veneration of the great thinkers of antiquity – Plato, Aristotle, Vergil, Cicero – even when they were known mainly through Arabic sources, was as great in the Middle Ages as in the Renaissance. The maxim, that 'a dwarf standing on the shoulders of a giant can see further than the giant himself', was invented (or re-invented) by Bernard of Chartres in the twelfth century. But as his near contemporary John of Salisbury observed, the maxim was meant to point out 'that we see more and farther than our predecessors, not because we have keener vision or greater height, but because we are lifted up and born aloft on their gigantic stature'. The maxim celebrated the ancient giants, not the medieval pygmies. William of Conches put it directly: 'The ancients were much superior to our contemporaries [*moderni*]' (Gurevich 1985: 125; Calinescu 1987: 15; Klibansky 1936).

The belittling of *moderni* and *modernitas* continued in the Renaissance. The words and their cognates entered the vernacular languages of Europe during this period to mean, as with the English *modern*, 'of or pertaining to the present and recent times; originating in the current age or period' (*Oxford English Dictionary*). But to be modern in this sense was not a cause for praise; rather the reverse. In Shakespeare's *As You Like It*, Jacques mocks 'the Justice, . . . full of wise sawes and moderne instances'. Shakespeare's slighting of the modern, as connoting the trite or commonplace, was the usual practice in the Renaissance.

This too, as with medieval Christianity, is at first sight surprising. Was not the Renaissance the birth of the modern age? Was it not the period that saw not just the rebirth of European civilization but its expansion into a New World which immeasurably broadened its horizons? Certainly the school history books and university history syllabuses still confidently date the Modern Period from the time of the Renaissance. The Middle Ages can then conveniently be delimited by the thousand years that separate the foundation of Constantinople in the fourth century from its fall in 1453. Before that, of course, comes Antiquity.

It was indeed the Renaissance that first made the division of western history into three epochs – Ancient, Medieval and Modern. Petrarch, the 'father of humanism', is credited with the invention in the fourteenth century of the notion of the 'Dark Ages': a period, a *medium tempus* supervening between the fall of Rome and the rebirth of society that he saw beginning in his own day. This gave the Middle Ages that characteristic quality of opprobrium that attached to it until well into the eighteenth century. Petrarch's *medium tempus* is an age of barbarism. It is a period of obscurity and backwardness that serves only to throw into greater relief the achievements of the preceding age of antiquity and, at the same time, to mark off the change of direction in modern times.

> Classical antiquity came to be associated with resplendent light, the Middle Ages became the nocturnal and oblivious 'Dark Ages', while modernity was conceived of as a time of emergence from darkness, a time of awakening and 'renascence', heralding a luminous future. (Calinescu 1987: 20; see also Mommsen 1942: 228, 241)

But it was a future largely conceived in terms of the past. This is the source of the Renaissance's uncertainty about its own status, its disposition to look upon its own times as imitative and uncreative. The 'rebirth' of the Renaissance was precisely that – a recovery of earlier forms, the thought and practices of the classical world. Classical antiquity had set the eternal standards. The Renaissance was indeed fortunate in being able to recover the treasures of that earlier time. That set it aside from the ignorance and superstition of the Dark Ages. But what it recovered, what it revered, was not something new, not something that it itself had invented. This was bound, at one level, to make it belittle its own achievements, as no more than strivings to reach the heights already attained by the ancients. So, at most: modern dwarfs, ancient giants.

There was a further consequence of the Renaissance worship of the classical world. It brought to the fore an interest in secular history, as opposed to the sacred history that had dominated medieval thought. The Christian philosophy of history was not ignored but it was relegated to a secondary position. Renaissance historians and political theorists accepted that the history of the Heavenly City had the linear, predestined form taught by Augustine; but, inspired by classical writers, their interest centred on the patterns of change in the Earthly City, the diverse states and empires of the human world. For Renaissance thinkers such as Machiavelli and Bodin, the great models for reflecting on this process were Plato, Aristotle and Polybius, together with such Roman historians as Livy. There was also the history of Graeco-Roman civilization itself, its rise and demise, that offered itself as a kind of paradigm of all world history. Both these sources were powerful inducements to a return to the ancient cyclical view of change. Hence the 'commonplace, that the rediscovery of the classical corpus during the Renaissance was accompanied by a revival of pagan cyclical conceptions of philosophical history' (Manuel 1965: 48).

It is this cyclical conception of history that is responsible for some of the many ambiguities of the Renaissance's idea of progress. The new time is indeed a revolutionary break with the stagnation of the Middle Ages; but it is a revolution conceived on the model of the ancients, as the movement of a wheel or circle that returns to its beginning. The new birth promised by the Renaissance is a return to a purer, more luminous time, the Golden Age of antiquity. The Dark Ages might be over, but what was to come was not something new and different, but a refurbished, a reborn past. 'When the darkness has been dispersed,' says Petrarch, 'our descendants can come again in the former pure radiance.' For Petrarch, at the birth of the Renaissance, the *moderni* were still men of the Dark Ages, but with an important difference: they knew that the future would restore the 'pure radiance' of antiquity (Mommsen 1942: 240).

It is not, then, to the Renaissance that we must look for the origins of modernity as we have come to understand it. Paradoxically, it was the very secular bent of Renaissance historical thought that prevented it from conceiving its own time as linked to the future in a radically new way. Its secularism, linked to the cyclism of admired classical models, turned its face backwards, to the past. In so far as it interested itself in the Christian idea of history, it held fast to the Augustinian view that the world was grown old and in a state of terminal decay (Nisbet 1970: 97–103). That too was unlikely to lead one to take much interest in the future, at least the earthly future. Western thought had to develop a different interest in the Christian philosophy of history before it could give modernity a meaning other than the second-hand, lacklustre activities of *i moderni*.

But there is a sense in which, indirectly at least, the Renaissance did contribute to our concept of modernity. The very vigour and vitality of Renaissance life gave Europeans a new confidence in their ability at least to emulate the ancients, if not to surpass them. More importantly, the Renaissance, in its attack on the authority of medieval thinkers and the medieval church, developed new critical and rational standards that could be turned against all forms of intellectual authority – that of the ancients included. This is what happened at the end of the seventeenth century.

The Birth of Modernity

It used to be generally held that it was in the seventeenth century that what we might call the modern idea of modernity, our idea of modernity, was born. This is especially apparent, the argument goes, in the so-called 'quarrel of the ancients and moderns' at the end of the century, in which the 'moderns' emerged victorious and so cleared the way towards a full-blown concept of modernity. 'Modern history,' said J. B. Bury in one of the best and clearest accounts of this kind, 'begins in the seventeenth century' (1955: 64; see also Schabert 1985: 8).

The milestones on this road are equally plain to see, according to this view. They are to be found in such works as Montaigne's *Essays* (1580), Francis Bacon's *Advancement of Learning* (1605) and *Novum Organum* (1620), and Descartes' *Discourse on Method* (1637).

Here, for instance, is Bacon's famous paean to the great inventions of modern times, printing, gunpowder and the compass, which have transformed the world in a way unimaginable to the ancients:

> For these three have changed the appearance and state of the whole world: first in literature, then in warfare, and lastly in navigation; and innumerable changes have been thence derived, so that no empire, sect, or star, appears to have exercised a greater power and influence on human affairs than these mechanical discoveries. (Bacon 1860: 446)

To this we can add Bacon's clever riposte to the traditional view that the ancients are the ripest in wisdom, and therefore we would do best to heed them. On the contrary, says Bacon, it is we modern who are the 'ancients', for it is we, not those we mistakenly call the ancients, who have benefited most from the longer history of the world. If truth is the daughter of time then it is we, not those earlier in point of time, who must be accounted closer to the truth.

> The wisdom which we have derived principally from the Greeks is but like the boyhood of knowledge, and has the characteristic property of boys: it can talk, but it cannot generate . . .
>   To speak the truth antiquity, as we call it, is the young state of the world; for those times are ancient when the world is ancient; and not those we vulgarly account ancient by computing backwards; so that the present time is the real antiquity. (Bacon 1860: 3, 49–50; cf. also Hobbes, in the *Leviathan* [1651]: 'If we will reverence the Age, the Present is the Oldest')[2]

Lastly we can take Descartes' 'declaration of the Independence of Man' (Bury 1955: 65) – his insistence that we clear the decks for the reconstruction of knowledge on the basis of human reason alone. This involved a rejection of all past systems of thought. There had to be a new beginning, based on a new method for searching out the truth. More uncompromising than Bacon, Descartes had none of his reverence for classical literature. He was proud of having forgotten the Greek he learned as a boy. In the first part of the *Discourse on Method* he tells why he abandoned the ancients:

> To live with men of an earlier age is like travelling in foreign lands. It is useful to know something of the manners of other peoples in order to judge more impartially of our own, and not despise and ridicule whatever differs from them, like men who have never been outside their native country. But those who travel too long end by being strangers in their own homes, and those who study too curiously

the actions of antiquity are ignorant of what is done among ourselves today. (Descartes 1968: 30–1)

All these attitudes were combined in the attack on the ancients in the late seventeenth-century 'quarrel of the ancients and moderns'. Borrowing a figure originally (though in a quite different spirit) advanced by Augustine, the history of collective humanity was compared to the development of a single individual, growing from infancy into adulthood, and increasing in wisdom and maturity with the years. In the works especially of French writers such as Pascal, Perrault, Fontenelle and the Abbé St. Pierre, the age-old tyranny of the ancient authors was challenged and overthrown. The moderns were not simply the equals of the ancients; by virtue of the progressive education of the race during its development since early times modern thinkers were capable of going far beyond their predecessors. Moreover Fontenelle added an important rider to Bacon's championing of modern times. Unlike the individual man, collective man

> will have no old age; he will always be equally capable of those things for which his youth is suited, and he will be ever more and more capable of those things which are suited to his prime; that is to say, to abandon the allegory, men will never degenerate, and there will be no end to the growth and development of human wisdom. (Quoted in Nisbet 1970: 104; see also Bury 1955: 69–153; Jones 1961)

But this brave affirmation of faith in the future was unusual. Commoner by far was the belief that, whatever the achievements of the modern, these did not exempt them from the general tendency of the world to decay. The very device that had given the victory to the moderns over the ancients suggested that fate. For if the 'present time is the real antiquity', then is it not also the prelude to the senescence of the world? Were we not in the old age of humanity? So Bacon seems to have thought. 'Mechanical arts and merchandise', he said, flourish 'in the declining age of a State'; learning has its infancy, its youth, its maturity and its old age, when 'it waxeth dry and exhaust'. The world had made great progress in knowledge, technique, trade and industry, but time was running out. Like any classical or Renaissance thinker, Bacon believed not in unending progress but in 'the vicissitudes of things' (Bacon 1906: 234).

Throughout the seventeenth and most of the eighteenth centuries there persisted the view that decay and degeneration were as much part of the human story as growth and progress. Knowledge, science and even the arts might progress, but this was generally at the cost of moral and spiritual progress. For Scottish moralists such as Hume, Ferguson and Smith, along with French thinkers such as Voltaire and Rousseau, the modern world had by no means escaped the cycles of growth, corruption and decline that had been the destiny of all past civilizations. Volney's *Ruins* (1791) was not simply a charming piece of Romantic artifice but expressed a widespread sentiment. 'Thus,' wrote Volney, contemplating the ruins of Palmyra, 'perish the works of men, and thus do nations and empires vanish away . . . Who can assure us that desolation like this will not one day be the lot of our country?' (Manuel 1965: 67–9; Nisbet 1970: 125–30; Koselleck 1985: 14–16).

Classical and Christian views of time and history continued to dominate the western mind until the second half of the eighteenth century. So long as this was so, there could be no true concept of modernity. The seventeenth century saw a powerful resurgence of apocalyptic and millenarian thinking, extending, as is now well known, even to such scientists as Isaac Newton. As in the Middle Ages, this view of time limited interest in the present to a period of waiting and preparation; the link with the anticipated future was providential, not the result of conscious human action.

The prevalence of classical concepts of history similarly worked against a present-oriented view of things. Employing the Augustinian figure of the Two Cities, thinkers up to Bossuet and beyond found little difficulty in fusing pagan concepts of history, applied to earthly affairs, with the linear Christian concept that portrayed mankind's path to salvation in the Heavenly City. So far as the human world was concerned – nature was another matter – there was no need to add much to the wisdom of the ancients. *Historia magistra vitae*, 'history is the teacher of life' – this Ciceronian maxim expressed the dominant view of history until the mid-eighteenth century. History, it was thought, was a rich storehouse of examples for instruction in moral and political matters. This presupposed a view of human life as fundamentally uniform, fundamentally unchanging, so that the experience of past generations could provide lessons for present purposes. 'Mankind,' said David Hume in his *Enquiry Concerning Human Understanding* (1748), 'are so much the same, in all times and places, that history informs us of nothing new or strange in this particular. Its chief use is only to discover the constant and universal principles of human nature.'

As Reinhart Koselleck puts it:

> History can instruct its contemporaries or their descendants on how to become more prudent or relatively better, but only as long as the given assumptions and conditions are fundamentally the same. Until the eighteenth century, the use of our expression [*Historia magistra vitae*] remained an unmistakable index for an assumed constancy of human nature, accounts of which can serve as iteratable means for the proof of moral, theological, legal, or political doctrines. Likewise, the utility of our topos depended on an actual constancy of those circumstances which admitted the potential similitude of earthly events. If there occurred a degree of social change, it took place so slowly and at such a pace that the utility of past examples was maintained. The temporal structure of past history bounded a continuous space of potential experience. (Koselleck 1985: 23; see also Collingwood 1961: 76–85)

It was this view of time and history that was gradually undermined in the second half of the eighteenth century, so opening the way to a new concept of modernity. A critical part was played by the Christian philosophy of history, which finally delivered up the idea of modernity that was inherent in it from the start. But it could only do so by being decisively secularized. What Kant called the 'moral terrorism' of Christianity – the apocalyptic expectation of the world's end – had first to be exorcised. This happened especially with the millenarian form that was so vigorous in the seventeenth century. In reflecting upon it, and its relation to the new scientific perspectives of the age, thinkers from the late seventeenth century onwards converted millennial beliefs into a secular idea of progress. The millennium became scientific and rational, the dawn of an era of unending human progress on earth. The idea of progress, as elaborated by Kant, Turgot, Condorcet and others during the eighteenth century, was the central building block of the new idea of modernity (Tuveson 1964; Becker 1932; Koselleck 1985: 241–2).

The eighteenth century did not just bring the Heavenly City down to earth. It secularized the Christian concept of time into a dynamic philosophy of history. The by now conventional divisions of Ancient, Medieval and Modern were elevated to 'stages' of world history, and these in turn applied to a developmental model of humanity that lent a special urgency and importance to the latest, the modern, stage. Modern times finally came into their own. No longer were they regarded as simply the inferior copies of earlier, more glorious, times; nor, again, as merely the last stage of an impoverished human existence that would thankfully end the human story on earth. On the contrary, modernity meant a complete break with past times, a fresh start on the basis of radically new principles. It also meant the entry into an infinitely expanded future time, a time for unprecedented new developments in the evolution of humanity. *Nostrum aevum*, our age, became *nova aetas*, the new age.[3]

Modern times become the pivotal point of human history. Modernity takes on messianic status. The past is meaningless expect as a preparation for the present. It no longer teaches us by example. Its only use is to help us to understand what we have become. History, wrote the German jurist Friedrich von Savigny in 1815, is 'no longer merely a collection of examples but rather the sole path to the true knowledge of our own condition'. This suggests that we can no longer make the old assumption of the constancy of human nature and the basic uniformity of human life through the ages. The past is indeed a different, an *other* country. Moderns are different from ancients. History changes human nature, as well as the forms of human social life. The later in time the greater the change.

Not only must the past be interpreted, and constantly re-interpreted, from the perspective of the present. At the same time its authority is abrogated. Age does not ennoble causes but rather throws a veil of suspicion over them. They are, most likely, the product of superstition and ignorance. The later the better, because the more enlightened. Even where this was not accepted, there was at least general agreement that one could no longer look to the past for illumination and instruction. Moderns live in a new world, and are thrown back entirely on themselves for ways of thinking and acting. It was fitting that it was the radically new republic of America that brought this most forcibly home to the young Alexis de Tocqueville.

> I go back from age to age up to the remotest antiquity, but I find no parallel to what is occurring before my eyes; . . . the past has ceased to throw its light upon the future . . . (Tocqueville 1988: 702; and generally see Koselleck 1985: 231–66; Habermas 1981: 4)

The sense of a new beginning infused new meaning into old concepts. The French Revolution of 1789 was the first modern revolution. It transformed the concept. Revolution no longer meant the turn of a wheel or cycle that inevitably returned a thing to its starting point. It now came to mean the creation of something absolutely new, something never before seen in the world. The French Revolution, it became common to say, had taken the world into a new era of its history. It marked the birth of modernity – that is, of a time that is constantly forming and reforming before our eyes.

Modernity as generally conceived is open-ended. It involves the notion of the continuous creation of new things. This is implicit in its rejection of the past as a source of inspiration or example. Modernity is not only the product of revolution – the American and French Revolutions especially; it is itself essentially revolutionary, a permanent revolution of ideas and institutions. Eventually this would lead modernity into an object-less relativism. But in its formative phase the prophets of modernity were convinced that there was a meaning to modernity. The modern age was in various ways seen as the culminating point of human development. It announced the secret of human history, hitherto concealed from the eyes of participants.

Here as in so many other ways the concept of modernity showed its dependence on and derivation from the Christian philosophy of history, particularly in its millenarian and Joachimite forms. This is especially marked in the German thinkers of the late eighteenth and early nineteenth centuries – Lessing, Fichte, Schelling, Hegel – who were responsible for some of the most influential statements of the modern credo. These thinkers, above all Hegel, transformed the Christian religion into a secular philosophy of history. History according to them is a process of the progressive revelation and self-realization of the human spirit. Modernity's task is nothing less than the discovery of God's purpose to man, and the conscious construction of God's kingdom on earth.[4] No doubt in Christian eyes this is the rankest heresy – Marxism, Arnold Toynbee once said, is the last great Christian heresy – but like all heresies it can claim to be grounded in the original inspiration.

> The Christian scheme of history and the particular scheme of Joachim created an intellectual climate and a perspective in which alone certain philosophies of history became possible which are impossible within the framework of classical thinking. There would be no American, no French, and no Russian revolutions and constitutions without the idea of progress and no idea of secular progress toward fulfilment without the original faith in a Kingdom of God . . . (Löwith 1949: 212)

To the philosophers of modernity, the French Revolution was one of the principal expressions, as well as one of the principal vehicles, of the new consciousness. It announced the aim of the modern period as the attainment of freedom under the guidance of reason. This was the meaning of the French Revolution. After it, declared Condorcet in 1793 at the high point of the Revolution's development, 'the word revolutionary can only be applied to revolutions which have liberty as their object'. Robespierre addressing his fellow citizens in the same year linked the fate of freedom to the realization of reason, and both to the fulfilment of the Revolution: 'The progress of human reason has laid the basis for this great Revolution, and the particular duty of hastening it has fallen to you.' Hegel later philosophized this moment as 'a glorious mental dawn'.

> Never since the sun had stood in the firmament and the planets revolved around him had it been perceived that man's existence centres in his head, i.e. in Thought, inspired by which he builds up the world of reality. (Hegel, 1956: 447; see also Kumar 1971: 18, 93; *Social Research* 1989)

If the French Revolution gave to modernity its characteristic form and consciousness – revolution based on reason – the Industrial Revolution provided it with its material substance. It is strange how rarely this obvious point is acknowledged in the literature on modernity. Perhaps because so much of it is written by philosophers and cultural historians, rather than sociologists, modernity is generally seen to be an affair of ideas: an ideology, a cultural style. And yet is it really possible to think of the modern world without considering that it is also *industrial*?

It is of course difficult to separate industrialism from the larger currents of modernity in which it is implicated. Its roots lie in the scientific revolution of the seventeenth century and, further back, in sixteenth-century Protestantism. So it is as much a matter of ideas and attitudes as it is of techniques. Moreover, in so far as modernity is related to capitalism, rather than industrialism in the narrower sense, the association between modernity and forms of economic life would again have to be traced back to the sixteenth century, and the world-wide system of commercial capitalism that originated then (see, for example, Wallerstein 1974).

Nevertheless it seems reasonable to argue that it was only with the British Industrial Revolution of the late eighteenth century that modernity received its material form. Partly this is because of the very explosiveness of the development – a speeding up of economic evolution to the point where it took on revolutionary proportions. Modernity has a before-and-after quality that is also the hall-mark of revolution. With the Industrial Revolution, such a quality increasingly became evident to contemporaries, to the extent that for many of them the only significant division in human

history appeared that between pre-industrial and industrial civilization (Kumar 1978: 45–63). So the connection between modernity
and revolution once more suggests itself, in the economic as much
as in the political or intellectual sphere.

But there is a more compelling reason for linking modernity
with industrialism. It is only with industrialization that western
society became, with increasing clarity, world civilization. It is
difficult to know, and perhaps idle to speculate, whether without
industrial technology the 'superiority' of the west over all other
countries would have become so manifest. Commercial capitalism
was an undoubted force, and the west had put itself at its centre
from the start. But the palm could well have passed to other
hands had it not been for the immeasurable strengthening made
possible by industrial technology. Industrialism turned societies
still largely poor and agrarian into concentrated centres of power
whose goods, guns and ships overwhelmed the resistance of all
non-industrial peoples. If Napoleon's armies carried the ideas of
the French Revolution all over Europe, British and French navies
carried the message of the Industrial Revolution all over the world.
The message was simple. In our times, modern times, there is only
one way to survive: become industrial. For the world as a whole
it became increasingly obvious that to be a modern society was
to be an industrial society. To modernize was to industrialize –
that is, to become like the west (Kumar, 1988c; cf. Gellner 1988:
162).

In yet another way modernity and industrialism are closely if
not intrinsically related. Our very image of modernity is formed
to a good extent of industrial elements. It is difficult to think of
the modern world without conjuring up steel, steam and speed.
From the Great Exhibition of 1851 in England to the World's Fairs
of the 1930s in America, industrialism trumpeted its achievements
and pronounced itself the salvation of humanity. The great cities
of modernity, especially American cities such as New York and
Chicago, are inconceivable without industrial technology. Tow-
ering skyscrapers, far-flung bridges, twenty-mile tunnels under
mountains and seas, supersonic air travel, satellites in space: all
these go to make up our picture of modernity, and all are the
fruits of industrialism. Writers such as H. G. Wells took these
emblems of modernity and made of them a new kind of fiction,
science fiction, a fiction of and for our times. For science fiction,
and the popular image of progress that it promoted, there was
neither present nor future that was not filled with the technological
marvels of industrial civilization.

Images can be as dangerous as they are inevitable. The close association of modernity with industrialism is one reason why there are thinkers today who proclaim the end of modernity. Industrialism, at least as conventionally understood, seems to have exhausted itself, to have reached its limits.

But these claims generally turn out to rest on a very narrow conception of industrialism, one inspired by its popular image. Industrialism is not simply large-scale technology, or economic growth, or even applied science in general. It includes these and goes beyond them. It is at one with modernity in having unleashed on the world a system that is in a permanent state of crisis and renewal. 'Constant revolutionizing of production, uninterrupted disturbance of all social conditions, everlasting uncertainty and agitation . . . All fixed, fast-frozen relationships . . . are swept away, all new-formed ones become antiquated before they can ossify.' It was in these, and similar, terms that in a famous passage in the *Communist Manifesto* (1848) Marx and Engels characterized capitalist industrial society. Destruction, even death, as Joseph Schumpeter in particular was later at pains to point out, are as much part of the industrial system as creation and growth. This includes important elements of the system itself, in its continual striving for survival. Nothing, it seems, cannot be dispensed with. Those who too readily announce the end of industrialism are perhaps seeing no more than the latest period of travail, the most recent of the cycles of renewal and decay that have been characteristic of industrialism throughout its still relatively short history. This, too, may be one of the reasons why many of the great nineteenth-century theorists of industrialism – Tocqueville, Marx, Weber, Simmel and Durkheim – still appear to have much to say to us about ourselves and our times (see, for example, Berman 1983; Frisby 1985; Sayer 1991).

History and Progress; Truth and Freedom; Reason and Revolution; Science and Industrialism: these are the main terms of the 'grand narratives' of modernity that the post-modernists wish to consign to the dustbin of history. They reached a point of crystallization in the great social theories of the eighteenth and nineteenth centuries. The French and Industrial Revolutions are their historical markers, the encapsulations of their tendencies and aspirations. Not in the vigour of the High Middle Ages; not in the creative outburst of the Renaissance; not even in the Scientific Revolution of the seventeenth century; but in the Age of Reason, in the second half of the eighteenth century, more than twelve hundred years after the Roman monk and scholar Cassiodorus first drew the distinction between *antiqui* and *moderni*, the idea of modernity was born.

Modernity and Modernism

Modernity is not 'modernism'. The idea of modernity once estab-lished at the end of the eighteenth century, came up against a complex reaction to it at the end of the nineteenth. This was the cultural movement of modernism. Modernism both affirmed modernity and denied it, both continued its principles and chal-lenged it at its very core.

'*Il faut être absolument moderne*', it is necessary to be absolutely modern, wrote the French poet Rimbaud – but modern in what sense? Matei Calinescu has identified 'two distinct and bitterly conflicting modernities' whose opposition came to the surface at some point in the first half of the ninteenth century. It was then that there took place the split in modernity's soul between modernity as a social and political project and modernity as an aesthetic concept. On the one side science, reason, progress, industrialism; on the other a passionate denial and rejection of these, in favour of sentiment, intuition and the free play of the imagination. On the one side 'bourgeois' modernity; on the other cultural modernity, 'with its outright rejection of bourgeois modernity, its consuming negative passion' (Calinescu 1987: 41–2).

Certainly it can be argued that the culture of modernity has been subversive of the idea of modernity from the start. Literature and the arts have been at the centre of that 'adversary culture' – that 'bitter line of hostility to [modern] civilization' – that Lionel Trilling sees as the hallmark of the modern age that began in the late eighteenth century (1967: 12, 19; cf. Kolakowski 1990: 11). Daniel Bell similarly sees a radical disjunction between the 'functional rationality' of the 'techno-economic order' of modern society and the anarchic and hedonistic impulse towards 'self-realization and self-fulfilment' that is the principle of its culture. In its ceaseless search for a 'new sensibility' of ever more intense and more complete modes of self-fulfilment, cultural modernity subverts the rational disciplined order that is the basis of the economy and the polity (Bell 1976: 14, 34).

The most obvious evidence of this early enmity – what Bell calls the 'cultural contradictions' of capitalist modernity – is the movement of European Romanticism, which can be dated from the late eighteenth to the mid-nineteenth centuries. The rehabilitation of the Middle Ages, and of the past generally, in the novels of Sir Walter Scott and the writings of Friedrich Schlegel, Burke, Chateaubriand and de Maistre; the claims on behalf of feeling and the imagination in the poetry of Blake, Wordsworth, Coleridge, Shelley, Keats and Byron; the fascination with violence and the exotic in the painting of Géricault and Delacroix: all these familiar features of Romanticism pitted it against the leading principles of modernity as expounded by the Enlightenment. Reason was opposed by the imagination, artifice by the natural, objectivity by subjectivity, calculation by spontaneity, the mundane by the visionary, the world-view of science by the appeal to the uncanny and the supernatural. The Romantic sensibility was the essential basis of the whole strand of moral and cultural criticism of industrialism that, in England, ran in the line from Blake and Coleridge, through Carlyle, Dickens, Arnold and Ruskin, to Morris and Lawrence (Williams 1963). An important aspect of this tradition was the recovery of past forms of experience in the life of pre-modern society, especially the Middle Ages. If modernity meant a sharp break with the past, and a decisive orientation towards the future, then Romanticism seemed inclined to find in the past the resources by which to criticize an inhuman and uncreative present.

So powerful and comprehensive a counter-movement to modernity have some critics found Romanticism that they have tended to see later movements, such as modernism and even post-modernism, as mere footnotes to the original impulse. Frank Kermode, for instance, treats the poet W. B. Yeats, who in most accounts is a central figure in the canon of modernism, as the exemplary Romantic (Kermode 1961). But this may lead us to ignore some other, equally distinctive, features of Romanticism. Romanticism, we should remember, was revolutionary not simply in its formal innovations but to a good extent, certainly in its early stages, in its social and political outlook as well. Many of the Romantic poets, such as Wordsworth and Shelley, were enthusiasts for the French Revolution, and looked forward fervently to a future of freedom, equality and justice. Byron, fighting for the Greeks against the Turks, gave his life for the new cause of nationalism, and became a nationalist hero throughout Europe. There was a strong utopian, even millennial, current in Romanticism that made it see its age as a time of new beginnings and boundless possibilities. In all these ways Romanticism went not against but along with the ideas and sentiments of modernity. Even the stress on subjectivity and the individual, which some have seen as most typical of the Romantic spirit, was by no means foreign to the modern mind. On the contrary, for some theorists it is precisely modernity's elevation of the ideal of the autonomous, self-determing individual, constantly re-making himself, that has led to the 'double bind' that it has imposed on itself (Bell 1976: 16).

In some of its expressions Romanticism came even closer to what many have seen as the characteristically modern attitude. This derived from the understanding of Romanticism as the aesthetically relevant aspects of Christian as opposed to pagan civilization. In such works as Chateaubriand's *The Genius of Christianity* (1802), the poetic and sublime elements of Christian art and thought – as seen, for instance, in the Gothic – were favourably contrasted with the rule-governed formalism and abstract rationalism of the world of classical antiquity. Eighteenth-century neo-classicism, the cultural style of the 'Augustan Age', had resumed the striving after universal ideals of beauty characteristic of ancient thought. In reacting against it, Romanticism, taking its cue from the romances, legends and epics of the Christian Middle Ages, put its stress on the 'interesting', the peculiar, the individual and the heroic. It focused on the historically specific and concrete, on all the variety and particularity of the life of the age. As against the universal and the timeless it concerned itself with the relative and the temporal. Romanticism in this sense is, declared the French novelist Stendhal, *'le beau idéal moderne.'* It is the awareness of contemporary life, of modernity. In his book *Racine and Shakespeare* (1823) Stendhal defined *'romanticisme'* as 'the art of presenting to the peoples literary works which, in view of the present-day state of their customs and beliefs, afford them the utmost possible pleasure.'

Calinescu has called this statement 'a kind of first draft of Baudelaire's theory of modernity . . . [F]or Stendhal the concept of romanticism embodies the notions of change, relativity, and, above all, presentness, which makes its meaning coincide to a large extent with what Baudelaire would call four decades later "*la modernité*". Romanticism, simply put, is the sense of the present conveyed artistically' (Calinescu 1987: 39–40). Add to this that Stendhal considered that the romantic artist would encounter great prejudices, and that he would need 'much courage' in confronting the artistic shibboleths of his time, and we can see that we have almost arrived at the concept of the avant-garde which is normally so firmly associated with late-nineteenth century modernism. The upshot of all this is paradoxical. Romanticism here is made to appear – as Kermode also argues – the parent of modernism. But at the same time both it and modernism are seen as close to the very aspects of modernity – as presentness, as ordinary everyday life – that they are generally held to have so vehemently protested against.

The paradox, or the ambiguity, has to do with the great importance of Charles Baudelaire, the French critic and poet, in the theory of modernity. Marshall Berman says that he 'did more than anyone in the nineteenth century to make the men and women of his century aware of themselves as moderns' (Berman 1983: 132). In the writings on modernity, no work is more frequently cited and quoted than his great essay, 'The Painter of Modern Life' (1863). Yet equally no work has been more frequently misrepresented. Baudelaire is said to celebrate the condition of modernity. He is a praiser of his own times, the 'lyric poet in the era of high capitalism'. He champions the painter of modern life, as against the academic painters of historical and mythological scenes. He delights in the life of the modern city, and in city types, such as the *flâneur* and the dandy. He is, on this view, on the side of the moderns against the ancients; he can be enlisted in the ranks of the prophets of modernity, along with such of his fellow countrymen as Condorcet, Constant, Saint-Simon and Comte.

But this account squares oddly with Baudelaire the admirer of Edgar Allan Poe and the author of *Les Fleurs du Mal*, the aesthete and decadent who in his later years was well-known for his implacable hostility to Positivism and the Idea of Progress. This hardly puts him on the side of Enlightenment modernity. It puts him, if anywhere, more fittingly among the modernists, for whom he has indeed always been a hero. This suggests as much a revulsion against modernity as a celebration of it. Once more we are led to examine the complex interplay between modernity and modernism, the positive faith and the negative passion.

For Baudelaire, the modern is the romantic. Here he follows Stendhal; here he seems to glorify the modern. In the 'Salon of 1846' he says that 'romanticism may be defined as the most up to date and the most modern expression of beauty.' The great artist of the day will be he who shows 'the greatest degree of romanticism possible'. This means a resolute rejection of the past: 'To call oneself a romantic and to fix one's gaze systematically on the past is contradictory.' The modern world, and especially the modern city, offers 'a new and particular species of beauty that is neither that of Achilles nor that of Agamemnon. Parisian life is rich in poetic and wonderful subjects. The marvellous envelops and saturates us like the atmosphere . . . ' At the end of the 'Salon of 1845' he had complained that the painters of the day remained transfixed by traditional subjects and ignored 'the heroism of modern life [that] surrounds and presses in on us'. 'The true painter we're looking for will be one who can snatch from the life of today its epic quality, and make us feel how great and poetic we are in our cravats and our patent-leather boots.' The 'Salon of 1846' ends with a paean to a modern writer who has done just that, and who therefore stands as an example to modern painters of how to portray 'modern beauty'.

> The heroes of the *Iliad* do not so much as reach up to your ankles . . . oh! Honoré de Balzac, you the most heroic and the most remarkable, the most romantic and the most poetical of all the characters you have drawn from your heart. (Baudelaire 1981: 107; see also 46, 51–2)

But if Balzac is romantic, so too is Delacroix, the artist who Baudelaire consistently championed throughout his life as the most romantic and therefore the best of the modern painters. Yet Delacroix conspicuously does not paint scenes of modern life. He chooses instead literary subjects, drawn especially from the works of Virgil and Dante. Or he paints exotic, Oriental scenes, some historical, some based on his visits to North Africa. At times he eschews human life altogether, preferring to portray the epic life of the animal world. In what sense then is Delacroix a romantic, and how is that related to modernity?

The answer is supplied when Baudelaire remarks that 'it is possible to make romantics of Romans and Greeks, if one is a romantic oneself' (Baudelaire 1981: 52). Here is a different, and deeper, sense of romanticism than a concern with modern life; or rather it expresses a concern with modern life in a different way. Romanticism in this conception is not so much a period, a historical epoch, nor is it even a style. It is rather an attitude of mind, and even more of feeling, peculiar to the modern age. Delacroix is a romantic and a modern because he displays qualities of intensity, imagination and passion – shown especially in his brilliant use of colour – that speak directly to the modern experience and outlook (Baudelaire 1981: 59–76). Given this attitude, and these abilities, an artist can display a modern romantic sensibility in his treatment of practically any subject, ancient or modern, from literature or from life, from nature or society.

It is with this dual concept of romanticism in mind that we need to approach Baudelaire's discussion of modernity in 'The Painter of Modern Life'. In this essay Baudelaire certainly heaps praise

upon the painter Constantin Guys for his vivacious painting of
contemporary scenes – whether of fashionable Parisian ladies at
their pleasure, the crowds in the streets, or the military in the
Crimea during the recent war with Russia. Part of the pleasure
we derive from the representation of the present, says Baudelaire,
is due 'to its essential quality of being the present.' Guys gives
us this pleasure. He reminds us that beauty is not 'a unique and
absolute' thing, but is 'always and inevitably compounded of two
elements'. There is the element that is 'eternal and invariable',
and there is a 'relative circumstantial element, which we may like
to call . . . contemporaneity, fashion, morality, passion. Without
this second element, which is like the amusing, teasing, appetite-
whetting coating of the divine cake, the first element would be
indigestible, tasteless, unadapted and inappropriate to human
nature' (Baudelaire 1981: 392). Guys serves up the divine cake
suitably sugared. A man of the world, a lover of life, 'he watches
the flow of life move by, majestic and dazzling. He admires the
eternal beauty and the astonishing harmony of life in the capital
cities . . . ' (Baudelaire 1981: 400).

But Guys is praised for more than his eye for the dazzlingly
variegated surface of modern life. His pictures are shown to have
a 'moral fecundity' that reveal the truth of things beneath the
appearance; he is concerned to display the ideal or the type that
underlies the particular scene of private or public life. Baudelaire
at one point compares him to Balzac, whom he describes as 'the
painter of the fleeting moment and of all that it suggests of the
eternal' (1981: 394). This is what the modern painter is after, or
should be after. 'The aim for him is to extract from fashion the
poetry that resides in its historical envelope, to distil the eternal
from the transitory' (1981: 402).

What this seems to mean is that modernity is only one aspect
of what the painter, or any other artist, should be concerned with.
This is made clear in the famous and much-quoted statement that
appears soon after: 'Modernity is the transient, the fleeting, the
contingent; it is one half of art, the other being the eternal and
the immovable.' Not only does this separate the modern from the
eternal, leaving it to the artist to marry the two in the achieved
work of art. It also makes it clear that modernity for Baudelaire
is essentially an aesthetic, not a historical, category. *Every* age has
its 'modernity'; there was, says Baudelaire, 'a form of modernity
for every painter of the past'. Every artist, at all times, has to
seek to represent the modern, the specific look and feel of his
or her own age. Every artist must incorporate in their work 'the

transitory fleeting element' or else risk falling into 'the emptiness of an abstract and indefinable beauty' (1981: 403).

We need to see that, however acceptable this may be as aesthetic theory, it is distinctly problematic as an element in most general theories of modernity. These have focused on modernity as a historical period, as an age – our age – with specific historical and sociological characteristics. But, as Berman says, Baudelaire's concept 'empties the idea of modernity of all its specific weight, its concrete historical content. It makes any and all times "modern times"; ironically, by spreading modernity through all history, it leads us away from the special qualities of our own modern history' (Berman 1983: 133).

We should of course beware of imposing our own preconceptions about modernity on others. It is perfectly proper for Baudelaire to be concerned with modernity as an aesthetic problem, even though neither he nor we can separate this entirely from the character of the age. It is interesting that at just about the same time the English critic and poet Matthew Arnold was advancing a similarly timeless concept of the modern, although with a broader social and cultural content than in the case of Baudelaire. In his inaugural lecture as Professor of Poetry at Oxford, entitled 'On the Modern Element in Literature' (1857), Arnold identified the modern with certain general intellectual and civic virtues which he purported to find conjoined at various times in European history. The modern element in literature, he argued, is not the product of mere contemporaneity but of attitude, the attitude of 'a significant, a highly-developed, a culminating epoch' (Arnold 1970: 60). A society is modern when it is tolerant, rational, critical and sufficiently possessed of the conveniences of life to allow the development of taste. By this definition Arnold finds Periclean Athens – 'in spite of its antiquity' – to be more modern than the England of Elizabeth, and Thucydides a more modern historian than Raleigh. By this definition we might equally judge the eighteenth century to be more modern than the nineteenth, and both more so than our own twentieth century. Arnold, in constructing so normative or prescriptive a concept of the modern, clearly meant to urge its qualities upon the society and culture of his own day. But what he emphatically does not do, and what his concept does not allow us to do, is to identify the modern with 'the modern age', that is, with the particular characteristics of the historical period that has come into being most recently.

No more than Baudelaire can Arnold be faulted for this. The

danger comes when such aesthetic or normative characterizations of modernity are lifted out of context and offered as historical or sociological descriptions of the modern age. That this has not happened so much to Arnold is partly because his concept is less well known, but more probably because it is less serviceable for most current purposes. Baudelaire, on the other hand, has suffered horribly from this fate. Whether he is seen as a celebrator of his age, or a critic of it, or both, he is thought to be an eminently suitable source of significant commentary on it. Again and again scraps from 'The Painter of Modern Life' and other writings are quoted in support of the view that modern society is fragmented and dislocated, that it has made some radical rupture with the past, that it is the theatre of 'the transient, the fleeting and the contingent'. More recently, and relying on much the same passages, Baudelaire has been pressed into the service of theories of post-modernity.

There can be no question of Baudelaire's importance in the theory of modernity. But there has to be a far greater awareness of the complexity of his attitude towards the modern. He at once admired the bourgeois and damned him. He fought for the Republic, even for socialism, then turned against both. He thrived on the life of the city and, like Guys, immersed himself in its crowds 'as though into an enormous reservoir of electricity'. But he could turn on that same city and those same crowds his unmitigated spleen (Clark 1973: *passim*; Berman 1983: 131–71).

Certainly there was no simple endorsement of his own age. Increasingly in fact Baudelaire distanced himself from what he saw as the dominant tendencies of the time. In finding a fellow-spirit in the American writer Edgar Allan Poe he saw himself as assailed by the same forces as had overwhelmed Poe. America was the outstanding example of the new type of modern society. It was utilitarian and materialist. It worshipped democracy and the rule of 'public opinion' – creating, according to Baudelaire, a 'new form of tyranny, the tyranny of beasts or zoocracy.' It believed in the idea of progress, 'that grand heresy of decrepitude', 'a kind of ecstasy for mugs'. Baudelaire joined himself to Poe in his fear of 'the rising tide of democracy which spreads everywhere and reduces everything to the same level.'

Prominent among its victims would be that admired social type, the dandy, which Baudelaire saw as 'the last flicker of heroism in decadent ages'. It was this belief in the hero, which he shared with Balzac, that according to Walter Benjamin ultimately puts both of them 'in opposition to Romanticism' – against, in other words, the spirit of their age (Benjamin 1973: 74; see also Baudelaire 1981: 163–6, 191–4, 421–2; Berman 1983: 138–42; Calinescu 1987: 55–8).

The Ambivalence of Modernity

Baudelaire's ambivalence towards the modern – what Berman calls his 'pastoral' and 'counter-pastoral' images of modernity – increases rather than diminishes his importance in the theory of modernity. Modernization – the social and economic processes of modernity – from the very beginning gave rise to modernism, the cultural critique of modernity. Rousseau, often said to be the first thinker to embody the modern sensibility, is best remembered for his passionate revolt against the rationalizing tendencies of modernity. Marx, the great theorist of capitalist modernity, was struck by the paradox that 'in our days everything seems pregnant with its contrary': material advance side by side with spiritual impoverishment, scientific knowledge alongside mass ignorance, the conquest of nature accompanied by the enslavement of men. 'We might even say,' remarks Marshall Berman in his splendid study of this paradox, 'that to be fully modern is to be anti-modern: from Marx's and Dostoevsky's time to our own, it has been impossible to grasp and embrace the modern world's potentialities without loathing and fighting against some of its most palpable realities' (Berman 1983: 14; cf. Anderson 1984: 104–6; Jameson 1992: 304).

Lionel Trilling has pointed to the changeability of the concept of the modern, its fluidity, so much so that it can swing round in meaning until it is facing in the opposite direction (Trilling 1967: 29). This has by no means been a unilinear process. The early revolts against modernity, in Rousseau, Romanticism and other developments of the early nineteenth century, yield nothing to later examples in their force and clarity. But, as we have seen with Romanticism, there is a real sense in which they have not given up hope. The modern world can be redeemed, and this will be in part with modernity's own tools, reason and revolution. For most of the first half of the nineteenth century, this confidence remained strong. In the writings for instance of Hegel and his successors, including Marx, the modern world is subjected to a rigorous and critical scrutiny. Its failings are exposed and denounced. But this is accompanied by the uncovering of those tendencies, equally modern, that will overcome those faults and deliver humanity into a new world of freedom and self-fulfilment.

The cultural critique of modernity increases in intensity with the progress of the nineteenth century. Or rather we might better say that the element of hope seems to diminish, and there is a corresponding increase in the element of despair, amounting sometimes to a kind of nihilism. This can be seen partly in the writings of Kierkegaard and Nietzsche, although they had to wait until the end of the nineteenth century for real appreciation. It can also be found in the writings of Dostoevsky, although here the Russian context makes it less easy to see him as representative of currents in Europe as a whole. More representative in this sense was the English poet and critic Matthew Arnold, with his fear of democracy, and his alarm at the effects on culture of the domination of society by the commercial middle classes, the 'Philistines'. Similar fears were voiced by the Swiss historian of culture, Jakob Burckhardt. The melancholy of both these thinkers, their stoicism in the face of what they clearly see as a lost cause, goes well beyond what one might be inclined to call the 'aesthetic' melancholy of Romantics such as Byron.

But it was the French, in the writings and persons of novelists and poets such as Flaubert, Baudelaire, Rimbaud and Verlaine, who most powerfully expressed the new mood of pessimism, cynicism, disgust and despair. In their personal lives this often took the form of exercises in what Rimbaud called 'the derangement of the senses', involving alcoholic excess and experiments with drugs and unorthodox forms of sexual behaviour. In their artistic works their feelings were expressed in radical experiments with form and new kinds of subject-matter. To their successors they bequeathed Symbolism, Imagism, Naturalism and even, in the last works of Flaubert, something approaching the 'anti-novel'. They, together with their counterparts in painting, the Impressionists, have in other words good claims to be regarded as the fathers of the movement of modernism that flourished between about 1890 and 1930.

Jean Baudrillard considers Baudelaire's 'The Painter of Modern Life' as 'the bridge between romanticism and contemporary modernity'. Modernism can, as we have noted, be seen as late Romanticism. But it goes so much further in its assault on modernity that we are entitled to regard it as something almost qualitatively different. There is a comprehensiveness in its sweeping rejection of all the idols of modernity that marks something new. In tone and manner there is a new urgency and fierceness, a savage desire deliberately to flout and offend. Baudelaire, says Baudrillard, introduces an 'aesthetic of rupture', a freeing of subjectivity and a ceaseless quest for the new. He is also responsible for the phenomenon of the cultural avant-garde, with its hostility towards all the received forms in the arts and, more generally, towards 'the authority and legitimacy of the received models of fashion, sexuality and social conduct' (Baudrillard 1987a: 68).

What is modernism? We can get an initial idea by simply setting out the principal names and aspirations in the period normally associated with modernism, the 1890s to the 1920s. In poetry there are Mallarmé, Valéry, Rilke, Yeats, Eliot, Pound and Stevens. These are associated with new metrics and modes like *vers libre*; they also radically develop the symbol and the image. They express too a sense of the crisis of language – a sense characteristic also of the modernist novelists, among whom one would include Proust, Kafka, Musil, Joyce, Woolf, Lawrence and Faulkner. The novelists raised questions about the traditional representations of reality. They broke with both Realism and Naturalism – themselves generally regarded as inventions of modernity – to introduce such techniques as the 'stream of consciousness', and to oppose standard ideas of plot and narrative. In drama Ibsen, Strindberg, Pirandello and Brecht challenged the technical conventions of the stage and, even more, the subjects traditionally treated by playwrights. They rejected the standard idea of character as whole and finished, showing instead multiple, frequently contradictory levels of personality and states of mind. In the Preface to *Miss Julie* (1888) Strindberg said that because his figures were 'modern characters' he had deliberately made them 'uncertain, disintegrated'.

> My characters are conglomerations of past and present stages of civilization, bits from books and newspapers, scraps of humanity, rags and tatters of fine clothing, patched together as is the human soul. (In McFarlane 1976: 81)

Fragmentation was also the effect, if not precisely the intention, of the musical innovations of the 'Second Viennese School', Schoenberg, Berg and Webern. Atonality and dissonance dissolved the expected regularities of harmony, leaving the listener unsettled and uncertain; the twelve-note system produced an effect severely at odds with the buoyancy and melodic flow of both classicism and romanticism. Fragmentation – of the figure, of the personality – also seemed the aim of the Cubist revolution in painting led by Picasso and Braque. In their pictures and collages human figures were composed literally of 'bits from books and newspapers'; in their relation to their social and natural environments these figures were shown, not as separated from them, as in naturalistic conventions of representation, but merged and dissolved in them – if, indeed, they were discernibly human at all.

It was not, of course, only in the arts that modernist tendencies asserted themselves. In the whole realm of philosophical, psychological, social and political thought the ground could be heard quaking and cracking. The dominant strands of rationalism, positivism and utilitarianism all came under attack. In the writings of Pareto, Mosca, Sorel, Le Bon, William James and Wallas, all the customary assumptions about political motivation and behaviour were questioned. Men were far from being simply the self-interested, utility-seeking, pleasure-maximizing, rational creatures of standard nineteenth-century political and economic theory. The attack on reason, the central tenet of modernity, was even more profound in the case of Freud and Bergson. The 'dethronement of reason', the revelation of the forces of the irrational and the unconscious, was perhaps the most devastating of the blows that modernism inflicted on modernity. It left the way open for the investigation, and to some extent the re-legitimation, of the forces of religion and mythology, and other 'pre-modern' forms, in the writings of Frazer, Durkheim and Weber. Modern society no longer looked so very different from 'primitive' or archaic societies. Freud in addition put a gigantic question mark against the modern idea of progress. Civilization, and *a fortiori* modern civilization was, he suggested, achieved at the cost of enormous psychic suffering and enfeeblement. This, in a different form, was also the message of Friedrich Nietzsche. Nietzsche, largely neglected up till this time, found an enthusiastic reception when in the late 1880s his work was drawn to the attention of the educated European public by the Danish critic Georg Brandes. His characteristic ideas seem to sum up some of the principal themes of the modernist movement in moral and social philosophy.

> His apocalyptic vision, his profound conviction that the history of man had arrived at a point of destiny, at the terminus of a long era of civilization, and that all human values must be subjected to total revision found a reverberant echo in the aspirations of western man in these years. By his violent assault on the tenets of Christianity, his advocacy of what Brandes . . . defined as his 'aristocratic radicalism',

his ruthless questioning of the nineteenth century's *idées reçus*, his total repudiation of traditional morality, he won a response from the generations of the *fin-de-siècle* and the First World War which gave him a uniquely influential role in the Modernist period. (McFarlane 1976: 79; see also generally Hughes 1958; Masur 1966; Bullock 1976; Biddiss 1977; Anderson 1984; Hobsbawm 1987: 219–275)[5]

We should remember the claim for Nietzsche as the prophet of modernism when we encounter him, as we frequently do, as the prophet of post-modernism. This suggests a degree of continuity, perhaps even of identity, between the two styles that is also strongly suggested by some other characteristic movements of modernism. These were the ones where the revolt against modernity was most spectacular, and most caught the popular imagination. Dadaism, which began during the First World War, reflected something of the disenchanted mood of the time but turned it into an exuberant, outrageous assault on all the official ideas and institutions that had conspired to produce the mess. The rage was directed however not at politics but at Art, the sacred cow of the establishment. The aim was to desacralize art, to question its purpose and its very possibility in these modern times. In the 'readymades' of Marcel Duchamp, Francis Picabia's representation of men and women as functionless machines, and the aggressive iconoclasm of Tristan Tzara's manifestos, the desire to mock and shock bourgeois taste and sensibility was carried to extravagant lengths. Irony and absurdity, scandal and subversion were the techniques by which the Dadaists sought to cure the age of its madness and restore a lost purity.

Surrealism, which borrowed both people and techniques from Dadaism, turned these ideas in a more political direction. For the Surrealists what was most hateful about modernity was its utilitarianism, and its capitulation to what Freud called the 'reality principle', as against the claims of the 'pleasure principle'. It had dehumanized existence by its acceptance of routine and its renunciation of desire and pleasure. It had deified reason and science and relegated fantasy and the imagination to the margins of society, as the sphere of children, primitives and the insane. Somewhat like the Romantics, Surrealists such as Breton, Aragon, Dali and Buñuel aimed to show that the fantastic was as real as the reality revealed by modern science. They took up Freud's ideas about the dream to turn it into a paradigm of the duality of human existence, a compound of logic and fantasy, conscious and unconscious processes. They celebrated pleasure and the imagination, exploring the erotic and the sensual and finding in magic and madness suppressed strengths and resources.

It has been argued that, 'for all its affinities with the past', Surrealism was 'an essentially modern aspiration' (Short 1976: 308). This is shown partly by the commitment of some of its followers to communism. Certainly it remained sufficiently potent and long-lasting to surface again as the main inspiration of the Situationists who, marrying Marx and Freud, elaborated a thoroughly modern idea of revolution in the events of May 1968 in Paris (Kumar 1988d). Generally it is right to stress that modernism was no simple rejection of modernity; it was rather a reaction, a critical response to it. In some of its aspects, as in Futurism and Constructivism, it showed a fascination and almost an obsession with the modern (Nash 1974). The charge here was that modern society was not modern *enough*. It was 'inauthentically' modern. It was too cautious, too cowardly, to accept all the implications of modernity. It preferred to harbour past relics, so preventing the realization of modernity's full potential.

Nowhere was this criticism so persuasively put, and so effectively practised, as in the Modern Movement in architecture. Modernist architecture was the clearest link between cultural modernism and the eighteenth-century idea of modernity. It denounced the age for its timidity and nostalgia, its constant revival of past styles, as in neo-classicism and neo-Gothicism. There had to be an architecture for the modern age, one that was in tune with modern life and modern technology. Inspired, oddly enough, by William Morris and the Arts and Crafts movement – usually thought of as a reversion to medievalism – modernist architects turned to new materials and new ideas of design.[6] They wished to work with truly modern materials – steel, glass, concrete. They wanted their buildings, and the cities they planned, to reflect the modern idea of reason. They should be based on scientific, universal principles. Form should reflect function; there was to be no useless ornamentation. In the work of Sullivan, Wright, Loos, Le Corbusier, Gropius and Mies van der Rohe, much of it incorporated in the practice of the Bauhaus, founded by Gropius in 1919; in cities such as Chicago and New York, modern buildings took on the familiar and characteristic features of the 'International Style': geometric, rectangular, streamlined (Scully 1961; Hitchcock 1968; Pevsner 1975).[7]

Modernism in architecture is important for our story because it was principally in architecture that the claims for 'post-modernism' were first seriously made. Hence post-modernism can be understood to some extent as a reaction against the kind of modernism represented by modernist architecture. But architecture is also important within the story of modernism itself. It indicates in the clearest possible way the diversity of modernism, its mix of conflicting and often contradictory tendencies. It could denounce the 'inauthentic' present in the name of the future, as in Futurism and Constructivism; and it could with equal force do so in the name of the past, as in the appeal to a time of lost wholeness in the novels of Proust, or to a former 'organic community' in the poetry of T. S. Eliot (not to mention in much, especially German, social theory of the time). It could attack reason and science, as in Dadaism and Surrealism, and it could embrace them with passion, as in Malevich's Suprematism and the *de stijl* and Bauhaus movements. It could at once reject modern technology and the industrial way of life, as in the primitivist painting of Henri Rousseau and the novels of D. H. Lawrence, and at the same time glory in them, as in Futurism and modernist architecture. It could celebrate the life of the modern city, as in much of the painting and architecture of the time, and equally find there desolation, isolation and alienation, as in Munch's paintings and the writings of Joyce and Eliot. It aimed to lift art and culture out of history, to make them timeless; and it simultaneously claimed that its works were the most intensely living expressions of its own, modern, times.[8]

The Austrian poet Hugo von Hofmannsthal wrote in 1893: 'Today, two things seem to be modern: the analysis of life and the flight from life . . . ' There was an urge to dissect, to understand all phenomena of nature and of the mind in the most ruthlessly scientific way. At the same time there was a profound revulsion from this, an 'instinctive, almost somnambulistic surrender' to dream and fantasy, a desire to escape from the modern world (McFarlane 1976: 71). The position was even more complicated in that the two things often co-existed in the same person, or the same movement. There could be in the selfsame expression both the embrace of modernity and the rejection of it. Joyce and Baudelaire revelled in the city life that they also damned. Cubism was both a critique of modernity and a fascinated exploration of modern, scientific, ways of seeing. Frazer and Freud showed reason to be engaged in a perpetual struggle with the irrational, and urged that we respect the claims of myth and the unconscious; they themselves remained firm rationalists, convinced of the rightness of reason and the need for it to prevail. Modernism, like Romanticism, had a split soul. But the split was deeper and more neurotic, as befitted a *fin-de-siècle* mood that could not escape a sense of crisis, a conviction that there was to be a cataclysmic end of things, even though this would be the prelude to new beginnings.

> If there is a persistent world-view it is one we should have to call apocalyptic; the modernism of the Nineties has a recognisable touch of this, if decadence, hope of renovation, the sense of transition, the sense of an ending or the trembling of the veil, are accepted as its signs. At such times there is a notable urgency in the proclamation of a break with the immediate past, a stimulating sense of crisis, of an historical licence for the New. (Kermode 1968: 2)

Modernism then had its own kind of confidence, its feeling of exhilaration in the midst of cultural despair. Its fascination with the new put it on the side of progress, and so connected it up with one of the central ideas of modernity. But the charge is made that this very obsession with novelty eventually broke that connection. Change came to be viewed as desirable for its own sake, rather than as the means towards the realization of greater freedom or more complete self-expression. Modernity, which had been defined as a 'break with tradition', itself became a tradition, the 'tradition of the new'. Under the impress of modernism, modernity came to be no more than endless innovation: endless changes of style, endless cycles of fashion. 'Bit by bit,' says Baudrillard, '[modernity] loses all the substantial value of progress which underlay it at the beginning, in order to become an aesthetic of change for change's sake . . . At the limit, it merges purely and simply with fashion, which is at the same time the end/aim [*la fin*] of modernity' (Baudrillard 1987a: 68–9; see also Rosenberg 1970: 23–4).

The end of modernity? Post-modernity? This clearly calls for a new chapter.

5

Modernity and Post-Modernity (II):
The Idea of Post-Modernity

*It is comforting . . . and a source of profound relief to think that
man is only a recent invention, a figure not yet two centuries old,
a new wrinkle in our knowledge, and that he will disappear again
as soon as that knowledge has discovered a new form.*
                                        Michel Foucault (1970: xxiii)

*Let us wage a war on totality; let us be witnesses to the
unpresentable; let us activate the differences and save the honour
of the name.*
                                        Jean-François Lyotard (1984b: 82)

*Post-modernity is modernity without the hopes and dreams which
made modernity bearable.*
                                        Dick Hebdige (1988: 195)

Post-Modernity and Post-Modernism

For modernity, it is possible, without stretching customary usage
too far, to distinguish between 'modernity' and 'modernism'. This
is useful in separating a largely political or ideological from a
largely cultural or aesthetic concept of modernity. They overlap,
of course, as we have seen especially in the case of architecture and
urbanism. But there is sufficient tension between them, amounting
at times to outright divergence, to make it helpful to consider
modernity in this dual aspect.

The same does not apply to the idea of post-modernity. There is
no tradition of use that we can fall back on to distinguish in any
consistent way between 'post-modernity' and 'post-modernism'.
Both are used more or less interchangeably. One might prefer, on
the analogy with modernity, to keep post-modernity for the more

general social and political concept, and post-modernism for its cultural equivalent. But this flies in the face of current usage, which refuses to make so sharp an analytical distinction – refuses, in most cases, to make any distinction at all.

This in itself tells us something important about the idea of post-modernity. It breaks down the dividing-lines between the different realms of society – political, economic, social and cultural. This is not new in principle. Nineteenth-century sociology, in the writings for instance of Marx and Durkheim, made its main contribution to the study of society by insisting on just this interconnection of realms. Marx's 'base' and 'superstructure' model, linking politics, religion and culture to the economic life of society, is the clearest example of this.

But post-modern theory goes beyond this. For despite sociology's concern with the social organism or the social system as a whole, it was in practice possible to regard modern society as sufficiently differentiated to make it useful to consider its parts or 'sub-systems' as relatively autonomous. For some sociologists, such as Herbert Spencer and Talcott Parsons, it was indeed one of the achievements of modernity so to differentiate society that different principles might apply in the different realms. The principle of 'achievement' and the ethos of utilitarianism, for instance, might dominate the economic system, while in the family and the kinship system 'ascription' and expressivity came into their own. For Parsons and his followers – implicitly criticizing the Marxists on this point – it was precisely in this differentiation and separation of spheres that modern society achieved its freedom and flexibility. It was in this that it most clearly distanced itself from the 'mechanical solidarity', the rigid integration of parts around a central core of values, that following Durkheim's influential account was held to characterize traditional societies.

Post-modern theory reverses this, once more collapsing the different realms into each other (cf. Lash 1990: 11). But the way it does this is different from both the conventional treatment of traditional society and sociology's account of the functionally integrated nature of modern society. The irreducible pluralism and diversity of contemporary society is not denied. That is what makes it modern as opposed to traditional. But that pluralism is not ordered and integrated according to any discernible principle. There is not, or at least no longer, any controlling and directing force to give it shape and meaning – neither in the economy, as Marxists had argued, nor in the polity, as liberals had thought, nor even, as conservatives had urged, in history and tradition. There is simply a more or less random, directionless flux across all sectors of society. The boundaries between them are dissolved, leading however not to a neo-primitivist wholeness but to a post-modern condition of fragmentation.

If there is a privileged sector, or at least a privileged discourse, among post-modernists, it appears to be cultural. That is perhaps why in the literature one more frequently encounters the term 'post-modernism' than 'post-modernity'. It suggests, what is largely true, that the impulse to post-modern theory came orginally from the cultural sphere, and that its principal concern was cultural modernism. It was then picked up by other thinkers – not to mention the mass media – leading to an ever-widening circle of social life being pronounced post-modern.

In the process elements of other theories, first elaborated elsewhere, were incorporated in post-modern theory. The theory of post-industrial society, usually associated with Daniel Bell, was one of the first to be absorbed. This highlighted the key role of knowledge in post-modern society, though the post-modernists see this in a quite different way from Bell's highly modernist, rationalist view of it. They similarly distance themselves from the euphoria that marks most accounts – Bell's included – of the information society, though sharing that theory's view of the importance of computers and the new forms of communication. Post-Fordism also features strongly in post-modern theory, especially in the stress on decentralization and dispersal, and the renewed importance of place. Once more though post-modernists reject the Marxist framework that generally goes with this approach.[1]

It would be wrong to see post-modern theory simply as a case of unashamed borrowing. As a powerful current of thought it has itself directly contributed to the sense of an ending, or of a new direction, which is to be found in other theories. The problem with it is of a rather different kind. Post-modern theory is as outrageously eclectic in its sources as it is synthetic and even syncretic in its expressions. This is one reason for its popularity; it is also the reason why it is so difficult to test or assess it in the usual way, or even to discuss it critically. For every feature you select for examination, another one bearing on the question can be offered with equal aplomb, even though it may point in an entirely different and even contrary direction. Earnest examinations of the fit between theory and reality are met with an ironic smile. Contradiction and circularity, far from being regarded as faults in logic, are in some versions of post-modern theory actually celebrated.

We will need to see if such open-armed generosity in a theory is justifiable, rather than, as is often the case, a cause for suspicion. Post-modernism, to be fair to it, must to some extent be assessed in its own, post-modernist, terms, according to its own self-understanding. But initially at least we need to be more modern and less post-modern in our approach. We have to ask historical questions, about origins and sources. We have to ask sociological questions, about the plausibility and validity of the assertions that are made about contemporary society: is post-modern theory *true*? We may even need to ask political and moral questions, about the attitudes and intentions of post-modern theorists. That many of these questions would be regarded as irrelevant or inapposite by post-modern theorists themselves cannot prevent their arising in the minds of most of us.

Origins and Development

It is helpful to begin with some reasonably clear definition of the post-modern. This admittedly is contrary to most post-modernist practice. Post-modernists are loath to define, partly for the reason that 'it is difficult to avoid giving a modern definition of the postmodern; in fact, virtually any definition of postmodernism will turn out to be modernist' (Nederveen Pieterse 1992: 26; see also Alexander 1994: 182). Definitions engage with those very qualities of rationality and objectivity that post-modernists are at pains to deny. Nevertheless, in the interest of promotion and propaganda, some have been willing to take the risk. Here is Charles Jencks, one of the foremost prophets of the 'post-modern age', and one of the most ardent proselytizers on its behalf.

> The Post-Modern Age is a time of incessant choosing. It's an era when no orthodoxy can be adopted without self-consciousness and irony, because all traditions seem to have some validity. This is partly a consequence of what is called the information explosion, the advent of organised knowledge, world communication and cybernetics. It is not only the rich who become collectors, eclectic travellers in time with a superabundance of choice, but almost every urban dweller. Pluralism, the 'ism' of our time, is both the great problem and the great opportunity: where Everyman becomes a Cosmopolite and Everywoman a Liberated Individual, confusion and anxiety become ruling states of mind and ersatz a common form of mass-culture. This is the price we pay for a Post-Modern Age, as heavy in its way as the monotony, dogmatism and poverty of the Modern epoch. But, in spite of many attempts in Iran and elsewhere, it is impossible to return to a previous culture and industrial form, impose a fundamentalist religion

or even a Modernist orthodoxy. Once a world communication system and form of cybernetic production have emerged they create their own necessities and they are, barring a nuclear war, irreversible. (Jencks 1989: 7)

This account is useful for a number of reasons. It shows clearly the overlap between theories of post-modernism and those of the information society. The emphasis on choice and pluralism also echoes a central tenet of post-Fordism. More importantly, Jencks makes it plain that post-modernism is primarily a response to cultural modernism. Its eclecticism is an acceptance of tradition, or at least of traditions, rather than, as with modernism, a defiant rejection of it. Instead of the 'Tradition of the New', there is 'the combination of many traditions', 'a striking synthesis of traditions'.

Between inventive combination and confused parody the Post-Modernist sails, often getting lost and coming to grief, but occasionally realising the great promise of a plural culture with its many freedoms. Post-Modernism is fundamentally the eclectic mixture of any tradition with that of the immediate past: it is both the continuation of Modernism and its transcendence. Its best works are characteristically doubly-coded and ironic, making a feature of the wide choice, conflict and discontinuity of traditions, because this heterogeneity most clearly captures our pluralism. (Jencks 1989: 7)

But modernism, as we have seen, has a complex relationship to modernity. Some aspects of it, as in Dadaism and Surrealism, seem to negate key features of modernity and, indeed, to look forward to post-modernism. Other aspects, as in architecture and urbanism, are continuations of modernity's basic rationalism. What, then, is the modernism that is both continued and transcended in post-modernism?

Here again Jencks is useful because he is an architectural historian, and it is architecture that most clearly enables us to see what many people mean by post-modernism. In an earlier work on architectural theory Jencks, in a direct echo of some famous remarks about the onset of modernism,[2] stated that

Modern Architecture died in St Louis, Missouri on July 15, 1972 at 3.32 pm (or thereabouts) when the infamous Pruitt-Igoe scheme, or rather several of its slab blocks, were given the final *coup de grace* by dynamite. (Jencks 1977: 9)

The dynamiting of Pruitt-Igoe is seen to represent, as an early and highly dramatic instance, the reaction against architectural modernism. Pruitt-Igoe was a typical – indeed prize-winning – example of the kind of high-rise building scheme that, developing out of the International Style, dominated the cities of Europe and North America in the post-1945 period. It was a style of urbanism that increasingly came under intense criticism in the 1960s and 1970s for its elitism and authoritarianism. It was accused of indifference to the neighbourhood and community contexts of its starkly modernist buildings, disdain for the preferences of ordinary people, and arrogance in its elevation of the architect-planner to the position of Corbusian demiurge (Jacobs 1965; Coleman 1985; Hall 1988).

The decisive rejection of this style inaugurates, for Jencks and others, the era of architectural and urban post-modernism. This is characterized by that eclecticism and pluralism, that often playful and ironic jumbling and fusing of traditions, that many take as typical of post-modernism in general. Often there is an air of theatricality or spectacle; the city is treated as a stage, a place for enjoyment and the exercise of the imagination as much as a utilitarian system of production and consumption. It is a site of fantasy; it embodies 'not just function but fiction'. The frequently-quoted examples, many of them American, include Faneuil Hall Marketplace in Boston, the similar waterfront development Harbor Place in Baltimore, the Westin Bonaventure Hotel in Los Angeles, the Piazza d'Italia in New Orleans, the Neue Staatsgalerie in Stuttgart, the new Lloyds Building in London (perhaps), the Musée d'Orsay in Paris (but *not* the Pompidou Centre). More generally, and more pointedly, post-modernist architects such as Robert Venturi have celebrated the 'aesthetic populism' of Disneyland and the 'urban populism' of Las Vegas (Jencks 1989: 16–19; Hall 1988: 347–51; Harvey 1989: 59–60, 66–98; Jameson 1992: 39–44).

Architecture is taken by many theorists to represent post-modernism not simply because it shows the clearest reaction to modernism but because it displays post-modernist features most palpably.[3] It is how and where most people are likely to encounter post-modernism in their daily lives. And this ordinariness is itself important to post-modernism. In its buildings and urban designs (not 'plans') it seeks to break down modernist distinctions between 'high' and 'low' culture, 'elite' and 'mass' art. In place of the autocratic imposition of a monolithic taste it accepts a diversity of 'taste cultures', whose needs it tries to meet by offering a plurality of styles. In Faneuil Hall Market there are art cinemas and representatives of the big chains; there are gourmet restaurants and fast-food bars; there are designer clothes shops and those selling mass-produced articles. It is assumed not only that different people will want different things but that the same people will, at different times, want different things.

A similar 'democratizing' impulse was at work in many of the cultural movements of the 1960s. Hence it is not surprising to discover that the term 'post-modernism' first established itself in the cultural criticism of these years. Here it largely reversed an earlier use, associated especially with the historian Arnold Toynbee. Toynbee had, in the later volumes of *A Study of History* (1954), identified a period of world history beginning in the last quarter of the nineteenth century that he called 'post-Modern'. The 'post-Modern Age' marked a rupture with the classic 'Modern Age' that had lasted roughly from the Renaissance to the late nineteenth century. As against the belief in progress and reason of the Modern Age, the post-Modern Age was characterized by the beliefs and sentiments of irrationality, indeterminacy and anarchy. These were linked to the advent of 'mass society' and 'mass culture' in our time. In Toynbee's philosophy of history, the post-Modern Age is a representative instance of a 'Time of Troubles', a period of disintegration and breakdown, although he saw some hope for the redemption of western civilization in a World State based on a synthesis of the 'higher religions' (Toynbee 1954: vol. 9, 182–9; see also Toynbee 1948).

The negative evaluation and connotation of 'post-modern' continued in some quarters in the 1960s. For defenders of modernism such as Irving Howe and Clement Greenberg, post-modernism represented a capitulation to kitsch and commercialism. In its unashamed populism, it repudiated the austerity and integrity, the striving after the aesthetic object for its own sake, that had been the hallmark of High Modernism (Howe 1970; Greenberg 1980, 1993; cf. also Eagleton 1985). Others such as Harry Levin and Lionel Trilling – followed later by Daniel Bell – saw in post-modernism's 'antinomianism' and 'anti-intellectualism', its unchained hedonism, a threat to the values of the (bourgeois) humanist culture that had hitherto held in check the potentially dissolving currents of modernity (Levin 1966; Trilling 1967; Bell 1976: 51–4, 120–45; 1980c).

But the stronger current was flowing the other way, away from this fear and suspicion and towards an emphatic endorsement of what increasingly came to be called post-modern culture. The 'counter-culture' of the 1960s enthusiastically adopted the banner of post-modernism. Its proponents saw themselves as embattled against everything that modernism stood for, whether in culture or politics. Pop art and pop music, the 'new wave' in cinema and the 'new novel' in literature, the 'happening' and the 'be-in', mass demonstration and contestation, the elision of the boundaries between 'art' and 'life', the cultivation of sensibility through sex and drugs rather than aesthetic contemplation or intellectual study, the elevation of the claims of the 'pleasure principle' over those of the 'reality principle': in all these ways the counter-culture assailed what it saw as the elitist, esoteric and autocratic world of modernism. In a euphoric essay entitled 'The New Mutants' (1965), the American critic Leslie Fiedler declared the world of the new movements to be not simply 'post-Modernist' but also 'post-Freudian', 'post-Humanist', 'post-Protestant', 'post-white', 'post-male', and several other 'posts' as well. As against the 'analysis, rationality, and anti-Romantic dialectic' of modernism, he celebrated the 'apocalyptic, antirational, blatantly romantic and sentimental' character of the new culture. In a later essay of 1970 he wrote:

> We are living, have been living for two decades – and have become actually conscious of the fact since 1955 – through the death throes of Modernism and the birth pangs of Post-Modernism. The kind of literature which had arrogated to itself the name Modern (with the presumption that it represented the ultimate advance in sensibility and form, that beyond it newness was not possible), and whose moment of triumph lasted from a point just before World War I until just after World War II, is *dead*, i.e., belongs to history not actuality. (Fiedler 1971: 461; see also 379–400; and cf. Berman 1992: 43–4).

In a similarly celebratory vein, though with a more systematic intent, another American critic, Ihab Hassan, was also in these years elaborating the distinction between modernism and post-modernism. Hassan, who was to become one of the leading prophets of post-modernism, saw in modernism the principle of 'Authority' and in post-modernism the principle of 'Anarchy'. The latter involved a tendency towards 'Indeterminacy', a compound of pluralism, eclecticism, randomness and revolt. Indeterminacy also connotes 'deformation', a stress on decreation, difference, discontinuity and 'detotalization' which together add up to 'a vast will to unmaking, affecting the body politic, the body cognitive, the erotic body, the psyche of each individual – affecting in short the entire realm of human discourse in the West.' Going along with Indeterminacy, and similarly promoting 'anarchy and fragmentation everywhere', is the tendency towards what Hassan calls 'Immanence' (the two together producing the post-modern condition of 'indetermanence'). Immanence is associated with such words as dispersal, diffusion, disseminatiion and defraction – but also integration, interdependence and interpenetration. Hassan seems here to echo something like Foucault's idea of 'the death of man-as-subject', and his reconstitution in discourses, symbols and images. Hence for Hassan, as for Bell and others, the importance of the media and the whole range of information technology in creating a new 'dematerialized' reality for post-modern man. In any case Indeterminacy and Immanence both tend towards the same end, Anarchy over Authority, 'the Many asserting their primacy over the One' (Hassan 1985: 126; a discussion which sums up many of Hassan's contributions of the 1960s and 1970s, for references to which see 1985: 130).[4]

The problem with all this is obvious. If one accepts the accounts of post-modernism offered by theorists such as Fiedler and Hasssan – as well as, in a more hostile tone, critics such as Bell and Trilling – it is difficult to see in what way there has been any real departure from modernism. The antinomian, anarchic, anti-systemic character of post-modernism seems at one with both the form and the spirit of much of what we understand as modernism, especially that aspect of it associated with the theory and practice of the avant-garde.

It is true that if we select certain modernist currents – the Modern Movement in architecture or Constructivism in painting, for example – we can reasonably represent post-modernism, as Jencks does, as a reaction against their typically modern rationality and functionality. One of the faces of modernism is indeed hieratic and hierarchical, austere and authoritarian. But in this case what we are really doing is pitting one side of modernism against the other. For it has been clear to many commentators that much of what has been proclaimed post-modernist can be found prefigured in some of the central movements of modernism, such as Dadaism and Surrealism. Thus Matei Calinescu can argue that 'antielitism, antiauthoritarianism, gratuitousness, anarchy, and finally, nihilism are clearly implied in the dadaist doctrine of "antiart for antiart's sake" (the formula of Tristan Tzara)' (Calinescu 1987: 143; see also Huyssen 1992: 49). Peter Wollen too sees post-modernism not as a rejection or replacement of modernism but as 'a belated surfacing of subordinate aspects of modernism that had always been there'. These include Surrealism and exotic tendencies such as Orientalism and Mexicanidad which, though tamed and relieved of much of their subversive character, retained enough distinctiveness to form the elements of a counter-tradition which 'implicitly challenged the ruling norms' of orthodox modernism (Wollen 1993: 205–10).

Most telling of all is the example of Jean-François Lyotard, one of the founding fathers of post-modernism. Lyotard vigorously rebuts many of the well-known accounts of post-modernism, such as Jencks's ('I have read that under the name of postmodernism, architects are getting rid of the Bauhaus project, throwing out the baby of experimentation with the bathwater of functionalism'). For Lyotard experimentation, the rejection of the comfort and solace of realism and representational art, is the essence of post-modernism. This more or less identifies post-modernism with the theory of the avant-garde – a prime modernist concept, as Lyotard acknowledges. But for him modernism has allowed itself to become ossified, bureaucratized and commercialized. It no longer challenges or threatens, as it should. Post-modernism is the form that modernism takes when it has lost its revolutionary élan. It is the aspect of modernism that constantly reminds it of its essentially subversive and disruptive purpose. Thus the postmodern 'is undoubtedly part of the modern. All that has been received, if only yesterday . . . must be suspect.' Post-modernism represents the ceaseless rupture with the past, however radical that past was in its own time. It is what gives modernism its meaning. A work becomes modernist by repudiating its past, by being 'post' something. Cezanne is modern because he is post-Impressionist, just as Duchamp is modern because he is post-Cubist. In the paradoxical language that the French make their own, Lyotard writes: 'A work can become modern only if it is first postmodern. Postmodernism thus understood is not modernism at its end but in the nascent state, and this state is constant' (Lyotard 1984b: 79).

We shall come back to Lyotard. But there is undoubtedly something here that presents a considerable challenge to the versions of post-modernism that we have been discussing so far. These turn out to be either varieties of modernism or, as combatively put by Lyotard, its very principle. Faced with this some theorists, such as Jencks, have tried to distinguish post-modernism from 'late modernism'. What Fiedler, Hassan and the conservative critics of the 1960s and 1970s were talking about – the counter-culture of the 1960s and its legacy – was, it is argued, not so much post-modern as late modern. It is this that makes Bell for example say that 'in the 1960s a powerful current of post-modernism developed which carried the logic of modernism to its farthest reaches' (Bell 1976: 51). A similar assumption, it is claimed, underlies Lyotard's avant-gardist concept of the post-modern. All of these understand post-modernism in terms of the 'tradition of the new' – a modernist principle – whereas post-modernism proper has a 'complex relation to the past'. It accepts and reworks the past, often in a playful, parodic or affectionate form, rather than rejecting it wholesale. It is concerned with context and continuity – and community – rather than rupture and discontinuity. The past, says Umberto Eco, 'must be revisited: but with irony, not innocently' (Eco 1992: 73). That is what he has done in his postmodernist novel, *The Name of the Rose* (1980), which uses the modern form of the detective story in a late medieval setting. Similarly the postmodernist architect Paolo Portoghesi ironically comments on the past in his Casa Baldi, which is a direct parody – 'ironically different', 'a critical revisiting', 'repetition with ironic distance' – of Michelangelo's Capella Sforza in the church of S. Maria Maggiore in Rome (Hutcheon 1988: 29; Portoghesi 1992). Post-modernism neither repudiates nor imitates the past; it recovers and 'expands' the past to enrich the present. Theorists such as Barth, Jencks, Hutcheon and Hassan too in his later writings, speak of the 'synthesis' or 'hybridization' of the old and the new, a dialectical 'sublation' of the past onto a new post-modernist plane which accepts 'the presence of the past'. The culture of the avant-garde gives way to the culture of the 'post-avant-garde'. If modernism – including 'late modernism' – is enamoured of the 'shock of the new', post-modernism is more likely to exhibit the 'shock of the old' (Jencks 1992c: 222; see also Jencks 1989: 32–8; 1992b; Hutcheon 1988: 22–36; Hassan 1992: 197; Barth 1992).

This attempt to save post-modernism by identifying a category of 'late modernism' gains some support from critical commentary on the cultural movements of the 1960s. Writing at the time Frank Kermode, for instance, made the distinction between 'palaeo-modernism' and 'neo-modernism', the culture of the 1890s and that of the 1960s. Modernism is for Kermode a matter of 'self-reconciling opposites'. Palaeo-modernism cultivated the occult, neo-modernism denied it; 'early modernism tended towards fascism, later modernism towards anarchism'. But both phases are extremist, both share the apocalyptic mood and a determination to break absolutely with the past. The culture of the 1960s does not therefore represent a rejection of modernism, as Fiedler and others claim. It is not post-modernist but neo-modernist, and the theoretical bases of neo-modernism are not revolutionary but are 'marginal developments of older modernism'. 'There has been only one Modernist Revolution', Kermode concluded, and 'it happened a long time ago . . . [C]ertain aspects of earlier modernism really were so revolutionary that we ought not to expect – even with everything so speeded up – to have the pains and pleasures of another comparable movement quite so soon' (Kermode 1968a: 23–6; see also 1989: 130–3).

Kermode however made the significant admission that 'the fact that defining the modern is a task that now imposes itself on many distinguished scholars may be a sign that the modern period is over' (Kermode 1968a: 28). This brings us back once more to the idea of some discontinuity, some new development or developments that call for a rethinking of the modern. It is easy to become irritated by the debates among literary critics and cultural historians as to whether we are living in a 'modern', 'late modern', 'post-modern' or some other similarly-labelled phase or period. Were it simply a matter of culture, in the sense of artistic developments, we might – at least as social theorists – be inclined to leave the whole thing to the cultural critics, if not to late night television programmes on the cultural channels. What continues to make the debates relevant and interesting is that they are part of a much wider debate on the contemporary condition and future direction of industrial societies.

Originating largely in the cultural sphere, the concept of post-modernism (or post-modernity) has spread to encompass more and more areas of society. There is talk not only of post-modern painting, architecture, literature and cinema, but also of post-modern philosophy, post-modern politics, the post-modern economy, the post-modern family, even the post-modern person. The suggestion is that industrial societies have undergone a transformation so fundamental and wide-ranging as to deserve a new name. The question then becomes, are we living not simply in a post-modern culture but in an increasingly post-modern society.

Post-Modern Culture and Post-Modern Society

There are some who would think that this question is improperly put. While they do not deny that the cultural changes that concern them are in some way connected to changes in society, they wish to reserve the term post-modern – in their usage generally un-hyphenated as 'postmodern' – exclusively for the cultural sphere. Postmodern culture is then linked to some new form of society, 'post-industrial' society being the commonly preferred concept. Postmodern is then to post-industrial as culture to society. Postmodernism is the culture of post-industrial society.

Thus the 'postmodern condition' that is the subject of Lyotard's influential study refers to the 'condition of knowledge' in the present, postmodern state of culture, which is in turn linked to the emergence of a post-industrial society. His 'working hypothesis' is that 'the status of knowledge is altered as societies enter what is known as the postindustrial age and cultures enter what is known as the postmodern age' (Lyotard 1984a: 3). Portoghesi similarly says that 'before a Postmodern culture, there . . . existed a "postmodern condition", the product of "post-industrial" society' (Portoghesi 1992: 208).[5]

A more sophisticated variant, coming from a more directly sociological, often Marxist, provenance, is to see postmodernism as the cultural face of capitalism in its more developed stages. Daniel Bell, who considers postmodernism to be simply an extension of modernism, sees it as part of the (anti-bourgeois, adversary) culture of capitalism in the era of mass consumption (Bell 1976: 65–72). For Fredric Jameson, drawing on Ernest Mandel's account of 'late capitalism', postmodernism is the 'cultural logic of late capitalism' (Jameson 1992; Mandel 1978). Scott Lash, who says that for him postmodernism is 'strictly cultural', a 'cultural paradigm', balks at the idea of 'logic' and prefers to speak instead of 'a relationship of compatibility' between postmodernism and 'an importantly post-industrial capitalist economy' (Lash 1990: 4; see also Eagleton 1985).[6]

This might seem a neat solution to nagging problems of nomenclature. Post-modernism can stand to post-industrial or late-capitalist society as modernism stands to industrial society in its modern or classically capitalist phase. Culture and society can be seen as complementary but distinct spheres, amenable to separate analyses. This indeed is the general practice of most literary critics and cultural historians dealing with the phenomenon of both modernism and post-modernism. It has also tended to be the practice of those sociologists, such as Lash, convinced of the rise of a new post-modernist cultural paradigm.

Unfortunately this convenient parallel between modernism and post-modernism will not work. Modernism was generally a cultural reaction to the main currents of modernity. In some of its forms it was a passionate rejection of them. The same cannot be said of the relation between post-modernism and post-industrial (or late-capitalist) society. All theorists, if they consider the relationship at all, see a convergence or complementarity between post-modern culture and post-industrial society. While therefore it may be proper to treat modernist culture as something distinct from modern society, in the sense that it represented a break or discontinuity within the general order of modernity, the same strategy cannot be applied to post-modernism.

But the problem is even greater than this. For not only is it difficult to consider post-modernist culture apart from its social context; in most of the attempts to do so it is clear that much of the content of post-modernism is derived from the theory's particular understanding of contemporary society. Culture and society are only apparently treated separately; in reality they are collapsed into each other.

Thus Lyotard's study of the changing character of knowledge – the 'postmodern condition' – is explicitly premised on a view of society in which 'knowledge has become the principle force of production' and the 'computerization of society' is taken as the underlying reality. Lyotard accepts, in other words, as his references make clear, the thinking of Bell, Nora and Minc and other theorists of the post-industrial information society (Lyotard 1984a: 3–7, 85–7). Knowledge, in its postmodern form, is not simply a cultural extrusion of post-industrial society; it is an aspect precisely of 'the knowledge society'.

So too Paolo Portoghesi ties his concept of postmodernism firmly to 'the age of information' made possible by 'the new electronic technology'. The very terms of postmodernist architecture are for him defined by the new 'organic' reality brought into being by the grid of information and communication. Postmodernist architecture mirrors the information society in being an 'architecture of communication'. The disembedded and abstract structures of modernism are replaced by the rediscovery of 'architectonic archetypes', which reflect the daily life and collective memory of mankind. These become literally the building blocks in re-establishing a relationship of community – 'communicating' – between buildings and their users (Portoghesi 1992: 211–12).

Neither Lyotard nor Portoghesi understand knowledge in the same way as Bell and the other theorists of the information society. For Lyotard especially, as we shall see, post-modern knowledge is quite different from the modernist understanding of it in the theory of the information society. The point though is that for both men the novelties they discern – in knowledge, in Lyotard's case, in architecture in Portoghesi's – are part of the very substance of the society as they describe it.

Something similar applies to the Marxist theories of post-modernism. Jameson purports to see postmodernism as the culture of a particular stage of capitalism, 'late capitalism'. He speaks of late capitalism rather than post-industrialism, he says, because he wants to indicate the new system's basic continuity with what preceded it, rather than, as with post-industrial theory, 'a break, rupture and mutation'.[7] 'Postmodernism is not the cultural dominant of a wholly new social order . . . but only the reflex and the concomitant of yet another systemic modification of capitalism itself.' Conventionally, and following the analyses of Marxists such as Mandel, Jameson lists the features of late capitalism as the trans-national business enterprise, the new international division of labour, 'a vertiginous new dynamic in international banking and stock exchanges', 'new forms of media interrelationship', computers and automation, and 'the flight of production to advanced Third World areas' (together with such social consequences as 'the emergence of yuppies' and 'gentrification on a now-global scale') (Jameson 1992: xii, xix; see also 260–78).

At the same time Jameson confesses to a certain uneasiness at the category 'late capitalism'. He admits to varying it with 'appropriate synonyms' such as 'spectacle or image society', 'media capitalism', 'the world system', and even 'postmodernism' itself. More significantly, from the point of view of retaining some distance between postmodern culture and (late) capitalist society, his account of the new stage of capitalism suggests a radically new relationship between culture and society. Late capitalism operates in an environment in which what Bell called 'the game against nature' has been superseded by 'the game between persons'. Its cultural correlate, postmodernism, is according to Jameson 'what you have when the modernization process is complete and nature is gone for good.' But this also installs culture at the centre of society, one in which '"culture" has become a veritable "second nature" '. Culture can now hardly be regarded as 'the reflex and concomitant' of society and the economic system. In the late capitalist stage, culture itself becomes the prime determinant of social, economic, political and even psychological reality. There has been, says Jameson, 'a prodigious expansion of culture throughout the social realm, to the point at which everything in our social life – from economic value and state power to practices and to the very structure of the psyche itself – can be said to have become "cultural" in some original and yet untheorized sense'. We are witnesses to 'an immense dilation' of the sphere of the cultural, 'an immense and historically original acculturation of the Real', 'a quantum leap in what Benjamin . . . called the "aestheticization" of reality'. Culture has become 'a product in its own right'; the process of cultural consumption is no longer merely an adjunct but the very essence of capitalist functioning (Jameson 1992: ix–x; 48).

We may choose if we wish to call this capitalism, and continue to regard post-modernism as its cultural expression or 'structure of feeling', to use the term of Raymond Williams's that Jameson likes. But we should have to admit that this is a capitalism profoundly different from its previous incarnations. It is one in which, as Jameson himself says, culture 'cleaves almost too close to the skin of the economic to be stripped off and inspected in its own right, . . . not unlike Magritte's shoe-foot.' It is a form of capitalism in which what Marxists would traditionally have called the 'superstructure' – knowledge and culture – seems to have moved to the core of the society, if not indeed to have become its 'base'. At the very least, as Jameson once again admits, in the late capitalist or postmodernist phase (seen as twin aspects of the same phenomenon) the two terms 'cultural' and 'economic' 'collapse back into one another and say the same thing, in an eclipse of the distinction between base and superstructure . . . ' (Jameson 1992: xv, xxi).

The example of Jameson is important, as his is the best-known and most sophisticated of the attempts to see post-modernism as the culture of a particular kind of society whose principle is found, initially at least, outside post-modernism itself. But other accounts, also mainly of a Marxist kind, show the same tendency towards the inflation of culture that is so marked a characteristic of all post-modernist writing. A kind of cultural imperialism asserts itself. What starts off as the part – post-modernist culture – ends up by becoming the whole – post-modernist society.

Scott Lash is another example. Lash ('I am not a postmodernist' – the protestation is already a warning) starts off in his study of postmodernism with the defiant intention of maintaining 'eminently modernist distinctions' between the cultural, on the one hand, and the economic and social on the other. Postmodernism will be seen as the culture of 'post-industrial capitalist society'. Not wishing to be too deterministic, Lash speaks of a relation of 'compatibility', or of an 'elective affinity', between postmodern culture and contemporary capitalist society. Drawing on his earlier work with John Urry (see chapter three, above), he diagnoses contemporary capitalism as 'disorganized', compared to the 'organized' capitalism of the last part of the nineteenth and the first half of the twentieth centuries. Disorganized capitalism includes most of the features we have previously looked at under the headings of 'post-Fordism' and the 'information society'. Lash here wishes to stress especially the fragmentation of working class cultures and communities, the decentralization of cities and social movements, and the resurgence of individualism. He also wants to point to the emergence of a 'new, "Yuppified" post-industrial bourgeoisie', with its base in the media, higher education, finance and advertising. This new middle class is disputing the primacy of society with the old bourgeoisie of organized capitalism. It cultivates and promotes its own culture, the culture of postmodernism, which unlike the culture of the older bourgeoisie makes no distinction between elite and mass, high and low. Just as modernism was the culture of, or at least compatible with, organized capitalism and its ruling bourgeois class, so postmodernism is the culture of disorganized capitalism and the new post-industrial middle classes (Lash 1990: 3, 16–18, 20–1, 37–8; see also Lash and Urry 1987: 285–313; Lash and Urry 1994).

So far, so straightforward. It is when we come to see what Lash means by postmodernism that this neat picture, as with Jameson, dissolves. Lash characterizes postmodernist culture – in what purports to be a cultural description – largely through a series of oppositions to modernism. Modernist cultural forms – from realist painting and literature to the 'autonomous' art work of high modernism – depended on a process of differentiation: of the cultural from the social, the aesthetic from the theoretical (or scientific), the sacred from the secular, science from religion. Each successive phase of modern culture involved a greater and greater degree of differentiation, culminating in the 'self-legislating', 'self-validating' claims for art in the modernist movement of the late nineteenth century (1990: 5–11; see also Habermas 1981: 9–10).

Postmodernism reverses this. It is the result of a continuing process of 'de-differentiation' whose origins are to be found in the social and cultural changes of the 1950s and 1960s. First, the different cultural spheres – the aesthetic, the ethical, the theoretical – lose their autonomy: 'for instance, the aesthetic realm begins to colonize both theoretical and moral-political spheres' (cf. Jameson's 'aestheticization of reality'). Secondly, 'the cultural realm . . . is no longer systematically separated from the social.' There is 'a new immanence in the social of culture': for instance social distinctions, as shown in the claims of the new middle classes, turn increasingly not on economic or political power but on the display of cultural symbols. Equally, and thirdly, the cultural is no longer separated from the economic. Culture and commerce interfuse, and feed on each other. This is most clearly shown in the central role of advertising in contemporary culture, and it can also be seen in the way in which artistic and sporting events, such as pop festivals and national and international football competitions, become the vehicles for promoting big business. Perhaps its would be better to say: *become* big business, because much of the business of the post-industrial economy is itself culture, concerned with the production of cultural goods and services. There has been, in other words, not just the familiar 'commodification of culture', extending now to 'elite' as well as 'mass' culture, but also a movement in the other direction in which culture has colonized the economy. Hence the importance to the economy of the 'culture industries': education, the mass media, tourism, leisure, sport.

Like Jameson, and pushed by the same logic of the analysis, Lash concludes that 'it is less useful in this context to speak in terms of the base-superstructure notion of "articulation" and instead consider culture as part and parcel *of* the economy . . . The new regime of accumulation [i.e. economic mode of production] is becoming itself progressively more and more a regime of signification [i.e. a cultural mode or paradigm] . . . The means of production are becoming increasingly cultural and [the] relations of production are becoming increasingly cultural. That is, relations of production are . . . not so often now mediated by material means of production, but are questions of discourse, of communications between management and employees . . . ' (Lash 1990: 38–9; see also 43–5; Lash and Urry 1994: 60–110).

There is much to commend in general in this comparison of modernism and postmodernism. It points to a good deal of what is going on in contemporary culture, and in contemporary society. But it is clearly highly problematic from the point of view of establishing that critical distance between culture and society – the 'modernist' standpoint – that Lash began with. Culture, far from keeping its distance or being merely 'compatible' with post-industrial capitalist society, seems to have all but taken over the society. This comes out even more strongly in Lash's final point of comparison between modernism and postmodernism. Modernism, he says, 'problematized' and 'destabilized' representation; while postmodernism problematizes and destabilizes reality itself. What this means is that modernist art questioned the whole way of representing reality, especially that embodied in the realist and naturalist traditions. It did not deny 'nature' or 'objective reality', it simply argued that art had its own autonomous reality, its own ways and forms, and that this should be the sole concern of the artist. Postmodernism, on the other hand, which has to some extent resurrected realist and naturalist modes of representation (for instance in pop art), casts doubt on the very nature of the reality represented. It suggests that this reality is no more than another set of representations or images – *simulacra*, in Jean Baudrillard's term. Andy Warhol's silk-screens, for instance, depict objects which themselves turn out to be images.

In this conception culture and society once more become one, or at least twin aspects of the same (insubstantial) thing. 'Our everyday life', says Lash, 'becomes pervaded with a reality – in TV, adverts, video, computerization, the Walkman, cassette decks in automobiles, and . . . CDs, CDV, and DAT – which increasingly comprises representations.' There is no distinction, or distance, between the 'signifier' (the image) and the 'referent' (the thing or external reality it purportedly represents). Both invade each other's space, both take over each other's function. The image or illusion mimics the real, and the real is illusory, composed of images. The real is as imagined as the imaginary. Postmodernism 'puts chaos, flimsiness, and instability in our experience of reality itself' (Lash 1990: 15; and generally 12–14).

Whatever our assessment of this position, the point is that it once more undermines the whole separation of culture and society that Lash like Jameson has been so anxious to establish. If postmodern culture is to be 'carried' by the economic and social system of post-industrial capitalism, it now appears that this system has been so penetrated by postmodern culture itself as to be a most fragile vessel. To put the matter differently, postmodern culture has to haul itself up by its own boot-straps. The social 'reality' supposedly underlying the 'illusory' realm of culture itself dissolves into illusion. Base and superstructure are collapsed into each other.[8]

It is the very plausibility of the accounts of both Jameson and Lash that makes it seem best to abandon the conventional Marxist or sociological models of the relation between culture and society. More than Lyotard or Portoghesi, they make a serious and systematic attempt to demonstrate the adequacy of their models. Their failure, in the light of their own analyses, is all the more convincing testimony to the need to consider the relation differently. We do indeed seem to be in an era in which culture has taken on an unprecedented potency in social life. Whether this is leading us into a new kind of society, post-modern society, is something still to be determined. But if we are to treat the claims seriously, the best model would seem to be something that might be called anthropological. Whether we talk about post-modern culture, or post-modern society, or the post-modern condition, or more generally a post-modern temper or sensibility, we should take it that we are dealing with a whole way of thinking, feeling and acting: culture as anthropologists generally understand the term. Another way of putting it is to say that, in present circumstances at least, we should prefer Hegel to Marx. Unlike Marx's privileging of the economic 'base', we should follow Hegel and regard culture and society as permeated by a common 'spirit', the spirit of post-modernism (however defined). If we follow the logic of most of the theories, it seems misleading even to speak of a convergence, or complementarity, or correspondence between post-modern culture and post-industrial society. What we have rather is a conflation of the two. Post-modernism appears an attribute of all aspects of society and it seems unwise, at least initially, to privilege any one part as cause or determinant. For post-modernists, what we seem to be witnessing is an extended explosion, or implosion, taking place across all sectors of society. That is why they, or other students drawn to their approach, have felt able to apply post-modernist perspectives in such a wide and varied range of disciplines: politics, geography, anthropology, history, even biology and physics – in addition to the more familiarly affected philosophy, sociology and cultural studies (see, for example, Gibbins 1989; Nederveen Pieterse 1992; Soja 1989; Rabinow 1986; Stone 1991; Griffin 1988).[9]

Charles Jencks and David Harvey are among those who have adopted the strategy of treating post-modernism as a comprehensive category of culture and society. The richness of their accounts, the wide-ranging links across different areas of society that they make, show the fertility of this approach. It really does not matter, in the end, whether we accept their claims or arguments. As compared with the narrowly-based, intellectually introverted literary and cultural accounts, they present us with a series of bold and provocative hypotheses touching on matters of interest to students in all the human sciences. For Jencks, post-modernism represents 'a pervasive shift both in world view and civilisation', 'a new era of culture and social organisation'. It includes, in addition to the cultural reaction to modernism, all the elements of what Bell earlier called the post-industrial society and later the information society. It also includes much of post-Fordism, and what in addition Toffler bundled together under the general heading of the 'Third Wave' (Jencks 1989: 43–56; see also Jencks 1992: 15, 34–6).

Harvey likewise treats 'the condition of postmodernity' through a bold series of contrasts between what he calls 'Fordist modernity' and 'flexible postmodernity'. As the terms show, he has collated the concepts and analyses of post-Fordist theorists (such as Lash and Urry) and post-modernist theorists (such as Hassan) to provide a comprehensive description of our current condition. Despite the subtitle of his book, 'An Inquiry into the Origins of Cultural Change', the postmodern condition he describes is one that has equally cultural, economic, political, philosophical and even psychological dimensions (Harvey 1989: 338–41).

Harvey's account is also important for another reason. He shows that taking the comprehensive view of post-modernity does not prevent one from adopting a Marxist or other kind of sociological approach to it. Only these have to be modified according to the new state of things. If one does not have to be locked into the categories of cultural post-modernism, equally one is not forced to adopt the separation of culture and society in the base-superstructure model. Post-modernity can be considered a kind of capitalism (as it is for Harvey), or a kind of industrialism (as it is for Jencks). The analysis can draw on all the theoretical tools available to students of these well-known systems. What has to be acknowledged, however, is that the systems have changed radically. They have thrown up new forces and new configurations. The old categories cannot simply be slapped on the new forms. However much contemporary societies may retain of their former principles – and the very terms post-modern and post-industrial indicate some continuity – these principles now operate in a new environment.

The Post-Modern Condition

In considering the question of how far we may be moving into a post-modern society as well as a post-modern culture, we should start by sketching the broad picture of post-modernity as it has been presented by its leading theorists. We can begin with the more familiar features, many of which we have already looked at in the chapters on the information society and post-Fordism.

Most theorists claim that contemporary societies show a new or heightened degree of fragmentation, pluralism and individualism. This is partly related to the changes in work organization and technology highlighted by the post-Fordist theorists. It can also be linked to the decline of the nation state and of dominant national cultures. Political, economic and cultural life is now strongly influenced by developments at the global level. This has as one of its effects, unexpectedly, the renewed importance of the local, and a tendency to stimulate sub-national and regional cultures.

The typical institutions and practices of the nation state are correspondingly weakened. Mass political parties give way to the 'new social movements' based on gender, race, locality, sexuality. The 'collective identities' of class and shared work experiences dissolve into more pluralized and privatized forms of identity. The idea of a national culture and national identity is assailed in the name of 'minority' cultures – the cultures of particular ethnic groups, religious faiths, and communities based on age, gender or sexuality. Post-modernism proclaims multi-cultural and multi-ethnic societies. It promotes the 'politics of difference'. Identity is not unitary or essential, it is fluid and shifting, fed by multiple sources and taking multiple forms (there is no such thing as 'woman' or 'black').

Post-modern society typically links the local and the global. Global developments – the internationalization of the economy and of culture – reflect back on national societies, undermining national structures and promoting local ones. Ethnicity receives a renewed impetus. There is an upsurge of regionalism and 'peripheral nationalisms' – the nationalism of small nations which have typically been incorporated in larger units such as the United Kingdom, France, Spain and other historic national groupings. 'Think globally, act locally', the slogan of the 1960s, applies to a good number of the new social movements, most noticeably the feminist and ecological movements. There is a similar link-up in some of the new movements of religious revival, such as Protestant and Islamic fundamentalism.

Post-modernity reverses or qualifies some of the typical spatial movements and arrangements of modernity. The concentration of populations in large cities is countered by a movement of de-concentration, de-centralization and dispersal. Much of this is related to post-Fordist developments. It is also the result of the 'de-industrialization' of many regions of western societies – with much manufacturing being exported to non-western societies – and a post-industrial 're-industrialization' based on high-tech, research-based concerns which have preferred new locations in suburban and ex-urban areas, especially those near university cities. Jobs and people move out of the big cities. Small towns and villages are re-populated. Post-modern architecture reverses the trend to high-rise offices and apartment buildings. The stress now is on small-scale schemes, linking people to neighbourhoods and aiming to cultivate the ethos of particular places and particular local cultures. A new, or renewed, importance attaches to place. There is a re-discovery of territorial identities, local traditions, local histories – even where, as with nationalism, these are imagined or invented.

These features of post-modern society are an amalgam of various elements deriving from some well-known accounts of contemporary western society. Post-modern society is thus far congruent with, if not identical to, post-Fordist society, the information society and 'late' or 'disorganized' capitalism as seen in a number of theories.[10] Even though many of these theorists would have no truck with concepts of post-modernity, they are not likely to find much to demur at in the picture so far sketched. What makes post-modernism so distinctive as an approach is that it goes beyond these familiar features to make wide-ranging and, to many people, outrageous claims about the very nature of society and objective reality. It makes assertions not just about a new society or social reality, but about our understanding of reality itself. It moves from history and sociology to philosophical questions of truth and knowledge.

Once more we can start with the familiar, but given an unfamiliar twist. Most theories of contemporary society attribute an important role to the media of mass communication, especially in the era of telecommunications and the computer. This is most obvious in the theory of the information society, but it is also strong in theories of post-Fordism and in Marxist theories of late capitalism.

For most of these theorists, just as information really informs – however distorted its uses – so the mass communication media really communicate, however distasteful their products or harmful their effects. Postmodernists – following here in the footsteps of Marshall McLuhan – see the effects of the mass media in a quite different way. For them the media today do not so much communicate as construct. In their sheer scale and ubiquity they are building a new environment for us, one which demands a new social epistemology and a new form of response. The media have created a new 'electronic reality', suffused with images and symbols, which has obliterated any sense of an objective reality behind the symbols. In the condition of what Jean Baudrillard calls the 'ecstasy of communication', the world, our world, becomes a world purely of 'simulation', 'the generation by models of a real without origin or reality: a hyperreal.' In hyperreality it is no longer possible to distinguish the imaginary from the real, the sign from its referent, the true from the false. The world of simulation is a world of *simulacra*, of images. But unlike conventional images, *simulacra* are copies that have no originals, or of which the originals have been lost. They are images which are 'murderers of the real, murderers of their own model'. In such a condition there can be no concept of ideology, no idea of 'the betrayal of reality' by signs or images. There are only signs and images, only the hyperreal. 'History has stopped meaning, referring to anything – whether you call it social space or the real. We have passed into a kind of hyperreal where things are being replayed *ad infinitum*' (Baudrillard 1987b: 69; 1988b: 166, 170, 182).

With the growth of an electronically mediated reality, the hyperreal is becoming the condition of the whole of the modern world. But postmodernists are particularly drawn to America as the capital, as it were, of hyperreality, the model of our future (once again). In such monuments of Americana as the Hearst Castle at San Simeon or the Forest Lawn cemeteries of California, in Disneyland and Disney World, in the desert cities of Las Vegas and Los Angeles, they find the the clearest instances of the reign of the hyperreal. Here the copy (or fake) substitutes itself for the real, becomes more real than the real itself. 'The American imagination', says Umberto Eco, 'demands the real thing, and, to attain it, must fabricate the absolute fake.' In the extraordinary illusion of realism created in these places, in their extravagant *bricolage* of styles and objects drawn from all countries and all histories, there is a 'fusion of copy and original'; the copy in fact 'seems more convincing than the model' (Eco 1987: 8, 19).

For Eco, as for many theorists, Disneyland is the apotheosis of the hyperreal, 'at once absolutely realistic and absolutely fantastic', 'a fantasy world more real than reality'. It is the truest art-work of America, its 'Sistine Chapel' (Eco 1987: 43–8). For Baudrillard too 'Disneyland is a perfect model of all the entangled orders of simulation.' It allows one to trace the 'objective profile' of the United States, the land par excellence of *simulacra*. But it is more than a 'digest of the American way of life'.

> Disneyland is there to conceal the fact that it is the 'real' country, all of 'real' America, which *is* Disneyland (just as prisons are there to conceal the fact that it is the social in its entirety, in its banal omnipresence, which is carceral).
>
> Disneyland is presented as imaginary in order to make us believe that the rest is real, when in fact all of Los Angeles and the America

surrounding it are no longer real, but of the order of the hyperreal and of simulation. (Baudrillard 1988b: 171–2; see also Marin 1984)

This stress on Disneyland not simply as a representation but as representative of American (hyper)reality is echoed in the observations on what are seen as typically postmodernist American cities. Just as earlier theories of modernity read the whole world through key modernist cities such as Paris and New York, so current theories of post-modernity read the contemporary world through American cities such as Las Vegas and Los Angeles which most clearly seem to embody post-modern patterns. Thus Las Vegas is for Eco (following Robert Venturi) 'a completely new phenomenon in city planning, a "message" city, entirely made up of signs, not a city like the others, which communicate in order to function, but rather a city that functions in order to communicate' (Eco 1987: 40).

The phantasmagoric quality of Las Vegas, its appearance as a desert 'mirage', is paralleled for Baudrillard by Los Angeles, 'a town whose mystery is precisely that it is nothing more than a network of endless, unreal circulation: a town of fabulous proportions, but without space or dimensions' (Baudrillard 1988b: 172; see also 1989: 102–4, 123–8). For Edward Soja, Los Angeles is a 'mesocosm of postmodernity', both the concentrated expression of, and, through its economic and cultural life, the leading contributor to global post-modernity. More than anywhere else in the world Los Angeles shows the urban form of post-modernity. Its 'hyperspace' is made up of a 'dazzling . . . patchwork mosaic' of over four hundred officially designated communities. Many of these – Venice, Naples, Hawaiian Gardens, Ontario – have names and ethnic groups that recall other cultures, other histories. First World (corporate capital) and Third World (migrant labour) mingle promiscuously; history and geography are jumbled up. 'Time and space, the "once" and the "there", are being increasingly played with and packaged to serve the needs of the here and now, making the lived experience of the urban increasingly vicarious, screened through *simulacra* . . .'

Once more, the illusory does not imitate the real, it becomes it. Los Angeles, says Soja, defies conventional descriptions of urban and suburban, community and neighbourhood. 'It has in effect been deconstructing the urban into a confusing collage of signs which advertise what are often little more than imaginary communities and outlandish representations of urban locality.' Underneath the 'semiotic blanket' of Los Angeles there is indeed an economic order – the most advanced in the world – but 'when all that is seen is so fragmented and filled with whimsy and pastiche, the hard edges of the capitalist, racist and patriarchal landscape seem to disappear, melt into air.'

> With exquisite irony, contemporary Los Angeles has come to resemble more than ever before a gigantic agglomeration of theme parks, a lifespace composed of Disneyworlds. It is a realm divided into showcases of global village cultures and mimetic American landscapes, all-embracing shopping malls and crafty Main Streets, corporation-sponsored magic kingdoms, high-technology-based experimental prototype communities of tomorrow, attractively packaged places for rest and recreation . . . (Soja 1989: 245–6)[11]

The state of hyperreality means not just the dissolution of objective reality, of something 'out there' to which signs and images refer. It also means the dissolution of the human subject, the individual ego that modernity took to be the autonomous thinker and actor in the world. For Baudrillard, as for Foucault, the individual subject – 'man' – was a temporary construct lasting for the few centuries of the modern period. He – and it was an almost purely masculine concept – was the Faustian or Promethean hero of Descartes' and Bacon's 'narratives' of modernity (Foucault 1973; Abercrombie et al. 1986).

The 'ecstasy of communication' has made such assumptions of an autonomous, sovereign individual impossible. The individual, says Baudrillard, no longer stands in an objective relationship, even an 'alienated' one, to his environment. He is no longer 'an actor or dramaturge but . . . a terminal of multiple networks', like an astronaut in his capsule, through which electronic, computer-controlled messages flow. 'With the television image – the television being the ultimate and perfect object for this new era – our own body and the whole surrounding universe becomes a control screen' (Baudrillard 1983: 127–8).

Baudrillard does not, unlike some celebrants of 'virtual reality' and 'cyberspace', rejoice in this condition. He finds it 'obscene', because it 'puts an end to every representation', obliterates all distinction and distance between the self and the environment. The oppositions subject/object, public/private lose all meaning; they collapse into each other. No secrecy, no interiority, no intimacy remains; everything, including the individual, 'dissolves completely in information and communication'. That is the 'ecstasy of communication', 'all functions abolished in a single dimension, that of communication'. For Baudrillard this is bringing into being 'a new form of schizophrenia'. It induces 'a state of terror proper to the schizophrenic: too great a proximity of everything, the unclean promiscuity of everything which touches, invests and penetrates without resistance, with no halo of private protection, not even his own body, to protect him anymore.'

> What characterizes him is less the loss of the real, the light years of estrangement from the real, the pathos of distance and radical separation, as is commonly said: but, very much to the contrary, the absolute proximity, the total instantaneity of things, the feeling of no defence, no retreat. It is the end of interiority and intimacy, the overexposure and transparence of the world which traverses him without obstacle. He can no longer produce the limits of his own being, can no longer play nor stage himself, can no longer produce himself as mirror. He is now only a pure screen, a switching center for all the networks of influence. (Baudrillard 1983: 132–3; see also 1987b: 70–1)

This image of despair – though admittedly not one that Baudrillard consistently presents in his writings – should remind us that many theorists of post-modernity are not celebrators of the condition they diagnose. Their attitude is more generally one of resignation, often tinged with ironic regret at the passing of the more confident modern era. Martin Jay (1993) has likened their feelings to those of clinical melancholia, as analysed by Freud. Certainly there is little of the exuberance exhibited by Marshall McLuhan (1967) in his similar reflections on the effects of the new electronic environment, still less the exhilaration of the new science-fiction explorers of cyberspace (for example, Gibson 1984).

Baudrillard's analysis of the impact of the new communications technology evidently takes him in a quite different direction from theorists of the information society such as Bell, Stonier and Masuda. Where they see an extension of human capacity and power, a Promethean expansiveness on a global scale, he sees the disappearance of the individual in networks of information. But for some theorists of post-modernity this very suppression of the individual contains the seeds of a possible future emancipation. For them it is wrong or impossible to go back to the subject-centred theories of modernity. We must build on the potentialities of the new era to find our freedom in a new way.

Mark Poster, for instance, like Baudrillard rejects Bell's theory of the information society. He finds it 'totalizing', in an old-fashioned modernist mode, and insufficiently attentive to the linguistic dimension of information and communication. He also very much goes along with Baudrillard in his view of the effects of the new electronic media on the traditional conception of the individual. In what he calls the 'mode of information' – paralleling Marx's mode of production – a new stage of 'electronically-mediated exchange' has been reached, accompanying and to good extent displacing orally- and print-mediated exchanges. In this third electronic stage 'the self is decentered, dispersed and multiplied in continuous instability . . . In electronically mediated communications, subjects now float, suspended between points of objectivity, being constituted and reconstituted in different configurations in relation to the discursive arrangements of the occasion.'

> In the [new stage of the] mode of information the subject is no longer located in a point in absolute time/space, enjoying a physical, fixed vantage point from which rationally to calculate its options. Instead it is multiplied by databases, dispersed by computer messaging and conferencing, decontextualized and reidentified by TV ads, dissolved and materialized continuously in the electronic transmission of symbols . . . The body is no longer an effective limit of the subject's position. Or perhaps it would be better to say that communications facilities extend the nervous system throughout the Earth to the point that it enwraps the planet in a noosphere, to use Teilhard de Chardin's term, of language. If I can speak directly or by electronic mail to a friend in Paris while sitting in California, if I can witness political and cultural events as they occur across the globe without leaving my home, if a database at a remote location contains my profile and informs government agencies which make decisions that affect my life without any knowledge on my part of these events, if I can shop in my home by using my TV or computer, then where am I and who am I? In these circumstances I cannot consider myself centered in my rational, autonomous subjectivity or bordered by a defined ego, but I am disrupted, subverted and dispersed across social space. (Poster 1990: 6, 11, 15–16)

One would have expected this assessment to lead Poster to a similarly melancholic state to Baudrillard's; and clearly he is by no means complacent. But he attacks Baudrillard for being, like Bell, totalizing. The phenomenon of the hyperreal is illegitimately expanded to incorporate the totality of social life. 'Baudrillard's totalizing position forecloses the possibility of new movements. Sunk in a depressing hyperbole of the hyperreal, he transgresses the line of critical discourse in sweeping, gloomy pronouncements as if he knows the outcome to a story that has not yet been imagined, much less written.' The dissolution of the subject in the new mode of information has for Poster emancipatory potential.

In the TV advertisement, for instance, although the subject is partly reconstituted as a spectator/consumer, he or she is also deconstructed as a 'centered, original agent'. Since such an agent in classic modernist theory tends to be 'the rational male bourgeois', this act of deconstruction is liberating. 'As a language/practice the TV ad undermines the type of subject previously associated with the capitalist mode of production and with the associated forms of patriarchy and ethnocentrism.' This is no guarantee of emancipation, of course. But 'in the TV ad a language has been made which leaves/urges viewers to regard their own subjectivity as a constituted structure, to regard themselves as members of a community of self-constituters . . . To the extent that TV ads (and, tendentially, the media in general) constitute subjects as self-constituters, the hegemonic forms of self-constitution are put into question' (Poster 1990: 66–8).

Poster explicitly bases himself on the thinking of the post-structuralists; and his account mirrors the ambivalence towards post-modernity shown by poststructuralist and deconstructionist theorists. This is a group that is generally held to include such French thinkers as Foucault, Derrida, Barthes, Lacan, Kristeva, Lyotard and Baudrillard. It also includes a group of mainly American literary critics – Paul de Man, Stanley Fish, J. Hillis Miller among them – who have been influenced both by these French thinkers and the writings of the Russian theorist Mikhail Bakhtin.

From the very beginning, since the 1960s, the poststructuralists have been linked with theories of post-modernism and post-modernity. But a consideration of them in this context is beset by a number of problems. Firstly they have tended to restrict themselves to questions of literature and philosophy. The implications for society and politics are left for others to draw. Secondly many of them – for instance Baudrillard – espouse poststructuralism or deconstructionism without committing themselves to a post-modernist position. The connections are, again, largely made by other thinkers. Thirdly it needs to be said that their writing, especially in the case of the French thinkers, is dense and difficult; quotations, especially in translation, are not often very illuminating.

The connection between these thinkers and theories of post-modernity has mainly to do with their announcements of the 'death of man' (Foucault), or the 'death of the subject' (Derrida), or the 'death of the author' (Barthes). In Foucault's account of the development of the human sciences, man as a subject of science is not, as is commonly thought, a preoccupation going back to the ancient Greeks. It goes back only as recently as to the birth of the modern age, in the late eighteenth and early nineteenth centuries. From that time man was placed at the centre of accounts purporting to uncover the truth of his being, his history and his future destination.

For Foucault this development of knowledge was illusory, based on a false 'anthropologization' of reality. It is not man, the 'knowing subject', who should be the ground of the human sciences; what needs to be studied are the discursive practices of the human sciences that constitute and construct man. Foucault gives his unstinted admiration to Nietzsche, who 'killed man and God both at the same time'. He put into question the whole status of man as agent and subject, showing the essential issue to be a matter of language. Man is a construct of linguistic practices, not the essential ground of knowledge and value.

> To all those who still wish to talk about man, about his reign or his liberation, to all those who still ask themselves questions about what man is in his essence, to all those who wish to take him as their starting-point in their attempts to reach the truth . . . to all these warped and twisted forms of reflection we can answer only with a philosophical laugh . . . (Foucault 1970: 342–3)

Foucault looks forward to the time when language will have regained its primacy in the study of the human condition. Then 'one can certainly wager that man would be erased, like a face drawn in sand at the edge of the sea'.

> As the archaeology of our thought easily shows, man is an invention of recent date. And one perhaps nearing its end . . . Man is in the process of perishing as the being of language continues to shine ever brighter upon our horizons. Since man was constituted at a time when language was doomed to dispersion, will he not be dispersed when language regains its unity? (Foucault 1970: 386–7)

Foucault's attack on the man-centred character of the modern human sciences is paralleled by Derrida's attack on the subject-centred character of modern philosophy, and modern western thought in general. Derrida, like Foucault, expresses his debt to Nietzsche, and also to Heidegger. His target is precisely defined in the following remark of Heidegger's, in his study of Nietzsche.

> That period we call modern . . . is defined by the fact that man becomes the center and measure of all beings. Man is the *subjectum*, that which lies at the bottom of all beings, that is, in modern terms, at the bottom of all objectification and representation. (In Habermas 1987: 133)

Derrida's response to the modern paradigm of knowledge is to propose a radical 'decentring of the subject'. Language does not have speakers with coherent, stable identities. Texts do not have authors with purposive design and intention. The subject or author as much as the text is a linguistic product – as Paul de Man puts it, we 'rightfully reduce' the subject to 'the status of a mere grammatical pronoun'. There is no distinction between literature and philosophy; all discourses flow into and interpenetrate each other; all are equally 'fictive', equally the products of particular signifying practices. There can be no privileged reading of a text or any other cultural practice, no universal or authentic meaning assigned to it. Texts are open, 'dialogic' structures, shot through with 'aporias' (ramifying contradictions) and 'heteroglossia' (a plurality of voices). Agreement on meaning can be reached, if at all, only in particular 'interpretive communities' – of critics or citizens – and remains internal to them. At any rate no author or reader, no agent or subject, can be the privileged carrier of meaning. Just as with Baudrillard the self is no more than the intersection of electronically-transmitted messages, and with Foucault the meeting-point in the flows (or discourses) of power, so with Derrida and the deconstructionists the self is the place where language criss-crosses in a spiralling arc (or abyss) of indeterminacy.[12]

Is there a clear connection between all this and a post-modern politics and social theory? Some have doubted it. Deconstructionism, they allege, is so relentlessly subversive that it subverts itself. Despite its insistence on difference, it conjures up a flattened, depthless, entropic world, devoid of all energy. Its radical rejection of the concept of subject or agent leaves society and history with no directional force. It leads to an apolitical detachment and resignation, an attitude of irony and amusement at the comic human drama (Alexander 1994: 181).

Moreover, although it proclaims that the concept of 'textuality' applies to the world, not just to the book, its aestheticization of reality and its obsession in practice with written language have seemed to some to bring it closer to modernism than to post-modernism. It appears to share in the modernist principle of the autonomous, separated world of culture (Huyssen 1992: 60; cf. Connor 1989: 226). It is not surprising therefore to find a high degree of ambiguity and uncertainty in the politics of many of the principal deconstructionsist – Derrida, for instance (Poster 1990: 104–6; but cf. Derrida 1994).

Nevertheless it is not too difficult, at least in principle, to connect up poststructuralism and deconstructionism with the social theory of post-modernity. They go along with the general emphasis on fragmentation and pluralism, and on the absence of any centralizing or 'totalizing' force, that is a feature of all theories of post-modernity. What they tend to see at the individual level, postmodern theory sees at the level of society. Deconstructionism's dissolution of the subject is paralleled – whether as cause or effect – by the post-modern dissolution of the social: not in the sense of denying society as such, but in denying its power as an embodied collectivity. Just as there is no responsible or active agent in deconstructionism – no author of a text, for instance – so in post-modern theory society cannot act, not at least in the manner assumed by Marx or Durkheim.

This can lead postmodern theorists towards a radical individualism, not easily distinguishable from the individualism of the contemporary radical Right. But it has also led some theorists on the Left to reconstruct such traditional concepts as democracy. Democracy can no longer, they argue, base itself on an 'essentialist' notion of a unitary and universal rational agent, the bearer of universal rights, as in classic liberal theory. It must accept, postmodern style, the plurality of perspectives and the differentiated identities that constitute individuals (or what may be called the 'non-individuality of individuals'). Democracy must adapt itself to the fact of this irreducible pluralism – by abandoning the idea of consensual politics, for one thing, or the view that the national 'sovereign' state must be the only arena of politics. Such a concept of democracy should prove, and has proved, attractive to several groups concerned with the politics of identity and difference – feminists especially, but also those active on behalf of subordinate ethnic groups and post-colonial peoples. Its appeal is that it does not abandon traditional leftist goals of liberation, but attempts to give a new meaning to that goal and proposes different means of achieving it (Laclau and Mouffe 1985; Mouffe 1993).

Moreover, even those such as Andreas Huyssen who argue that poststructuralists are primarily modernist, in their overwhelming concern with language and culture, see a critical difference between the older and newer forms of discourse. Modernism believed in the power of art, uncontaminated by extraneous considerations of politics and commerce, to keep alive certain pure values. It contained implicitly, if not always explicitly, a critique of modern society, especially in its bourgeois form. That is why ardent champions of modernism such as Clement Greenberg could also be Marxists (Clark 1982). Poststructuralism rejects this belief in the redemptive power of culture. Art cannot save the individual or change the world. Such a vision of redemption was always illusory, and is any case no longer credible.

It is in such a 'retrospective reading' of modernism, its awareness of 'modernism's limitations and failed political ambitions', that poststructuralism shows its affinity with post-modern theory (Huyssen 1992: 61). More than this, perhaps. In its radical scepticism, its urge to deconstruct and dissolve everything, its fundamentally anti-messianic and anti-utopian character, poststructuralism connects up directly with one of the central tenets of post-modernity: what Lyotard calls the 'incredulity toward metanarratives' (1984a: xxiv). This is one of the best-known and most generally accepted attributes of post-modern theory. It unifies what would otherwise be a hopelessly diffuse and dispersed series of propositions. In doing so, it shows where the theory of post-modernity gets its main thrust from: not in the announcement of something new, in a positive sense, but in the rejection of the old, the past of modernity.

The 'metanarratives' or 'grand narratives' that Lyotard talks about are the great historico-philosophical schemes of progress and perfectibility that the modern age threw up. Though narratives, being prescriptive and practical, are distinguished by Lyotard from 'science', which is concerned with truth and truth-claims, there cannot be any doubt that much of the appeal of the metanarratives of modernity turned on their association with science and the scientific method. From Kant to Hegel and Marx, from Saint-Simon to Comte and Spencer, the advancement of reason and freedom was linked to the progress of modern science. Science was both a way of understanding the world and a way of transforming it.

It is indeed the crisis of science that may partly account for the attraction of post-modern theory at the present time. The rejection of 'grand narratives' had started, at least in the west, some time ago. Already in the 1940s and 1950s books such as F. A. Hayek's *The Road to Serfdom* (1944), Karl Popper's *The Open Society and Its Enemies* (1945), Jacob Talmon's *The Origins of Totalitarian Democracy* (1952), and Isaiah Berlin's *Historical Inevitability* (1954) had launched powerful and highly influential attacks on the philosophical and historical presuppositions of much nineteenth-century social theory. The grand narrative of Marxism in particular, as the most conspicuous and successful survivor of nineteenth-century thought, was assailed for its theoretical shortcomings and its historical implausibility.

But not only did this leave the grand narrative of liberalism largely unscathed. More importantly science remained untouched. In fact it was further elevated as the only true method of inquiry, while its presence in society – in the form of scientists amd scientific institutions – was declared by some such as Sir Charles Snow to be the sole guarantor of future progress and prosperity. Hence, though it was widely proclaimed that 'ideology', in the sense of systematic social philosophies, had been discredited, this did not prevent a quite powerful ideology of progress from attaching itself to such ideas and practices as 'modernization' and 'industrialization'. In this guise the grand narrative continued to enjoy a flourishing career, in the west and the world at large.

The downfall of communism in eastern Europe, and its retreat in most other parts of the world, has inevitably further weakened the credibility of grand narratives (though arguably nationalism was waiting in the wings to inherit the mantle). But it is perhaps more significant that modernization and industrialization are now also under attack, together with the whole idea of progress that sustained them. There are a number of reasons for this, but a principal one is the spread of ecological consciousness. Ecology throws a pall of gloom over all theories of progress through further industrialization. The crisis of confidence has extended to the scientists themselves. Not only do they now question the wholesale application of science to the world; they also raise disturbing questions about the very status of science as a privileged method of understanding (see, for example, Griffin 1988). With the rise of the 'new indeterminacy' – not to mention the repeated assaults of the sociologists – science itself seems subject to the same subjectivity and relativism that are characteristic of all narratives. 'The game of science is . . . put on a par with the others . . . Science plays its own game; it is incapable of legitimating the other language games' (Lyotard 1984: 40–1; see also 53–60).

This is a turnabout indeed, by any measure – if it is true – one of epochal proportions. Modernity was associated – even if mainly retrospectively – with the Scientfic Revolution of the seventeenth century (Kolakowski 1990: 7). It was this that gave moderns the confidence that they could match and even surpass the achievements of the ancients. Out of this confidence came the grand themes and theories of Progress, Reason, Revolution and Emancipation. In one form or another, covertly or explicitly, they shored up most of the politics of the western world from the late eighteenth to the mid-twentieth centuries.

Now, if the post-modernists are right, they are empty, high-sounding words, no longer capable of inspiring commitment or action.[13] It is not simply that 'there aren't any good, brave causes left' to fight for anymore, in the aggrieved tones of the protagonist of John Osborne's play of 1956, *Look Back in Anger*. The point seems to be that there *cannot* now be any great causes left to fight for. Philosophy, whether in the form of Popper's anti-historicism or Derrida's deconstructionism, has undermined the pretensions of most social theories to be objective, scientific accounts of the world. Politics, in the form of the failure of communism as well as of other explicitly ideological experiments in social reconstruction, has undermined confidence in the power of politics to re-make the world. The rot has now spread to liberalism as well. The rational, autonomous individual of liberal theory has been dissolved – 'deconstructed' – into a multiplicity of overlapping and mutually inconsistent persons possessing different identities and interests. The rational pusuit of goals by self-interested, utility-maximizing individuals becomes a chimaera. The question, whose or what interest, properly applies, it is claimed, as much to the many-headed individual as to the plural society. In these conditions 'reason' or 'truth' become impossible, because unreal, objectives (see Pangle 1992: 19–56).

The post-modernists can support their case by pointing to a widespread disengagement and disillusionment with politics, both in the newly-emergent democracies of eastern Europe and the older democracies of the west. This suggests a withdrawal and a scepticism consonant with the discrediting of 'grand narratives'. Others too, without necessarily accepting the post-modern diagnosis in its own terms, have concurred to the extent of seeing in this condition a new, more profound 'end of ideology'. Such is the position of Francis Fukuyama, whose much-discussed statement on 'the end of history' (1992) was commonly misinterpreted as a triumphalist vindication of western liberalism against all other ideologies. In fact Fukuyama finds liberalism almost as unattractive as its rivals. Its practical victory in the conflict with communism heralds not a new era of freedom and creativity but an end to the dialectic of ideas that gave history meaning. It means the reign of passive consumerism and privatized existence. In his melancholy Nietzschean vision of the 'last man', Fukuyama conjures up a future world as lacking in meaningful striving or purpose as any of the scenarios of the post-modernists (Fukuyama 1992: 287–339). The death of grand narratives may mean less fanaticism but it also means the death of passion, and the loss of the cultural creativity that comes of the struggle of ideologies.

Lyotard himself puts a brave face on all this. The lack of a 'universal metalanguage' that can validate the great narratives does indeed imply that we must abandon the Enlightenment goals of universal emancipation and the rational society. Nor can these goals be saved in the manner attempted by Jürgen Habermas, who looks to the achievement of a rational 'consensus' through a dialogue between free and equal actors. Such a hope still rests on the Enlightenment belief in humanity as 'a collective (universal) subject', which attempts to achieve its 'common emancipation' through finding a structure of agreed or general rules governing all forms of interaction. But there are no such universal rules of the game – of *all* games – and no prospect therefore of consensus. We have to acknowledge that 'any consensus on the rules defining a game and the "moves" playable within it *must* be local, in other words agreed on by its present players and subject to eventual cancellation' (Lyotard 1984: 66).

Here are the grounds for some kind of optimism. The abandonment of grand narratives leaves the way open for the free play of 'little narratives' (*petits récits*). Little narratives are for Lyotard the stuff of 'imaginative invention', in science as well as social life. They are forms of 'customary' or 'local' knowledge, with the contextuality, provisionality and boundedness that this suggests (cf. Geertz 1983). Little narratives – as in truth all narratives, shorn of their scientfic pretensions – do not depend on external, objective validation but are internal to the communities within which they occur. They determine their own criteria of competence and define what has the right to be said and done – that is, they are self-legitimating. Unlike the scientific claims of grand narratives, which are couched in homological universals, little narratives are 'paralogical', which means that they accept what according to the canons of scientific logic would be called false reasoning and illogical arguments.[14] They show a 'sensitivity to differences' and a willingness to 'tolerate the incommensurable'. In this as in most other respects they are like the popular stories recited in traditional societies, as in Homeric Greece (Lyotard 1984: xxv, 18–23, 60).

The political vision underlying this is, as in much of Lyotard's writing, rather vague. It strives towards an ideal of an 'open community' based, among other things, on the 'temporary contract'. This, says Lyotard, 'corresponds to the course that the evolution of social interaction is currently taking; the temporary contract is in practice supplanting permanent institutions in the professional, emotional, sexual, cultural, family, and international domains, as well as in political affairs' (1984: 66). This echo of post-Fordism is not altogether reassuring, as Lyotard himself admits. It leaves room for exploitation and insecurity as much as for flexibility and freedom. But it seems for Lyotard to spell out the forms of the future. No more permanent institutions and organizations, encased within the rigid framework of the nation state. No more 'totalizing' ideologies, setting distant goals within the context of pseudo-scientfic blueprints for the future. Instead a network of loosely connected communities, inventing their own forms of life and finding their own means to express them. Not social systems governed by metalanguages, but 'the "atomization" of the social into flexible networks of language games' (Lyotard 1984: 17). Not scientific 'laws' of society, but local customs and usage; not 'legislators' but 'interpreters' of culture who seek to make communities mutually intelligible (cf. Bauman 1987; 1992: 1–25). Not Marx – but Proudhon?

A New Society? A New Epoch?

Lyotard's gesture towards the future raises the question, finally, of post-modernity and time. Where or how does post-modernity situate itself in history? Does it see itself as a new period? Does it herald the coming into being of a new society or civilization? What does the 'post' of post-modernity mean?

The 'post' prefix in social theory has always been ambiguous. The term 'post-industrial' is a good example. For some writers, especially economic historians, it has meant the society created after and as a result of the Industrial Revolution of the late eighteenth century. In that sense they have used it to refer to what most sociologists have called simply 'industrial society'. For sociologists such as Daniel Bell, on the other hand, 'post-industrial' refers to the society emerging out of and succeeding classic industrial society. For him post-industrial is *after* industrial society. As we have seen, he eventually came to give the new society a name, the 'information society'.[15]

Nevertheless even with Bell there is some ambiguity. 'Post-industrial' evidently comes out of industrial. It carries its mark. The very name implies a degree of continuity, as if the new society can only define itself by a backward look. How much continuity? For some people what Bell saw as post-industrial they saw as 'super'- or 'hyper'-industrial society, so struck were they by the high degree of continuity (see, for example, Kumar 1978).

Postmodernism and post-modernity raise the problem of period and new beginnings in an even more acute form. There are certainly some, such as Charles Jencks and Ihab Hassan, who are confident that a new culture and civilization is emerging, one that goes beyond modernity. Less clearly, and certainly less optimistically, there are thinkers such as François Lyotard who define a post-modern 'condition' still tied to a predominantly modern industrial principle of 'performativity'. This is a post-modernity struggling to be born, to throw off the incubus of the past (in Lyotard's case, partly in order to recover the subversiveness of the original movement of modernism).

But the more typical case is more ambiguous still, as exemplified by writers such as Fredric Jameson and Scott Lash. Both of these formally reject the idea of a new, post-modern, society. Postmodern *culture*, which they acknowledge, they regard, in Jameson's words, as 'the cultural dominant of the logic of late capitalism' (Jameson 1992: 46; cf. Lash 1990: 3, Lash and Urry 1994: 15). But not only do they both, as we have seen, elevate culture to a new centrality in the economy and society. Their whole account of 'late' (or 'disorganized') capitalism suggests that we are in a radically new situation, one that marks it off decisively from past society.

For Jameson, just as realism in culture corresponds to market capitalism, and modernism to monopoly capitalism or imperialism, so postmodernism corresponds to late or multinational capitalism. This historical typology already expresses a sequence of stages and periods. But Jameson goes further in demarcating them in such a way as to emphasize the discontinuities and differences between them. They may all be capitalist, but this seems minor by comparison with what distinguishes the different stages or orders of capitalism.

Thus late capitalism inaugurates the 'Third Machine Age', one in which the new technology of information and communication comes to occupy a dominant position in the economic infrastructure, relegating manufacturing technology to a subordinate role. It establishes 'a network of power and control . . . difficult for our minds and imagination to grasp: the whole new decentered global network of the third stage of capital'. Again and again Jameson dwells on 'the incapacity of our minds, at least at present, to map the great global multinational and decentered communicational network in which we find ourselves as individual subjects'. He speaks of 'the as yet untheorized original space of some new "world system" of multinational or late capitalism', 'some as yet unimaginable new mode of representing' its new 'world space' (Jameson 1992: 35–6, 38, 44, 50, 54). We are still manifestly, according to Jameson, in a capitalist world. But everything he says about the third stage – the new global reach of capital, the pivotal importance of media and communication, the enhanced role of culture, the loss of the sense of history – points to a new era.

Lash's position is similar. His later work with John Urry goes even further in sketching the outlines of a new society of 'signs and space', a society in which signs have replaced things, and objects – both people and images – are caught up in a ceaseless world-wide flow (Lash and Urry 1994). This is still 'disorganized capitalism', to use their earlier term. But they do not hesitate to talk about 'post-industrial society' and the 'postmodernization of contemporary political economies'. More strikingly they point to the growth of a high degree of 'reflexivity' or self-consciousness among the populations of contemporary industrial societies, to the point where it is creating new possibilities for social relations in a wide variety of spheres – 'for intimate relations, for friendship, for work relations, for leisure and for consumption' (Lash and Urry 1994: 31). Once again the 'end of organized capitalism' seems to throw us into a new situation, where the old rules no longer apply and new ways of thinking and acting have emerged. 'Post-modernity' as generally characterized does not seem too misleading a description of this new condition – especially if we bear in mind that post-modernity and capitalism, as we have seen with David Harvey, are not necessarily antithetical concepts.

Jameson and Lash exemplify another important feature of writing about post-modernity. Like a number of other theorists they do not identify themselves with a post-modern approach. But they are so sympathetic to its basic concepts, and elucidate them with such understanding, that they appear in practice to embrace a post-modern view of the world. They are in effect closet post-modernists. That is often the case with post-modernists. It is very hard indeed to find anyone who declares unequivocally for the post-modern position. One of the curiosities of the much-publicized post-modern party is how few fully paid-up members its appears to have. Most of the French thinkers associated with the theory, for instance, either publicly distance themselves from it, or avoid referring to it in their writings. Those, like Jencks, who declare themselves full-blooded post-modernists lay themselves open to considerable critical attack, not to say ridicule. It is a dangerous provocation to be a post-modernist, in academic circles at least. There are far more books and articles telling us what is wrong with post-modern theory than there are statements in its favour – or even, for that matter, telling us clearly what it is.

But post-modernity has more friends than this might make us

think. There are in fact a good number of closet post-modernists. Leaving aside the out-and-out opponents of post-modern theory (for example, Callinicos 1989; Norris 1991), there are a considerable number of commentators like Jameson and Lash whose very involvement and fascination with post-modern phenomena seem half-way towards an acceptance of a post-modern position.[16] They are the fellow-travellers of post-modernity, if not full party members. To that extent they lend support to the idea that we are indeed in a new, post-modern period of history.

There is an alternative position, which has been persuasively put by Zygmunt Bauman, Andreas Huyssen and others. This, while generally denying that post-modernity represents a new era, accepts that we are in a new situation to the extent that we can now, for the first time, look back at modernity. We can reflect upon it. The 'post' of post-modernity refers not so much to a new period or society coming 'after' modernity as to the view of modernity possible after the completion of modernity – or at least as much of it as could be completed in its own terms. Post-modernity means that modernity can now be inspected 'as in the rearview mirror' (Nederveen Pieterse 1992: 26). As put by Matei Calinescu, post-modernity is not 'a new name for a new "reality", or "mental structure", or "world view", but a perspective from which one can ask certain questions about modernity in its general incarnations' (Calinescu 1987: 278).[17]

This is an attractive view. It seems to capture well what many post-modernist critics and theorists are in fact doing. It is also satisfyingly historical in the way that it places post-modernity at the end of the period of history – roughly the last two hundred years – during which modernity can reasonably be said to have worked itself out. Hegel-like it declares that it is only now, as dusk settles on the modern project, that we can see what it really looks like, what it was all about. Knowledge and understanding come *post factum*. Post-modernity is modernity recollected, if not in tranquillity at least at the end of the working day. The concept of post-modernity, says Bauman,

> supplies a new and external vantage point, from which some aspects of the world which came into being in the aftermath of the Enlightenment and the Capitalist Revolution (aspects not visible, or allotted secondary importance, when observed from inside the unfinished process) acquire saliency and can be turned into pivotal issues of the discourse . . .
>
> Postmodernity may be interpreted as fully developed modernity taking a full measure of the anticipated consequences of its historical

work . . . modernity conscious of its true nature – *modernity for itself.* (Bauman 1992: 102–3, 187; see also 23–4)[18]

For Bauman this perspective means that we are now more aware of the limits of modernity, its over-ambitious and to some extent tyrannical enterprise. The postmodern condition is 'modernity emancipated from false consciousness'. In particular, intellectuals now realize that their role cannot be that of laying down absolute rules and standards for society, in accordance with some notion of the principles of universal truth and reason. No such principles exist. Intellectuals must accept the more modest role of interpreters and brokers of customs and cultures, using their skills to help communities to understand one another. While this may seem a come-down from the high position of modernist 'legislators', it is not only more realistic but has the advantage of restoring to individuals 'the fullness of moral choice and responsibility'. Individuals and societies are far less determined, far freer to shape their own destinies, than the classic social theory of modernity allowed them. In that sense post-modernity, as a perspective, releases some of the hidden potential of modernity. It uncovers the modern spirit that modernity aspired to check and restrain through the construction of a perfected, rational society, governed by experts. 'The postmodern state of mind is the radical . . . victory of modern (that is, inherently critical, restless, unsatisfied, insatiable) culture over the modern society it aimed to improve through throwing it wide open to its own potential' (Bauman 1992: viii, 188).

Huyssen, too, sees postmodernism as an opportunity, an opening to new possibilities that were always latent or inherent in modernity. This prospect was opened up by the recognition of the limits of modernism within the mode of modernity; the perception that there had been a confusion of modernism and modernization. It was, he says, 'only in the 1970s that the historical limits of modernism came into sharp forcus'. Hence the rise of postmodernism as a cultural movement. Postmodernism thus expresses the crisis of modernism. But it does not mean the end of modernity, or even of modernism. Postmodernism does not make modernism obsolete; on the contrary 'it casts a new light on it', and appropriates many of its techniques and strategies for its own purposes. But it forces us to reject the 'one-way history of modernism which interprets it as a logical unfolding towards some imaginary goal'. It makes us see that modernism is open-ended, necessarily incomplete, full of possibilities that were excluded by the received ideologies of modernity (Marxist as well as bourgeois). What has become obsolete, therefore, are 'the codifications of modernism . . . which are based on a teleological view of progress and modernisation' (Huyssen 1992: 67). It is this space that is now occupied by postmodernism, with its radically different conception of progress and history.

What further enhances the appeal of this general position – post-modernity as the questioning and loosening of modernity – is that it corresponds quite closely to some other influentially expressed-views on the current state of modern societies. In these cases there is an explicit disclaimer of a post-modern analysis, but what is advanced seems not very different from Bauman and Huyssens. Anthony Giddens and Ulrich Beck are the best-known advocates of the view that modern societies, while not usefully thought of as 'post-modern', have reached a stage of 'high' or 'radicalized' modernity in which the dominant characteristic is a high degree of 'reflexivity'. By this they mean that modern societies have reached a point where they are forced to reflect on themselves, and at the same time have developed the capability of reflecting *back* on themselves. Giddens tends to emphasize personal, individual self-reflexivity – the 'life plan'; while Beck emphasizes societal self-reflexivity – social monitoring and social movements. But both share the view that the long-standing patterns of development of modern societies have now thrown up such fundamental problems and dilemmas that they call into question any further movement along those lines. Modernity must now take stock of itself and become self-conscious about its future. 'We have not moved beyond modernity but are living precisely through a phase of its radicalisation' (Giddens 1990: 51; see also 150–73; Giddens 1991; Beck 1992; Beck, Giddens and Lash 1994).[19]

In Beck's case the argument takes the unusual form of a con-cern with the high degree and high number of 'risks' thrown up by modern society – risks connected with such matters as environmental pollution, the hazardous use of nuclear power, and the industrial treatment of food and farming. What this portends, however, is not the end of modernity but the rise of a self-conscious 'risk society' that takes upon itself the task of modernizing the principles of modernity. Modernity has hitherto seen itself narrowly as 'industrial society'. Industrial society is however only imperfectly modern; it is 'a semi-modern society', not so much because of the persistence of feudal remnants as because its own practices and institutions deny the universal principles of modernity as conceived by the Enlightenment. The risk society acknowledges that to continue along the lines of classic industrialism is to run the danger of self-destruction. The requirement now is less industrialization and more modernization – more application of the principles of modernity to the dangerously limiting practices and perspectives of capitalist industrial society. The result – as also conceived in the post-modernist perspective of Bauman and Huyssen – would be to free modernity from its neurotic thraldom to a limited part of itself, to unleash its full potential for rational reflection and all-round development.

> Just as modernization dissolved the structure of feudal society in the nineteenth century and produced the industrial society, modernization today is dissolving industrial society and another modernity is coming into being . . . Today, at the threshold of the twenty-first century, in the developed western world, modernization has *consumed and lost its other* and now undermines its own premises as an industrial society along with its functional principles. Modernization within the horizon of experience of *pre*-modernity is being displaced by *reflexive* modernization . . . Modernization *within* the paths of industrial society is being replaced by a modernization of the *principles* of industrial society . . . It is this *antagonism* opening up between industrial society and modernity that distorts our attempts at a 'social mapping', since we are so thoroughly accustomed to conceiving of modernity *within* the categories of industrial society . . . We are witnessing not the end but the beginning of modernity – that is, of a modernity *beyond* its classic industrial design . . . Reflexive modernization means not less but more modernity, a modernity radicalized against the paths and categories of the classical industrial society. (Beck 1992: 10, 14–15; see also 57, 81–2, 87, 104, 153–235).

Bauman and Huyssen talk about post-modernity and post-modernism; Giddens and Beck about late modernity and reflexive modernization. The fact that, despite this, they can agree substantially on what they all regard as the central feature of contemporary industrial societies is an indication that the idea of historical stage or period is not crucial to the postmodern debate. This is shown even more by the relative insouciance postmodernists themselves display towards the problem of periodization. Hassan, for instance, one of the foremost advocates of the post-modern position, has explicitly denied that this means that we must speak of a new era or period succeeding the modern. Postmodernism is as hybridized as any period or style; only perhaps more so.

> History moves in measures both continuous and discontinuous. Thus the prevalence of postmodernism today . . . does not suggest that ideas

or institutions of the past cease to shape the present . . .

Modernism and postmodernism are not separated by an Iron Curtain or Chinese Wall; for history is a palimpsest, and culture is permeable to time past, time present, and time future. We are all, I suspect, a little Victorian, Modern, and Postmodern, at once . . . This means that a 'period' . . . must be perceived in terms *both* of continuity *and* discontinuity, the two perspectives being complementary and partial . . . (Hassan 1985: 119, 121)

Hassan does however suggest that, unlike terms such as romanticism and classicism, baroque and rococo, the word postmodernism 'evokes what it wishes to surpass or suppress, modernism itself. The term thus contains its enemy within . . .' (1985: 121). This suggests a greater degree of dependency of the postmodern on the modern than is normally implied in the succession of types or historical periods. The suspicion that we might be thinking in the wrong terms about postmodernity is heightened by the frequent reference in the postmodernist literature to those whom Hassan calls 'prepostmodernists': the ancestors and precursors of contemporary postmodernism (Hassan 1992: 198). All movements have their heroic predecessors; but critics have protested at the unusually wide historical diffusion as well as the immense variety of those that make up the genealogy of postmodernism (see, for example, Berman 1983: 351). It is one thing to see in such relatively recent thinkers as Nietzsche, Simmel, James, Heidegger and Levinas the seeds of postmodernist thought. It seems to be stretching things rather too far to find among literary precursors not just Borges and Gertrude Stein, not just Baudelaire and the Brontes, not just Sterne and Blake, but Rabelais and Cervantes and even Homer – not to mention the artists and thinkers of the Baroque.[20] Hassan guilelessly remarks that 'there is some evidence that postmodernism, and modernism even more, are beginning to slip and slide in time' (1985: 121); but such a promiscuous jumbling of historical epochs, stretching over a period of two thousand years, not only casts doubt on the novelty and distinctiveness of postmodernism but suggests that its proponents do not take seriously the task of historical placing. It seems so much like a typical post-modernist game.

But we should remember that, at least so far as cultural postmodernism goes, they are doing little more than following wellknown practices in cultural history. It has been common, for instance, to recover or discover 'neglected' classics from the past, or to see in established classics the seeds of future forms. There is nothing wrong in finding postmodernist elements in Sterne's

Tristram Shandy, or in retrospectively renaming Joyce or Kafka or even Flaubert as postmodernsist writers. All movements – political as well as cultural – 'reinvent their ancestors'. A style, just like a period or mode of production, can only trace its ancestry, its genealogy, once it has reached a certain stage of development. Only then can it be clear what its main features are. The finding of numerous 'prepostmodernists' might then be taken as some evidence of the reality of postmodern culture.

But, in the end, the cheerfully cavalier attitude which the proponents of post-modernity display towards the past is an indication of their fundamental indifference to it. Or rather, their indifference to the past as real history. We have already seen, in architecture, their essentially eclectic manner of dealing with past forms, their love of pastiche and parody. The past is something to be played with, to be cannibalized for aesthetic purposes. Literary examples would include the new kind of 'historical' novel, as in John Fowles's *The French Lieutenant's Woman* (1969) and E. L. Doctorow's *Ragtime* (1975). Here there is no attempt to reconstruct the historical past, in the manner say of Walter Scott or Victor Hugo. Instead images or stereotypes of the past – Victorian prudery, the jazz age – are self-consciously and knowingly employed to create special effects, often of an ironic kind. There is no idea of fidelity to the past, or any attempt to treat the past as an organic part of the present (see Jameson 1992: 16–25; also Hutcheon 1988: 105–23).

The post-modern rejection of grand narratives also devalues the past. The past is no longer a story within which we can situate ourselves – whether that story be one of growth, progress and emancipation, or one of growth, maturity and decline. We have no grounds for reading such significance in history. The past is essentially meaningless. Hence the pointlessness of talking about post-modernity as an era or period 'succeeding' modernity.[21] That would still suggest some significance, some idea of development or even progress, in the historical record. In the postmodernist view all periods are equal – equally full and equally empty, equally interesting and equally uninteresting. 'In the postmodern, the past itself has disappeared (along with the well-known "sense of the past" or historicity and collective memory' (Jameson 1992: 309; see also Harvey 1989: 54). What takes its place are *simulacra*, images or representations of the past – but with no sense of the past that is represented.

When the 'death of the past' was announced some time ago, it had as one of its purposes the repudiation of speculative or 'philosophical' history, and its replacement by sober, 'scientific' history – by what was seen as real history (see, for example, Plumb 1973). The post-modern rejection of the past goes far deeper. It has no time for sober, scientific history either. It lives in what Jameson calls a 'depthless present', without a sense of the past or of the future. The modernist obsession with the New was only possible when the old, the past of pre-modern society, was still sufficiently present to act as a foil and a contrast. That old has now completely gone, at least in the west, and the new no longer has the capacity to excite and stir the imagination (Jameson 1992: 307–11; see also Anderson 1984). The end of the 'tradition of the new' also means the end of a sense of the future as something constantly accelerating away and distancing itself from the past. What persists, what alone gives us material for contemplation, is a timeless present.

With the devaluation of time comes the elevation of space. The plane of the timeless present is the spatial. If things do not get their significance from their place in history, they can receive it only from their distribution in space. Post-modernity traffics in the contemporaneous and the simultaneous, in synchronic rather than diachronic time. Relations of nearness and distance in space, rather than in time, become the measure of significance.

The spatial implosion brought about by the global informational and communicational network is one example. Not to be a part of it is to be cut off from a significant section of contemporary life. The multinational networks of global capitalism are another example, the other face of the decentralization and dispersion that are the most obvious features of the post-Fordist economy. In both cases individuals are inserted in new sets of social relations, both at work and beyond it, to each other. Then there is the new importance of landscape and townscape, the heightened awareness of urban space and the need to regulate the countryside. The activities of ecological groups and other social movements concerned with urban forms and natural spaces is one obvious indication. There is also the novel development of 'post-modern' cities such as Los Angeles, with their radically decentred urban communities. This throws into relief the de-industrialization of the older cities, and the predicament of new groups of the urban 'underclass' trapped in their decaying inner areas. All this calls for a new kind of 'cognitive mapping', a new way of perceiving the spatial relations between neighbourhood, city and the global systems of information and economic organization (see on all this Soja 1989; Harvey 1989; Agnew and Duncan 1989; Carter et al. 1993; Lash and Urry 1994; Jameson 1992: 364–76, 410–18).

The domain of the spatial, it has been argued, extends even to the sense of self and personal identity. The 'de-centred subject' of post-modern theory no longer thinks of his/her identity in historical or temporal terms. There is now no expectation of continuous life-long development, no story of personal growth over time. Instead the post-modern self considers itself as a discontinuous entity, as an identity (or identities) constantly made and re-made in neutral time. No one identity or identity segment is privileged over the other; there is no development or maturation over time. This seems to require a metaphor of the self conceived in spatial terms – or, to put it in another way, in schizophrenic terms, 'the pure and unrelated presents in time' experienced by the schizophrenic, unable to unify past, present and future (Jameson 1992: 27). Personal biography becomes a matter of discontinuous experiences and identities, rather than a story of a developing personality. The post-modern individual does not experience the 'sentimental education' and personal growth of Goethe's Wilhelm Meister or Dickens's David Copperfield. He or she is more likely to feel a resemblance to Luke Reinhart's dice-man, ceaselessly changing roles and identities in an eternal present.

We are here in Foucault territory, so perhaps it is fitting that Foucault should be allowed the last word on the rise of the spatial:

> The great obsession of the nineteenth century was, as we know, history: with its themes of development and suspension, of crisis and cycle, themes of the ever-accumulating past, with its great preponderance of dead men and the menacing glaciation of the world . . . The present epoch will perhaps be above all the epoch of space. We are in the epoch of simultaneity: we are in the epoch of juxtaposition, the epoch of the near and far, of the side-by-side, of the dispersed. We are at a moment, I believe, when our experience of the world is less that of a long life developing through time than that of a network that connects points and intersects with its own skein. (In Soja 1989: 10)

So here we have the post-modern world: a world of eternal presentness, without origin or destination, past or future; a world in which it is impossible to find a centre, or any point or perspective from which it is possible to view it steadily and to view it whole; a world in which all that presents itself are the temporary, shifting and local forms of knowledge and experience. Here are no deep structures, no secret or final causes; all is (or is not) what it appears on the surface. It is an end to modernity, and all that it promised and proposed.

Is this our future? How does it differ from the visions of the theorists of the information society, or the projections of the post-Fordist theorists? It is time now to assess the three approaches together, and to consider in what ways they might help us to think about our present condition and future prospects.

6

Millennial Themes: Endings and Beginnings

The fall of Communism can be regarded as a sign that modern thought – based on the premise that the world is objectively knowable, and that the knowledge so obtained can be absolutely generalized – has come to a final crisis.

Vaclav Havel (1992: 15)

What we are experiencing is not the crisis of modernity. We are experiencing the need to modernize the presuppositions upon which modernity is based. The current crisis is not the crisis of Reason but that of the . . . irrational motives of rationalization as it has been pursued thus far.

André Gorz (1989: 1)

The point is that we are within *the culture of postmodernism to the point where its facile repudiation is as impossible as any equally facile celebration of it is complacent and corrupt.*

Fredric Jameson (1992: 62)

Apocalypse and Millennium

Theories announcing some dramatic shift, some new direction, in western history, are not new. They accompanied the Renaissance and Reformation. They were present in the eighteenth century, at the birth of modernity. They were prominent at the end of the last century, in the 1890s and 1900s. From our point of view it is these more recent ones that are the most interesting. They show some striking parallels with our own condition. Not only did they occur, as ours do, at the end of a century. They also have something of the same character. Then as now there was the same mixture of hope and despondency, confidence and despair.

Apocalyptic pronouncements of decline and degeneration were matched by ringing declarations that never before had western civilization reached such heights of prosperity and progress. Just as now, while some deplored the impact of western societies and the spread of western materialism throughout the world, others gloried in the fact that western civilization – western values and institutions – had apparently become the only acceptable model to the rest of the world's societies (Adas 1994).

Fin-de-siècles, in the western tradition at least, have a tendency to inspire this kind of prophetic thinking. 'Our sense of epoch,' Frank Kermode has said, 'is gratified above all by the ends of centuries' (Kermode 1968b: 96; see also Schwartz 1990). This presumably has something to do with the tangled legacy of millennialism in western thought. Although this mainly concerned the Second Coming of Christ and his thousand-year reign on earth – *the* millennium – it also applied to the prophecy of the end of the world at the end of the (first) millennium after Christ's first appearance in this world. The passing of the year 1000 without this terminal event notwithstanding, western thought continued to be fascinated by the idea of the ends of millennia or – analogically – centuries as being somehow peculiarly revealing of the nature of things and of our destiny to come.

Typically therefore the millennial feeling concentrated on fin-de-siècles contained two things. There was the sense of an ending – originally, the end of the world and of earthly history; and there was the heightened expectation of a new beginning, a radically new era of peace, freedom and happiness – the original Christian millennium. Apocalyptic terrors connected to the end of the world – the fire and sword imagery of the Book of Revelation – were mixed with millennial hopes and expectations that out of that storm would come a great peace and joy, 'a new heaven and a new earth'. Endings and new beginnings were linked in a single structure of thought, though it was always open to particular ages and thinkers which feature they chose to dwell on.

It would be wrong to suggest that current theories of change in industrial societies are solely bound up with this fin-de-siècle feeling. The first of them, the original theory of post-industrial society as formulated by Daniel Bell, surfaced as long ago as the mid-1960s. Since that time there has been a steady stream of such theories, of which the ones considered in this book have been the principal varieties. So we are talking about theories that have occupied the whole of the last third of this century. Moreover, as compared with past fin-de-siècles, the current views of the coming century are peculiarly lacking in élan, distinctly low-keyed. The announcement of the end of this or that project or period – 'modernity', 'history' – brings with it little excitement or hope, little sense of a new beginning or something to look forward to in the future. Many commentators seem sunk rather in a mood of resignation or melancholy (Kumar 1995a).

Nevertheless, the onset of the end, not just of another century but of another millennium, is bound to have an effect on the theories under consideration. It clearly affects their appeal, as is shown in the popularity of slogans about post-modernity and post-history, and the publicity given to their utterance. It is responsible for a growing volume of books, conferences and television series which focus on the fin-de-siècle and the millennial turn. These give to the more academic theories a greater resonance with the temper of their times than is customary. It has the effect also of encouraging their proponents to strengthen and to an extent simplify their pronouncements, to chime in with the popular mood of apocalyptic expectation. Despite some disavowals, few have been able to resist the temptation of thus gaining some additional publicity for their views. So even though many of the theories were elaborated before a strong sense of fin-de-siècle came upon us, they have come to be identified with its mood and to shape themselves, in part at least, according to its expectations.

There has been another, more immediate and in some ways more compelling, cause of this. The approaching end of the century has witnessed one of the most significant developments of contemporary history, perhaps of modern history as a whole. This is the failure and eclipse of communism in central and eastern Europe, and the decline of Marxism as an ideology throughout the world. There may be, there must be, an element of pure historical accident in this coincidence of events, the end of communism and the end of the century. There seems no obvious reason why, if communism was destined to fail, it should choose to do so in so spectacular a fashion precisely in the last decade of the twentieth century. But the coincidence is a palpable fact, and the idea that there might be some hidden connection between these two stirring events has been almost impossible to resist. Since, at the same time, many of the explanations for the downfall of communism have drawn in particular upon theories of the information society and of post-modernity (see Kumar 1995b), this too has served to confer upon such theories of change many of the customary features of fin-de-siècle prognostications. The end of the century, the end of communism, and the end – say – of modernity, seem to possess at least an 'elective affinity' for one another, even if we would be hard put to specify causal links.

Still, there may be no need to attempt to make the millennial connection in understanding the appeal of our theories. In some cases, as with the concept of the information society, their utopian character is sufficiently developed by the thinkers themselves not to need any help from fin-de-siècle sentiment. Even where, as with several of the theorists of post-modernity, there is little enthusiasm for the state of things described, the scope and nature of the claims made can scarcely be considered modest or lacking in grandeur. We are faced, at the end of the twentieth century, with a series of pronouncements and declarations that, taken either singly or together, amount to the claim that the western world is undergoing one of the most profound transformations of its existence.

We are at the end of modernity; we are at the end of history. Socialism is dead, utopia is dead. Even nature has died. More cheerfully, we are entering a new post-industrial age, the age of information and communication. We are moving into a post-Fordist era of small organizations and revivified craft work. We can look forward to a post-modern world that has renounced the errors of modernity and opened the way to a new freedom.

This is only a selection of the claims currently being made for our times. On all sides one hears the expression of convictions that things have fundamentally changed in one way or another. The modern nuclear family has disintegrated, to be replaced by a diversity of individual arrangements. Class society has dissolved, leading to fragmented groupings and movements based on ethnicity, gender or locality. The nation state, the classic political embodiment of modernity, has gone, assailed by a combination of global and local forces. Parliamentary democracy has broken down; the age of mass electorates and mass political parties has passed. Democracy and citizenship have to be rethought; older concepts such as 'civil society' may have to be revived, and re-applied to current conditions. At the most elevated level of all is the persistently voiced conviction that the whole of our industrial way of life, the legacy of the 'Great Transformation' of the industrial revolution, is fatally flawed. Allowed to cover the earth unchecked, as it is currently in the process of doing, it will not merely render social life intolerable, it will destroy the planet itself.

Many of these claims, again, are not new; they go back some time, in some cases to the mid-century or even earlier. They have not all emerged as a unified chorus at the very end of the century.

Moreover there are some obvious difficulties in attempting an overall assessment of them. They are made at very different levels of generality, and they are directed at varying levels of society. At one level are the assertions concerning changes in family life, gender and sexuality. These have essentially to do with new forms of personal identity. At quite another level are the assertions about globalization and planetary devastation. These engage the ideologies and economies of western and, indeed, world society. The problem is not only one of connecting the various levels, for instance those of the family and the economy. Most theorists are aware of this need, where relevant, and meet it with greater or lesser degrees of success. More forbidding is the formidable range of material, and the variety of skills and techniques, that would have to be drawn upon in attempting a general assessment of so numerous and varied a set of claims. The danger is of a descent into vacuousness.

One way of trying to avoid this danger is to limit the scope of the theories examined. The theories we have been considering in this book are mainly concerned with changes in the culture, politics, and economic and social institutions of contemporary western societies. That hardly makes them narrow – their ambitiousness indeed is one part of their appeal, and a good reason for their claims on our attention. But it does make them more manageable than if we try to take on change at all levels of the global system, not to mention those of the eco-system.[1] This does not mean that we have to ignore those levels. Post-modernity, for instance, evidently touches on questions of personal identity as much as it does on the impact of global processes. So too, though more indirectly, do the theories of post-Fordism and the information society. Any of these theories can, depending on interest, be pursued at a number of different levels, from the most intimate to the most global, from the most cultural to the most material. But there should also be a way of handling them that makes them more amenable to the kinds of discussion traditionally engaged in by sociologists.

That, at any rate, is the main intent of this chapter. But none of this is meant to make us ignore the larger picture. The theories we have been considering are clearly part of a widespread feeling, among intellectuals and the general population alike, that western societies, and perhaps the world at large, have undergone fundamental changes. Such a feeling may be in some ways misplaced but we cannot disregard it. The constant stream, over the past twenty to thirty years, of new theories of change cannot all be put down to the machinations of the media industry. It must reflect something real in the experience of these societies, a real sense of disruption and disorientation. We need to keep this in mind, and to consider what it might mean, whatever our assessment of the particular theories under consideration.

The Information Society and the Home-Centred Society

We have questioned, in chapter 2, the idea of a movement to an information society. If this is meant – as it is by thinkers such as Daniel Bell – to refer to the coming into being of a new society, replacing the society of classic industrialism, then this is an exaggerated and mistaken claim. There is no question of the significance of the new information technology in large areas of social and economic life. This does not amount to the establishment of a new principle of society, or the advent of some 'third wave' of social evolution. In most areas, information technology has speeded up processes begun some time ago; it has aided the implementation of certain strategies of management in organizations; it has changed the nature of work for many workers; it has accelerated certain trends in leisure and consumption. But it has not produced a radical shift in the way industrial societies are organized, or in the direction in which they have been moving. The imperatives of profit, power and control seem as predominant now as they have ever been in the history of capitalist industrialism. The difference lies in the greater range and intensity of their applications made possible by the communications revolution; not in any change in the principles themselves.

But we also noted that simply to characterize the information society as (still) 'capitalist' or 'industrial' was not the end of the story. Capitalism is not a timeless category. It has a history, with changing forms and features. Even its spatial extensions, as in the current phase of global capitalism, develop in time, at particular moments of capitalism's evolution. So 'informational capitalism', if we can swallow the term, has its own specific contribution to make to that evolution. Like kindred terms such as 'late' or 'post-industrial' or 'post-Fordist' capitalism, it points to a way of doing things that may look and feel very different from previous forms of capitalism.

The impact of information technology on such matters as employment, the functioning of capital markets, and the re-structuring of cities has been amply documented and discussed

(Castells 1989; Hepworth 1989; Sassen 1991; Mulgan 1991; Carnoy et al. 1993; Lash and Urry 1994). All the studies make it clear that capitalism now works through informational networks that have transformed many of its key operations. The compression of space and time made possible by the new communication technology alters the speed and scope of decisions, enhancing the capacity of the system to respond rapidly to changes but by the same token rendering it more vulnerable through a tendency to amplify relatively minor disturbances into major crises (for example, the global stock market crash of 'Black Monday', November 1987). Organizations can decentralize and disperse, with high-level decision-making remaining in 'world cities' – New York, London, Tokyo – while lower-level managerial operations, linked to the centre by communication networks, can take place virtually anywhere on the face of the earth. Cities and regions now have to compete to establish their positions in the global flows of information, or miss out on the most dynamic developments. 'People live in places; power rules through flows' (Castells 1989: 349).

But it is in the sphere of leisure and consumption, rather than work and production, that we can see the most direct and dramatic impact of the revolution in information technology. Perhaps that is why social theorists, traditionally concerned more with the nature of work and economic organization than with non-work activities, have tended to stress the continuities with past forms of capitalist society. Informational capitalism has restructured work and industrial organization, but in ways mostly consistent with the existing principles of Taylorism and scientific management (not to mention those of capital accumulation). The reshaping of consumption, according to the principles of what has been called 'social Taylorism' (Webster and Robins 1989), also follows the familiar logic of capitalism. That is, it is concerned with bringing ever more areas of social and cultural life within the purview of capitalist activity and market rationality. But partly owing to the relative novelty of the process itself, partly because of the particular areas that have been opened up to capitalist penetration, the effect is in this case to push society in unfamilar and what are in some ways new directions.

The most significant of these is the move towards a 'home-centred society'. Information technology, directed by a whole host of big business interests, has been increasingly put at the service of home-based consumption. Entertainment is the most obvious example. 'Going out' has been replaced by 'staying in'.

Instead of visits to the pub or the cinema, families – collectively or separately – watch video-cassettes at home or choose from around thirty channels of broadcast, satellite or cable television. Home computers supply the facility for an endless array of electronic games. Backed up by microwaveable TV dinners, one of the many attractions of staying in is its relative cheapness compared to going out – compare, for instance, the cost to a family of hiring a video and having a TV dinner at home, with the cost of buying cinema tickets and having a restaurant meal afterwards – and this leaves out the cost of transport and perhaps a baby-sitter.

Other services apart from entertainment are equally seeking the home as their base. 'Tele-banking' has made significant progress with the various forms of 'direct banking', allowing for 24–hour banking by telephone from the home. As with home entertainment, it is cheapness and convenience, as compared with traditional banking, that partly explain this success. Similar claims have been made for the fast-growing practice of 'tele-shopping' – not just in the old-fashioned form of mail-order shopping, but more in the newer form of shopping by television. Armed with a credit card and a telephone, the customer chooses from the panoply of goods displayed on the TV screen and orders accordingly. Shopping becomes a 24-hour a day, 7-days a week activity, lending some credibility to the (supposedly postmodernist) slogan, 'I shop, therefore I am'.

Taken with the development of a range of home diagnostic machines for health care, and the spread of various forms of 'distance learning' – 'tele-education' – on the model of Britain's Open University, there is considerable evidence for the move towards a home-based 'self-service society' (Gershuny 1978; Miles 1988a). But it is not just as consumers that information technology is encouraging us to remain at home and provide for ourselves what we previously sought outside the home. This echo of pre-industrial times has also been heard in the claims for the rise of what Alvin Toffler calls the 'prosumer', the person who consumes what he or she herself produces. Toffler is pointing to the growth of home-based production as well as consumption. Since many workers in the service economies of post-industrial societies make or handle information rather than goods, it is becoming increasingly possible for many of them to work at or from home, rather than making expensive and time-consuming journeys to offices in the crowded centres of cities. Most homes can be fitted with low-cost 'work stations' composed of a home computer and modem which are connected by the telephone to national and international computer networks. The 'electronic cottage' then becomes the base for a number of new homeworkers, especially professionals in such fields as architecture, accountancy, advertising, computer programming, business consultancy, higher education and the law. It can also be made attractive – through its combination of work and family responsibilities, for instance – to a variety of other workers, such as secretaries, sales people, and bank and insurance employees (Toffler 1981: 194–207, 265–88; see also Hakim 1988; Popcorn 1992: 52).

The precise extent of these developments towards a home-centred society is difficult to determine (see the exchange between Forester 1988 and Miles 1988b). But there seems no doubt of the intention of many of the most powerful actors on the world stage to urge is in this direction. The Nippon Electric Company, one of the information technology giants, speaks in one of its publications of its aim to 'make home a comfort haven', 'a treasured sanctuary'. Home will be a place where 'boredom is unheard of' thanks to 'remote-control video recorders, giant 60–inch video screens . . . air conditioners that gauge the temperature automatically, stereos that remember your favourite music, appliances that do more as you do less, even home security systems to safeguard these valuables. Eventually . . . computers will be part of this scenario, controlling your environment and freeing your time further for other leisure pursuits' (in Webster 1986: 412).

The focus on the home, as the site of our fullest sense of ourselves and the theatre of our most fulfilling activities, is the result of a number of convergent intellectual and social tendencies in late twentieth century society (see Kumar 1995c). But it is fair to say that one of its major sources is the idea of the information society. This not only points to the technological feasibility of home-based work and leisure. It also in some sense provides the ideological driving force for the return to the home, after the centuries of industrialization that broke up the pre-industrial household and drove people to seek both their work and their pleasure outside the home. The advocates of the information society make much of the ability of the new information technology to break up the large centralized structures of industrial society. Knowledge can be dispersed, work and learning decentralized, rural areas regenerated by the transfer of many economic and cultural activities away from the large cities. The home, as the focus of most people's primary loyalty and interest, is the institution best fitted to benefit from these potentialities. It can gather them all up in one place, reuniting activities previously dispersed by the industrial revolution. It can reintegrate and strengthen the family around shared work and leisure. The home, says Toffler, can once more be 'the center of society'. It becomes the focal point of all the changes unleashed by the Third Wave.

> I believe the home will assume a startling new importance in Third Wave civilization. The rise of the prosumer, the spread of the electronic cottage, the invention of new organizational structures in business, the automation and de-massification of production, all point to the home's re-emergence as a central unit in the society of tomorrow – a unit with enhanced . . . economic, medical, educational and social functions. (Toffler 1981: 354; cf. Naisbitt 1984: 281–2; Saunders 1990: 311)

But why should these changes stop at the threshold of the home? Why do they benefit mainly the family unit? The home may indeed be the beneficiary of the new developments. It is where they are most easily concentrated. It is also the area targeted by the information technology corporations. But the home as a place is different from the home as a family, or as a centre of shared activities. The true tendency of the information society is to free and strengthen the individual, not the family. This is implicit in much of what the information society theorists say about the potentiality of the new technology. The ultimate promise of the computer, linked to the global networks of communication, is to put the whole world of knowledge and information in the hands of the single individual. The increasing miniaturization, portability and cheapness of information goods is making it possible for every individual, in principle at least, to instal themselves at the centre of information networks. There is no need, and no place, for collective or group activities here – not, at least, such as might take place in the home with other members of the family. Ensconced in the privacy of his or her own room, seated at a computer terminal, the individual entertains himself, educates himself, communicates with other people on the information highway, and provides for himself by undertaking the necessary work in the information economy.

If, as Philippe Ariès argued, the individualism of western society was contained by the modern nuclear family (Ariès 1973: 393), then the attitudes and artefacts of the information society threaten that containment. They aspire to liberate the individual from the fetters not just of the work group or mass cultural institutions but of the family as well. The home becomes the preferred site of individual activities, but it generates no collective purpose or sense of shared family values. Individuals can effectively choose to live their lives independently of and in isolation from each other. The home becomes less a 'haven in a heartless world' for the family, more like a hotel for paying (and non-paying) guests.

The information society, paradoxically, is the private or privatized society – one might almost say, the narcissistic society. This is in the face of its claims to be producing a new 'world *oikoumene*' (Bell 1980b: 62), or a 'global village' (McLuhan 1967), or a 'virtual community', a new 'electronic agora', of world users of the Internet, the computer-based global information network (Rheingold 1994). What kind of village is it that is global? What kind of community where people communicate with each other only electronically? The 'information superhighway' is traversed by isolated selves. The forty million people currently wired into the Internet may share some common sense of engaging in an exciting new enterprise but their involvement begets no feeling of real community, no new *gemeinschaft*. The links between them are for the most part segmental and resolutely one-dimensional. Not even a human voice connects them, merely a scatter of written messages, some scraps of disembodied humour, a number of useful technical services, and a vast quantity of electronic junk mail.

The ideologues of the Internet make much of the dispersal of the subject, postmodern style, in the networks of electronic communication. A new 'collective subject' is emerging in the 'virtual reality' of 'cyberspace'. We float in cyberspace as new entities, neither human nor machine, neither mind nor body, neither self or other. We become integrated human machines, 'cyborgs', able to invent our identities, as single or collective, male or female, more or less at will (Robins 1994; Heim 1994).[2]

This may be all right in virtual reality, but in actual reality it sounds like nothing so much as narcissistic or schizoid fantasies of power (Raulet 1991: 51). The free-floating surfers of the Internet engage in wish-fulfilment on a dramatic and, in some cases, highly self-damaging scale. Cyberspace may lead to the creation of new forms of art, as in the intriguing new science fiction genre of cyberpunk. But it does not lead to the creation of new communities, not at least in the sense of people who know each other in the round and engage in communal action. It is not surprising to discover that the French Minitel, the most elaborate national communication network in existence, is most heavily used by lonely individuals seeking amorous adventures. What is even more telling is that most of them do not even want to meet their cyberspace correspondents in the flesh. That would be too much like painful reality. 'Virtual sex', we know, is one of the offerings on the Internet (Foden 1994). A *New Yorker* cartoon nicely illustrates both the possibilities and the limitations of depersonalized communication in cyberspace. Speaking of his cyberspace chum, a dog seated at a computer says to another dog: 'On the internet, she doesn't know I'm a dog.'

The idea of the information society has grown in a period that has seen a widespread decline in the vitality of public life. Membership of voluntary organizations has plummeted; participation in politics, local and national, has shrunk. There is the evidence of a heartfelt cynicism and alienation from public life in all western societies (and, after a brief halcyon period of hope, in the new east European democracies as well). The public sphere, it is felt, has been colonized by the commercial mass media and political power-mongers. This is a process that arguably has been going on for most of this century (Habermas 1991a, 1992). But its most concrete expression, as shown by declining participation rates and a widely-remarked turn to private life and private pursuits, has become readily visible only in the last quarter of the century (Slater 1976; Mulgan 1994; Putnam 1994).

The information society idea appeals powerfully to this privatized existence. It suggests that even though we may be losing control over our immediate social environment, we gain ample compensation for this in the global citizenship that is within the reach of everyone with access to a personal computer. We can overstep the boundaries of our class, our race, our nation. Moreover we can do so as individuals, in our own person and in our own private space. We do not have to join parties or movements. The information society puts the power of knowledge at our fingertips, at the touch of a computer keyboard. It allows us to communicate with thousands of people across the globe. States are powerless in the face of the new technology. At a stroke their regimes of censorship and surveillance are undermined – or at least by-passed as impotent (hence, according to this view, the collapse of east European state socialism in the era of the information society). The eighteenth-century dream of cosmopolis can be realized – without the need of a world state. Information technology substitutes for the cumbersome bureaucratic structures of world organizations. It allows for direct global democracy.

It is difficult to exaggerate how attractive this vision must appear in the current condition of western societies. We have become accustomed to regarding our immediate social environment as threatening and intractable. To step outside our homes is to encounter a world that is increasingly uncomfortable, dirty and dangerous. Whether our personal safety is actually more at risk now than in the past is doubtful, but, equally, many people believe it to be so and are confirmed in this by the pronouncements of politicians and publicists. Moreover there seems to be little that either we or the same politicians and publicists can do about it. The causes of our discomforts and discontents appear remote and impersonal, almost like natural forces. Crime, unemployment, mysterious health hazards, uncivilized cities and spoilt beauty spots all seem resistant to any practical action we could take. They result apparently from the arcane operations of faceless multinational companies and foreign governments whose policies we are powerless to affect. Even more distantly, they come from processes of environmental decay whose global nature makes them difficult even to comprehend, let alone control.

How comforting it must be, then, to feel that this whole frightening and frustrating environment can be ignored. Like some latter-day alchemist or science fiction hero, the lone individual can sit at his computer console and manipulate the world. The mythology of clever teenage 'hackers' and daring raids on the files of banks and government departments add to this fantasy of power. If we cannot get our politicians to do what we want, if our politicians cannot in fact do what we want, we will make direct contact with like-minded people the world over and hatch our schemes. H. G. Wells, at the beginning of the century, called for an 'Open Conspiracy' of active thinkers and doers which would by-pass the anachronistic statesmen of the day and bring into being the peaceful and scientific world civilization that was waiting to be born.[3] Now at the end of the century the open freemasonry of the Internet appears to some to be delivering just this world community. In both cases the wish is father to the thought; but, as Marx said, it is not enough that thought tend towards reality, reality itself must tend towards thought. There is as yet little sign of that.

We should accept that, like all ideologies, the ideology of the information society meets certain needs and expresses certain important aspects of the everyday reality of contemporary societies. Computers have become a feature of most people's lives whether or not they themselves are users. It will not be difficult to habituate many people to tele-shopping, tele-banking, tele-education, electronic mail, perhaps even electronic newspapers and magazines. The combined television and computer in the corner of the room, controlling much of household entertainment, information, management and security may well become a familiar sight in the not too distant feature. At work, too, whether in the home or in a shop, office or factory, people will come to accept a computerized environment as routine. And we should not neglect, because too difficult to gauge exactly, the unconscious effects of information technology. There is, for instance, a distinct fetishism of information goods – all those glossy and caressing computers, cassettes, CDs, VCRs, videodiscs, fax machines, and the rest of the paraphernalia of the computer supermarkets.

The information revolution is a reality, and we inhabit that reality. It has affected the way we see the world and the way we live in it. The flow of images and information does indeed give rise to the sense of the 'hyperreal', as Baudrillard and Eco claim. We do live in the 'society of the spectacle', as the Situationists of May 1968 in France were already proclaiming. Our image-saturated world, ceaselessly fed by the electronic media, does change our perceptions of what is real, and makes it less easy than formerly to distinguish image from reality.

But an information revolution – a speeding up of the supply and use of information goods – is not the same thing as an information society. The information revolution may be changing our attitudes to politics, work, family life and personal identity in complex ways but so far this does not seem to add up to a new form of society. We have some good accounts of the effects in particular areas – for instance, the effect of television in breaking down our sense of place (Meyrowitz 1986). But it is significant that no coherent or comprehensive view has emerged that has demonstrated an overall pattern of change. Certainly we have no warrant for accepting the claims of Bell, Stonier and the other theorists of the information society that we have entered a new phase of social evolution, comparable to the 'great transformation' ushered in by the industrial revolution. That revolution achieved a new relationship between town and country, home and work, men and women, parents and children. It brought in a new ethic, and new social philosophies. There is no evidence that the spread of information technology has caused any such major changes. On the contrary, the bulk of the evidence indicates that what it has mainly done is to enable industrial societies to do more comprehensively what they have already been doing.

But that may turn out to be more significant than is generally thought. Quantitative changes can sometimes lead to qualitative ones. By generalizing and intensifying certain of the tendencies of industrialism, the information technology revolution may set in train developments whose outcome it is at the moment impossible to foresee. The globalization of information and communication suggests possibilities for a new framework of citizenship and democracy that has so far barely been thought about. At the same time the increased privatization and individualization that information technology have also promoted point in a different and almost opposite direction: towards the evacuation and diminishing of the public sphere of contemporary western societies. What may come out of this mixture of tendencies may be easier to speculate about when we have considered some of the other views of contemporary change.

Post-Fordism and Post-Marxism

Post-Fordism is fundamentally about the fate of Marxism. In its different guises it attempts to save Marxist analysis in an era when various Marxist projects have seemed to falter or fail. What it purports to describe is a restructuring of capitalism that has taken place in the last third of the twentieth century. Mass production and mass organization have come to an end, or at least reached their limits. Mass working-class movements have broken up, and their parties reformed or rejected altogether. The dominant framework of national, 'organized', capitalism has been breached. What increasingly takes their place is flexible, customized, production in dispersed units; new social movements, often of a local kind; and a complex interplay of global and local developments in a new global economy. The new order is still capitalist; but post-Fordists, following the lead given by Gramsci in his analysis of Fordism, speak of an 'epochal' (*New Times*) transition in the development of capitalism, a 'second industrial divide' (Sabel and Piore) comparable to the transformation of capitalism in the late nineteenth century.

To try to save Marxist analysis is not necessarily to commit oneself to an optimistic outcome, in traditional Marxist terms. Certainly some post-Fordist theorists, such as the British *New Times* group, do look forward to new forms of opposition to capitalism, and are not inclined to give up what is often referred to as 'the emancipatory project' of Marxism (here as in so many other ways the legatee of the Enlightenment). And Charles Sabel and Michael Piore, the champions of 'the second industrial divide', see in the renaissance of craft production a hopeful and humanizing development within late capitalism. It contains for them the potential for a 'collective individualism' that includes many of the features that Marxists traditionally looked forward to.

But Scott Lash and John Urry are far less sanguine about the prospects for socialists in the era of 'disorganized capitalism'. Despite an increased 'reflexivity' on the part of the populations of industrial societies, what the present mainly displays to them is the constant flux that characterizes capitalism, and its tendency to transform itself in such a way as to give itself more space, and more time. This capacity for renewal is also the theme of thinkers of the Regulationist school of Marxists, such as Michel Aglietta and Alain Lipietz. In their very choice of the term 'neo-Fordist' they indicate that the features which have often been glossed as 'post-Fordist' are for them more the signs of a redeployment of capitalist energies and enterprise in the age of globalization. This suggests continuity rather than change, and strength rather than vulnerability.

In any case, we should remember the momentous events that have occurred since the main elaboration of post-Fordist theory in the mid-1980s. With the revolutions of 1989 in central and eastern Europe, and the collapse of the Soviet Union in 1991, the fate of 'actually existing socialism' was sealed. The majority of the world's societies that had proclaimed themselves socialist or communist now ceased to do so. This did not mean the end of Marxism, as many commentators were quick to point out. But there could be no doubting the severe blow dealt to socialism by the events in eastern Europe. An early indication of this was the demise of most of the Communist parties in the west, following the example of their eastern European counterparts. Among them was the British Communist Party. One consequence was that the party's theoretical journal, *Marxism Today*, ceased publication in 1991, only two years after its promotion of post-Fordist theory had led to the party's post-Fordist *Manifesto for New Times*.

Post-Fordist theory does not necessarily come out badly because of these developments in eastern Europe. One of its most important contributions was precisely to suggest that the quintessentially Fordist organization of state socialist societies was likely to lead to their collapse, in competition with a capitalism that had invented new and more dynamic post-Fordist forms (see, for example, Hall and Jacques 1989b: 16). Moreover, post-Fordists did not have to wait until 1989 to see the proof of this. Already the changes in Hungary and Poland in the early 1980s, and above all Mikhail Gorbachev's desperate experiment in *glasnost* and *perestroika* in the Soviet Union, had revealed the need for socialist societies to throw off the Fordist mantle. The years 1989 and 1991 merely revealed that they were unable to do so without at the same time casting off their communist clothing as well.

So the eastern European revolutions do not render post-Fordism obsolete simply by virtue of its generally socialist or Marxist orientation. Post-Fordism is about changes in capitalism, and Marxism is pre-eminently a theory of the development of capitalism. That the socialist outcome hoped for and predicted has not and may not come about does not by itself invalidate post-Fordist or any other Marxist analysis of contemporary changes in capitalism.

But the failure of socialism in eastern Europe, in however grotesque a form it was practised there, cannot help affecting western socialism. Some may say that socialism, like Christianity, has never really been tried, and that the fate of socialism so-called in eastern Europe is therefore irrelevant to the desirability and possibility of establishing a true socialism in modern societies. For these people it might have been better if socialism had never been attempted in eastern Europe, since the backward condition of societies there – especially in Russia – made it inevitable that what would emerge would be a corrupt and bastard socialism.

But socialism, of a kind, *was* tried, and failed. No amount of learned commentary can prevent most people from feeling that the socialist experiment in eastern Europe has a bearing on anything that might be attempted in the name of socialism in the future. Fairly or not, socialism has been tarred with the eastern European brush. The continuing revelations of what socialist regimes did to the society and ecology of eastern Europe have made it infinitely harder for socialists to appeal to the populations of western societies. All sensible socialists acknowledge this.

Post-Fordism therefore, in so far as it is predicated on a socialist future, is inevitably affected by this historic blow to socialism. As we have seen, though, some post-Fordists are content to use the tools of Marxism simply to dissect current changes, and are agnostic or even pessimistic as to whether these changes favour a socialist outcome. It is probably impossible for Marxist analysis to dispense with the socialist project altogether – as Rosa Luxemburg once said, Marxism as a theory is shaped by its expectation of a socialist revolution – but there is no doubt that it can mute or put aside for the time being the issue of the prospects for a future socialist society. The question must be to what extent post-Fordism even of this less commited kind is affected by the current condition of socialism. More generally, is what has happened to socialism a comment on the essential tenets of post-Fordism? Are the kinds of things that have brought socialism to its current predicament relevant for assessing the the validity or plausibility of post-Fordist analysis?

We have already, in chapter 3, considered some of the objections to post-Fordist theory. The reliance on the example of the 'Third Italy', it has been argued, is dangerous and misleading. The pattern of economic and social development there depends on a complex of historical and cultural factors that are unique to the region – even in the context of Italy, let alone the industrial world as a whole. Even though the Third Italy continues to fare remarkably well (despite – or because of? – the political chaos at the centre of Italian politics), we should be wary of generalizing its experience to other countries. 'Industrial districts', though they share certain general features, are also heavily stamped by the political character and historical traditions of the regions in which they develop. Not every local 'informal economy' is an industrial district, nor capable of becoming one. Former industrial districts, once they have lost the local culture and institutional networks that sustained them, cannot readily be regenerated by the injection of certain technical instruments or new organizational forms. Sheffield or Birmingham, once the centres of thriving industrial districts, cannot now easily be turned into Parma or Prato (see further Amin 1994).

Another set of objections charges post-Fordist theory with too rigid a division of the history of industrialism into binary opposites – Fordist vs. post-Fordist, mass production vs. flexible specialization. The argument here is that, at least within the last century or so of capitalism, different modes of 'regulation' or accumulation have not displaced but have overlapped one another. Fordism is found alongside post- (or neo-) Fordism, mass production along with flexible production. A key example here is Japan, by general agreement the most successful industrial economy in the second half of the twentieth century. Japan's pattern of 'flexible rigidities' (Dore 1987) shows a thriving system of mass production co-existing with a high degree of the 'vertical disintegration' usually associated with flexible specialization. By comparison with western economies, it is also a very organized form of capitalism, involving strong linkages not only between the big firms but between big firms and their many small sub-contractors. By any measure of significance, Japan is more central to the world economy than the Third Italy, the model type of post-Fordist practice. Its presence, even allowing for certain peculiarities of its economy, suggests not only that Fordism and post-Fordism are inextricably mixed up but that the future may lie more with a modified Fordism than with anything that looks like post-Fordism.

The hybrid quality of Japan's economy serves also to cast doubt on some of the central concepts of post-Fordist theory. We have noted the uncertainties surrounding the term Fordism itself, the way in which it is made to mean a number of different and some-times inconsistent things. It has even been argued that, contrary to the claims of post-Fordists, Fordism and mass production cannot be equated, or, more precisely, that Ford's practice at his Highland Park plant lacked many of the features later mythologized as Fordist mass production. If there is no real Fordist model of mass production, this calls into question the idea of a post-Fordist successor (Williams et al. 1992).

'Flexibility', another key term, also appears ambiguous, too flexible for its own good. It has several meanings, some of which carry no implication of the coming of a new form of industrial organization. Some forms of flexibility, in fact, are not only not incompatible with mass production but actually strengthen it (and not simply by the imposition of unsociable hours of work and job insecurity). In any case, many of the problems of mass production in the west, the immediate spur to post-Fordist theory, arise not from internal problems of Fordist organization but from external causes, from the the increased competition in mass produced goods coming from Japan and the 'newly industrializing countries' (Taiwan, South Korea, Singapore, Hong Kong, Mexico, etc.).

Then there is the idea of small batch production replacing mass production. This, it is argued, far from being a novelty or discontinuity, is implicit in the general tendency of capitalism to multiply the number of different kinds of commodities over time. Capitalism grows by the creation of new needs, which it then seeks to satisfy by increasing the range and diversity of its products. Small batch customized production reflects no more than the current phase of consumerism, which has gone beyond the earlier phase of mass consumption to demand greater variety and individuality. (For a summary of these various objections, see Meegan 1988; Sayer and Walker 1992: 191–223.)

Taken together, these criticisms of post-Fordist theory amount to a comprehensive rejection of the idea that we are moving into a new society, a 'new world', as Stuart Hall and Martin Jacques claim (1989b: 20). For these critics, who are also mostly Marxists, though of a more traditional kind, post-Fordism is not some new order of capitalist society. Even if it is identifiable, it betokens no new principle. In so far as new features can be distinguished, they are simply the expressions of capitalism's well-known disposition to change and modify its practices in accordance with the requirements of survival and growth.

Even to say this is of course to say quite a lot. It is the old problem of whether the glass is half full or half empty. There are very few abrupt changes in society. Leaving aside political revolutions, where the tendency is to exaggerate the changes, discontinuities in other spheres of society are often perceived only some time after they have begun to occur. This was as true of the scientific revolution of the seventeenth century as of the industrial revolution of the nineteenth.

None of the post-Fordists is claiming change on this scale. We are in any case too much in the midst of things to be able to judge confidently whether a genuinely new economic order is emerging. But we can see major changes in the character of industrial organization, and in the nature of work. Much of this has to do with the new international division of labour, capitalism on a global scale. That too, though arguably a seed implanted from capitalism's earliest days, may now have reached such a point as to be giving capitalism a quite different face. Historic centres of industry are being displaced and new ones created at unnerving speed. The mobility of capital has achieved unprecedented levels, effacing national boundaries and enabling capitalists to make entirely new kinds of agreements with local labour forces and local power structures. Unions are forced to engage in plant bargaining at the local level, losing much of their national effectiveness. For large numbers of workers, the idea of secure lifetime employment is vanishing. Men find themselves displaced by women, as the newer 'flatter' organizations seek more 'flexible' workers able and willing to work part-time and for less pay. Skills become rapidly obsolescent and new ones have to be learned. The educational system in all industrial societies is under extreme pressure to reshape itself to respond to these requirements.

This adds up, whichever way one chooses to look at it, to quite a formidable degree of change. Post-Fordists are, as we have seen, divided as to how far these developments are to be seen as threats or opportunities. Clearly they put a lot of strategic power in the hands of capital, though at the expense of the security of the individual capitalist, who has to operate in a far more volatile and unstable environment than in the era of 'organized capitalism'. Moreover we have to remember that these economic changes are only part of what is comprehended by post-Fordism. Post-Fordists connect these changes to a more far-reaching general move away from large-scale organization, centralization, bureaucracy and hierarchy. They are concerned that the greater flexibility and choice opened up by this development should not, as they have tended to do, benefit only right-wing parties and their supporters. In pursuit of this they have urged the left not mechanically to oppose the current changes but to see in them the possibilities of real gains. New coinages, such as 'socialist individualism', have expressed an aspiration that goes beyond the traditional horizons of the left.

It is important to see that, from a social democratic perspective, there have been some genuine successes. The left in the west has largely thrown off its traditional male-orientated 'productivist' or 'workerist' stance, and engaged with men and women more roundedly in their roles not simply as workers but also as family members, consumers, and citizens of the welfare state. It has aimed to forge alliances going beyond the work-place, to recognize people's interest in their homes, their health, their schools, and the places where they go for rest and recreation. It has encouraged new forms of social action, outside the party and the trade union, in such areas as housing, race relations, education and the environment (in Britain a notable success in an action of this kind was the nation-wide protest against the poll tax).

In other ways, too, post-Fordists of the 'New Times' variety might feel that the future does not belong entirely to their enemies. Organizations have been forced to become more responsive to the needs and demands of their customers and clients. Public institutions in particular have been pushed into abandoning much of their traditional secrecy and inaccessiblility. There is a new attitude of irreverence towards authority which, while it can breed cynicism, also encourages independence. The very idea of a 'citizen's charter', however imperfect in implementation, is a concession to a new mood of popular demand for openness and accountability.

Even the strong revival of individualism, which has been one of the most marked features of western societies in recent years, has not worked entirely against traditional left-wing goals. Socialism and individualism have always had a troubled relationship but there can be little doubt that, as Durkheim argued in the late nineteenth century, they are ultimately close bedfellows. At any rate the drive towards individualization has encouraged a greater freedom in the relations between workers and employers, men and women, parents and children. Traditional forms of deference have given way to a new assertion of individual rights, backed up if necessary by recourse to the courts. The new individualism seems to have had a particularly strong effect on women, in stimulating them to achieve more in business and professional life, and to be more prepared to make their way in society independently of men. Generally the increased 'reflexivity', or self-consciousness and awareness of social processes, that many have seen as characterizing contemporary societies, might be regarded as an expression of this heightened individualism.

So the changes which have generally been termed post-Fordist can reasonably be held to have had some positive effects for the left. But the very case of individualism illustrates well just how problematic too those changes must appear, and what kind of challenge they pose to the left. Individualism has many faces, and one of those is that of unprincipled social irresponsibility. Individualism in recent years has most strongly run in the form of market or economic individualism. This has not only entailed a drive towards commercialization in all sectors of society. It has also encouraged a selfish, devil-take-the-hindmost attitude throughout society (see, for example, Marquand 1988). With this, and perhaps as a reflection of it, there has also been a move towards the privatization of society. This refers not only to the process of selling off state enterprises to private buyers, as in British Conservative policy in the 1980s and 1990s. It also refers more generally to the withdrawal into private life, and especially the life of the home, that we have already discussed.

Individualization and privatization are the master themes of contemporary western life. They are redrawing the boundaries between state and society, the public and the private sphere, society and the individual. Their ramifications are complex, as are the evaluations of their effects. For some they empower the individual, for others they enfeeble society. But whatever the emphasis there seems no question that they are bringing about a historic shift in the character of western societies. Many traditions, not just of socialism but of civic republicanism and similar philosophies of the public realm, find themselves severely under challenge (see Bellah et al. 1985; Weintraub and Kumar 1995).

Individualization and privatization are central to post-Fordist analysis. What concerns many of the theorists is the need to harness them to the socialist cause, rather then regarding them, as is traditional on the left, as antagonistic to it. But they would be the first to admit that the main beneficiaries of these tendencies in recent years have been the parties and movements of the right. Left-wing parties and ideologies everywhere have been tagged with the collectivist and statist label, and suffered accordingly in electoral competition with a right that has redefined itself as primarily individualist. Even where, as in France and Spain, the left has maintained some presence, it has done so mainly by taking on board substantial parts of the baggage of its right-wing opponents.

It has also been clear that the tendencies which have been unpropitious for the left in the west have been equally significant in the rejection of socialism in eastern Europe. The explosion of market thinking and rampant individualism that has occurred in the region since 1989 is some indication of the forces that had been pent up by state socialism. This explosion of feeling can by no means all be attributed to the agents of the World Bank and western business schools. Eastern Europe has its own traditions of individualism and entrepreneurship. More to the point, however, and the explanation at least in part for the downfall of socialism there, is that throughout the 1970s and 1980s western-style individualism and consumerism made significant inroads into the countries of eastern Europe. There was nothing mysterious about this process. Travel between east and west, in both directions, had been getting progressively easier. In the information age it was virtually impossible for eastern European governments to control the flow of ideas and images across their borders. The western mass media could be picked up in one way or another in almost all the communist countries. When communism crashed in eastern Europe it was for much the same reasons that socialist parties in the west found themselves increasingly ignored.

It is in this way that the fate of socialism in eastern Europe reflects back on the post-Fordist analysis in the west. It suggests that the post-Fordists are right to stress that many of the old assumptions of industrial societies are breaking down. There has been a widespread reaction against large-scale organization and centralization, especially in their statist forms. Individuals are witholding their allegiance to many of the established forms of authority. They are coming to rely more on informal networks of family and friends than on institutional arrangements. They are putting the emphasis on individual rather than collective rights, as a surer protector of freedom and security.

In the wake of 1989, many people were trumpeting the death of socialism. It remains to see whether this is so. Socialism is about more than a nationalized economy and a welfare state (Kumar 1993). But it seems undoubted that socialism will have to modify its collectivist ethos considerably if it is to come to terms with the new attitudes. The more so, as eastern Europe also suggests, since these attitudes exist if not world-wide at least on a very wide scale, going well beyond the societies of the west. A gale of individualist thought and practice seems to be blowing through the entire developed world. Why this should be so is not entirely clear. Probably it has something to do with the kinds of developments that are considered in the theory of the information society, as well as that of post-modernity. Once more the overlaps between the three theories suggest themselves. We should turn now therefore to the most comprehensive of these theories, for a fuller assessment of the changes.

Modernity versus Post-Modernity

At the end of his series of magisterial reflections on post-modernism, Fredric Jameson writes:

> I occasionally get just as tired of the slogan 'postmodern' as anyone else, but when I am tempted to regret my complicity with it, to deplore its misuses and its notoriety, and to conclude with some reluctance that it raises more problems than it solves, I find myself pausing to wonder whether any other concept can dramatize the issues in quite so effective and economical a fashion. (Jameson 1992: 418)

It is this dilemma that haunts most discussions of post-modernity. Is post-modernity simple a slogan, a fashionable dinner-party tag much deployed on the media, a catch-all concept so vague and all-embracing as to be vacuous? Or is it, or something like it, actually necessary in the current condition of contemporary western societies? Does it describe a real new state of society, one which requires a new term?

The problem, as we have seen, does not stop there. Even if the new term is desirable, what does it purport to describe? Does it, as its name initially suggests, point to a state of things 'after' or 'beyond' modernity? Or is it rather a form of reflection on modernity, a new way, as one commentator has put it, of 'relating to modern conditions and their consequences' (Smart 1993: 152)?

We have, as seems logical, set our discussion of post-modernity against a background of the concept of modernity. Whatever meaning post-modernity may have must derive in some way from an understanding of modernity.

We have also, as have many others, made the distinction between modernity and modernism. Modernity refers to the economic, technological, political and in many respects intellectual creations of western societies in the period since the eighteenth century. ('Modernization' may then be thought to be the process by which this modernity was brought into being, and hence made imitable by other, non-western, societies). Modernism is a cultural movement that began in the late nineteenth century. Though in some ways continuing the impulse of modernity, modernism more significantly constituted a reaction against some of the dominant features of modernity.

No comparable distinction can be made between post-modernity and post-modernism, for reasons that we have indicated. But we should remember Charles Jencks's account of post-modernism as a 'double-coded' phenomenon, at once continuing and opposing (or 'transcending') the tendencies of both modernity and modernism.

It is partly because of the existence of such a plurality of terms, each with shifting meanings, that there can be so much fertile ground for disagreement: a boon to publishers but a nightmare for social theorists. We need to accept that whatever verdict we might pass on the idea of post-modernity will depend to a good extent on our highly challengeable definitions of it. Things, in other words, are not as they are with the information society or post-Fordism. In those cases there is a reasonable degree of consensus on their meanings; nothing of the kind applies to post-modernity. If, in the end, we agree with Jameson that post-modernity is a useful and even perhaps indispensable term, it will be because the account that we have given of it in the previous chapter highlights certain aspects of the theory that appear particularly promising and valuable. Our definition of the 'field of meaning' surrounding post-modernity suggests uses and perspectives, a map of our current condition, that more conventional descriptions do not match.

The confusions of the debate on post-modernity are well illustrated in the celebrated riposte to the postmodernists by the German thinker Jürgen Habermas. Habermas accuses the postmodernists of a defeatist and escapist conservatism in face of the still unfulfilled promise of Enlightenment modernity. But the 'postmodernists' he has in mind are cultural conservatives or 'neoconservatives' such as Daniel Bell, whose *Cultural Contradictions of Capitalism* is singled out for treatment as a postmodernist tract. Along with these neo-conservatives are nostalgic 'old conservatives' and a group Habermas labels 'the young conservatives'. This group includes Foucault and Derrida, namely, the very people normally associated with postmodernism. For Habermas though these thinkers are not so much postmodernist as anti-modernist.

He sees them as following in the footsteps of the original exponents of 'aesthetic modernity' at the turn of the century. But their view of a de-centred subjectivity, and their attacks on reason, take them 'outside the modern world.' 'On the basis of modernist attitudes, they justify an irreconcilable anti-modernism' (Habermas 1981: 13).

It is probably fortunate that most commentators have not followed Habermas's usage in the debates on post-modernity. What they have rightly taken seriously, however, is his attack on post-modernity as fundamentally a conservative, anti-modern ideology. For Habermas it is too early to renounce modernity. He accepts that Enlightenment rationality contains many perils, some of them powerfully exposed by Habermas's own mentors Max Horkheimer and Theodor Adorno in their book *Dialectic of the Enlightenment* (1944). The main problem is the reliance on a concept of 'subject-centred reason', developed most influentially by Kant. This privileged the solitary, individual ego, seeking to comprehend the world in its totality from the viewpoint of the individual mind. The danger is of a solely instrumental, calculative concept of reason, which can lead to an attitude of domination and exploitation towards both nature and society. But, argues Habermas, the Enlightenment had already provided its own antidote. Already in the critics of Kant, in Schlegel, Schiller, Fichte and a whole line of thinkers culminating in the Young Hegelians and Nietzsche, this concept of reason had come under vigorous attack. Thus from the very beginning modernity supplied its own 'counterdiscourse'. Our contemporary radical critics of reason, the deconstructionists such as Foucault and Derrida, 'suppress that almost 200–year counterdiscourse inherent in modernity itself . . . The intention of revising the Enlightenment with the tools of the Enlightenment is . . . what united the critics of Kant from the start' (Habermas 1987: 302–3; cf. Giddens 1990: 48–9).

From this critical tradition Habermas develops, in opposition to subject-centred reason, the concept of what he calls 'communicative reason'. In this the perspective of the all-knowing individual subject is subordinated to the consensual agreement that is reached through communicative interaction between equals. For Habermas this avoids the potentially 'terroristic' implications of subject-centred reason, the focus of the attacks of contemporary postmodernists. Our problem is not, as they assert, reason itself but the dominance hitherto of a particular, one-sided, version of it. We suffer indeed not from an excess but 'a deficit of rationality'. The task is to disinter alternative traditions of reason buried within the legacy of the Enlightenment. Capitalism, the chief carrier of modernity, has in this respect been ambivalent. 'The communicative potential of reason has been simultaneously developed and distorted in the course of a capitalist modernization.' Habermas is the least starry-eyed of thinkers, and is aware of the immense difficulties of releasing this potential in the face of the powerful technological and bureaucratic structures of capitalist rationality. The instrumental rationality of these structures has gone far in colonizing the 'lifeworld' that is the sphere of communicative interaction. But he equally remains convinced of the greater dangers of the 'totalizing repudiations of modern forms of life'. We are not, whatever the postmodernists say, at the end of modernity, nor can we simply renounce it. To reject the 'grand narratives' of modernity is to render ourselves powerless in the face of instrumental rationality. We are in modernity; modernity is our fate. The challenge now remains essentially what it was for Hegel, and for Marx: how to to fulfil modernity's promise of universal 'self-consciousness, self-determination and self-realization' (Habermas 1987: 338; see also Bernstein 1985; Ashley 1990).

Habermas's view that Enlightenment modernity itself offers us the tools with which to deal with its perplexities ('aporias') is shared by a number of other writers who are equally hostile to theories of post-modernity. Albrecht Wellmer, who comes from the same school of Critical Theory as Habermas, argues that what appears today as a rejection or supersession of modernity is mainly a form of 'self-critical' modernism. The critique of modernity has been implicit in the modern project since its inception; at most postmodernism has 'redirected' this critique, removing the remaining vestiges of utopianism and scientism. Thus cleansed, we are left with a 'post-metaphysical modernism', a modernism that Wellmer regards as 'an unsurpassable horizon in a cognitive, aesthetic and moral-political sense'. Moreover the denial of the utopian component does not detract from the persisting moral or political appeal of the original promise of modernity. 'A postmetaphysical modernity would be a modernity without the dream of ultimate reconciliations, but it would still preserve the rational, subversive and experimental spirit of modern democracy, modern art, modern science and modern individualism' (Wellmer 1991: viii; see also 91–4; and cf. Bürger 1992: 44–5).

The most spirited defence of modernity, and the most defiant rejection of post-modernity, is to be found in Marshall Berman. For Berman, like Habermas, modernity is double-edged. Its very power and dynamism means that it destroys as much as it creates.

'To be modern is to find ourselves in an environment that promises adventure, power, joy, growth, transformation of ourselves and the world – and, at the same time, that threatens to destroy everything we have, everything we know, everything we are.' Modernity unites all mankind, but it is 'a paradoxical unity, a unity of disunity: it pours us all into a maelstrom of perpetual disintegration and renewal, of struggle and contradiction, of ambiguity and anguish' (Berman 1983: 15).

But whether we are more impressed by modernity's destructive or its creative capacities, we have no choice but to live with it. It is 'the only world we have got.' Both anti-modernism and what is claimed as postmodernism are doomed attempts to escape our fate. Berman has some sympathy for the exuberant 'postmodernism' of 1960s America, as expressed by Leslie Fiedler and other exponents of the pop and counter-culture. As against the official custodians of modernism, they had in fact a better claim to the 'spirit and honour of modernism'. But he is scathing about the French thinkers of the 1970s and 1980s who represent the second wave of postmodernism. He accuses them of a retreat into an esoteric intellectual world divorced from all political and social reality. 'Derrida, Roland Barthes, Jacques Lacan, Michel Foucault, Jean Baudrillard, and all their legions of followers, appropriated the whole modernist language of radical breakthrough, wrenched it out of its moral and political context, and transformed it into a purely aesthetic language game.' Contemporary postmodernists are the heirs of the failed hopes of May 1968 in France. They have 'dug themselves into a grand metaphysical tomb, thick and tight enough to furnish lasting comfort against the cruel hopes of spring' (Berman 1992: 42–6).

In any case, says Berman, the postmodernists are irrelevant. They are a side-show. The main drama on the world stage is still modernity, and it is destined to hold its place for as long as we can see. We are in fact most likely still only in the early stages of modernization. Large sections of the world are only just beginning to feel its full impact. It is for this reason that Berman thinks we can still draw inspiration from the great nineteenth-century writers on modernity – Marx, Nietzsche, Baudelaire, Dostoevsky. Living in the earliest and most formative years of modernity, they were able to grasp its contradictions – the losses and the unprecedented possibilities – more profoundly than we seem able to. 'To appropriate the modernities of yesterday can be at once a critique of the modernities of today and an act of faith in the modernities . . . of tomorrow and the day after tomorrow'

(Berman 1983: 36; see also 345–8). What links the positions of Habermas, Wellmer, Berman and similar thinkers is the conviction that modernity is still unfinished business – an 'unfinished project', as Habermas puts it. It has potential still to be realized. One can make this point in a spirit of celebration, as with Berman, or in a more guardedly hopeful way, as with Habermas. Or one can simply be pragmatic about it. One might make the point that, as a matter of empirical fact, modernity – seen as an expression of Enlightenment rationality – is what most of the world seems to want, to the exclusion of other modes of thought and practice.

Ernest Gellner, for instance, is quite prepared to concede that belief in Enlightenment reason is ultimately a form of faith. Enlightenment rationalism is the product of a particular culture at a particular time: eighteenth-century western civilization. By virtue of its success in conferring enormous economic and political power on those who adopted it, it has become the preferred mode of thought of most educated people in the world. 'Enlightenment Secular Fundamentalism' has become the path to scientific-industrial civilization, and that is the path chosen by the majority of the world's societies. The relativism of the postmodernists may be philosophically tenable but apart from the fact that it leads to nihilism it is practically irrelevant. It remains the fashionable plaything of western intellectuals. The attacks on 'rationalist fundamentalism' fall on deaf ears. 'We happen to live in a world in which one style of knowledge [Enlightenment rationality], though born of one culture, is being adapted by all of them, with enormous speed and eagerness, and is disrupting many of them, and is totally transforming the milieu in which men live. This is simply a fact' (Gellner 1992: 78).

It is important to see that there is a certain correspondence between these views of modernity and the position of at least one important strand of postmodern theory. Clearly for the champions of modernity – whether in Gellner's stoical acceptance of it as a matter of fact, or in the more desire-laden conviction of Habermas and Berman that modernity still has to fulfil its emancipatory promise – modernity cannot be declared over, at least in a temporal or historical sense. But that is not the same as saying that it has not changed. Such an understanding is especially implicit in Habermas's and Berman's account of modernity as driven by the process of capitalist industrialization. Two hundred years may not be a long time in civilizational terms, but it is long enough for modernity to reveal a good deal of its character. This is particularly so with a social form as inherently unstable and dynamic as all agree is the case with modern capitalist civilization. We should remember the position of postmodernists such as Bauman and Huyssen. They do not regard post-modernity as a new historical stage but rather as the culmination of modernity, a vantage point from which critically to assess its performance and, presumably, its remaining potential, if any. Post-modernity on this view is a modernity become conscious of its principles and practice, a self-conscious modernity. Such an interpretation accords well with that of thinkers such as Agnes Heller, who is generally hostile towards theories of post-modernity. If the concept of post-modernity has any meaning it cannot, she says, refer to 'a new period that comes after modernity'. It should be understood rather as equivalent to 'the contemporary historical consciousness of the modern age'. 'Post-modern is not what follows after the modern age, but what follows after the unfolding of modernity. Once the main categories of modernity have emerged, the historical tempo slows down and the real work on the possibilities begin' (Heller 1990: 168–9; see also Heller and Feher 1988: 1).

There are of course postmodernists, such as Jencks and Hassan, who believe that a new era has dawned. But it is equally clear that we should be careful not to draw too hard and fast a line between theories of modernity and post-modernity. For many thinkers on both sides of the divide the difference is mainly one of emphasis, when it is not simply terminological. Modernists stress the persistence of past characteristics, and the relevance therefore of past analyses of modernity. Postmodernists do not deny continuity but are more struck by the fact that we are now in a position to take stock of the whole experience of modernity, in a way not possible before. Hegel and Marx may have acute insights to offer but writing as they did in the first century of modernity they could not be expected to see how things would work out in the long run.

This seems a valuable corrective to the standard accounts of modernity. The modernity of the late twentieth century is different from that of the early nineteenth century. This obvious point is often obscured in those treatments – Berman's in part – in which modernity appears as a perennial or timeless order, a once-and-for-all achievement that then produces relatively minor variations on the main theme (see Anderson 1984). Modernity, like the capitalism with which it has been closely associated for much of the time, has a history. Even if the concept of post-modernity were to do no more than point to that, it would have achieved something important. It alerts us to features of late modernity that might otherwise escape our attention. We are enabled to see new things, or things not previously noticed, or developments that may have appeared unpromising in the earlier stages of modernization and have unexpectedly survived or revived. The ecological crisis produced by the world-wide expansion of the industrial way of life; the fragmentation of national cultures, and the revival of 'small nationalisms' (or 'tribalism'); the persistence of religion, in old and new forms; the historic impasse that socialism seems to have run into; the declining appeal of traditional political ideologies, and of politics and the public sphere generally: in all these and other ways postmodern theory points to unexpected developments and significant discontinuities in the history of modernity. This may not mean the end of modernity but it does seem to mean that we should rethink the modern project, ask again what it was all about.[4]

A recognition of this fact, and an attractive response to it, lies in the thinking of the American philosopher Richard Rorty. Rorty is often accounted a postmodernist, and he does not seem particularly troubled by the label. But his position is more interesting for attempting to steer a path between the modernists and the postmodernists. With Lyotard and the postmodernists he accepts the 'death of metanarratives'. With Habermas and the modernists he argues that nevertheless we need not and should not give up on political commitment.

Rorty agrees with Lyotard that, contrary to Habermas's claims, there is no abstract and universal 'narrative of emancipation' that can be discerned in the project of modernity. If emancipation of a (fitful) kind has emerged in the course of modernization, this is because of local and particular moral and political 'narratives' in the west that have produced western liberal democracy. No supra-historical concept of 'reason' and its realization need to be invoked in order to understand this outcome. If modernity has a principle, it is simply the confidence to be 'self-assertive' – a 'willingness to center our hopes on the future of the race, on the unpredictable successes of our descendants'. Out of this modern confidence has come the 'reformist politics' and the 'social engineering' that have produced tolerance, a free press, universal education, parliament and the rest of the apparatus of liberal democracy. We are certainly free to call this 'progress', so long as we do not assume that everyone the world over shares our (western) view of progress, nor that this progress is a realization of 'reason' (for which there are in any case no universal criteria), nor that it is is logically determined in any way, as the 'secret history' of modernity. Parliamentary democracy and the welfare state are good but not because 'these institutions are truer to human nature, or more rational, or in better accord with the universal moral law, than feudalism or totalitarianism'. In Lyotard's terms, we must drop 'metanarratives' but 'keep on recounting edifying first-order narratives' (Rorty 1985: 170; 1992: 60).

As this account already suggests, Rorty is not prepared to follow Lyotard and the postmodernists into a nihilistic rejection of all forms of political belief and commitment. Lyotard's position is that the absence of a universal concept of reason or of a common human nature must make us treat all political programmes as potentially terroristic and totalitarian. There is no common or universal subject of human history, hence there can be no 'universal history of humanity.' There exist only local cultures whose ways and beliefs are mutually incomprehensible and probably also incompatible.

But as self-confessed Deweyan pragmatist Rorty protests that 'we need not presuppose a *persistent* "we", a trans-historical metaphysical subject, in order to tell stories of progress. The only "we" we need is a local and temporary one: "we" means something like "us twentieth-century western social democrats".' There is no reason why that 'we' should not continue to press for the 'pragmatist utopia' in which all opinions and options are 'thrashed out in free and open encounters.' This goal does not depend on 'the revolutionary rhetoric of emancipation and unmasking' but rather 'the reformist rhetoric about increased tolerance and decreased suffering'. If we accept the primacy of the (relativist) idea of tolerance, there is nothing to stop us ('twentieth-century western social democrats') from attempting to persuade more and more of our fellow humans to join us in the enterprise to achieve a world society based on liberal institutions. We may or may not succeed, and we have no basis in 'human nature' or 'the moral sense of mankind' to force this outcome on anyone. But it is a rationally defensible goal.

> We see no reason why either recent social and political developments or recent philosophical thought should deter us from our attempt to build a cosmopolitan world society – one which embodies the same sort of utopia with which the Christian, Enlightenment and Marxist metanarratives of emancipation ended . . .
>
> Deweyan pragmatists urge us to think of ourselves as part of a pageant of historical progress which will gradually encompass all

of the human race, and are willing to argue that the vocabulary which twentieth-century social democrats use is the best vocabulary the race has come up with so far . . . But pragmatists are quite sure that their own vocabulary will be superseded – and, from their point of view, the sooner the better. (Rorty 1992: 62, 68; see also 1985: 171–2)

This is undoubtedly an attractive position, one that attempts to 'split the difference' between Lyotard and Habermas (Rorty 1985: 173). From our point of view what makes it appealing is that it takes the most persuasive part of the postmodern critique while refusing to accept its more nihilistic or apocalyptic conclusions. There has clearly been a loss of belief in the kind of transhistorical or universalist ideology that sets the goal towards which all mankind is tending. Neither the socialist nor the democratic utopia seems preordained. The Hegelian idea, so influential in a variety of guises, that human history is essentially the history of freedom, no longer commands widespread assent. To that extent the 'incredulity towards metanarratives' is a plausible claim. But this does not leave us as helpless as Lyotard and some other postmodernists suppose. Liberal democracy, and no doubt certain varieties of socialism, can be defended in other terms than as 'metanarratives'. This then can suggest forms of contemporary identification and action that, with appropriate modesty, seek to realize some of the goals of Enlightenment modernity. We need not give up on the 'emancipatory' promise or programme of modernity. We must simply acknowledge its pragmatic, culturally-limited, time-bound character; and in attempting to carry it out we must proceed by persuasion, constant argument and constant experimentation.

There is a further aspect of Rorty's discussion of modernity that is helpful to our purposes. Rorty even-handedly charges French thinkers with an obsession with revolutionary politics, and German thinkers with an obsession with the philosophical bases of modernity. The French concern in fact derives from their acceptance of the German definition of the problem. If revolutionary politics cannot be philosophically justified, there is no politics. The choice for them is either total revolution or total nihilism. It is beneath their dignity to consider 'mere reformism'. Since revolution cannot be justified, because there is no rational basis for it, postmodernist intellectuals such as Foucault and Lyotard retreat to the avant-garde salons of the academy.

German thinkers generally accept this position – hence Habermas's desperate attempt to hold on to some concept of reason.

But their main concern has been to trace and reflect on the philosophical tradition, from Kant (or Descartes) to Nietschze and beyond, that has grappled with problems of truth and validity. This for them is the essential underpinning of modernity. Modernity for them has been fundamentally about finding a rational basis for society to replace the religion that previously supplied social meaning and social integration. Hence their concern with the 'diremptions' and 'alienations' of western society that have followed upon the loss of religion. The main problem, for Habermas and the whole German school of Critical Theory, is that the 'subject-centred reason' that we inherit from Kant and the Enlightenment has not been adequate to the task. It has not been capable of supplying a new principle that finds a rapprochement, while acknowledging the differences, between the three spheres of science (truth), morality (goodness) and art (beauty) identified by Kant as the modern successors to a unified religion. From this failure follows the spectre of post-modernity that Habermas has tried to exorcize with his concept of 'communicative reason' (Rorty 1985: 169–70; 1992: 68–71).

But what, asks Rorty, if this whole enterprise is misguided? What if this whole obsession with 'subject-centred reason', and generally with questions of epistemology, has obscured other, perhaps more important, perspectives on modernity? Rorty suggests that 'that famous "subjectivity" which post-Kantian historians of philosophy, anxious to link Kant with Descartes, took as their guiding thread', has misled us as to 'the principle of the modern'. That principle is better suggested not by Descartes, the prophet of 'self-grounding', but by Bacon, the prophet of 'self-assertion'. From Bacon derives the whole modern project of social experimentation and 'social engineering' that has been far more consequential than philosophic attempts to find an agreed basis for reason. Bacon takes us back to the real as opposed to the speculative history of modernity. He leads us away from the abstract, a-historical Platonic concern with 'clear and distinct ideas' to the actual technological, social and political accomplishments of modern societies, and the blessings and headaches they have brought. Rorty points to

> the various rosy prospects which appear once one suggests that working through 'the principle of subjectivity' (and out the other side) was just a side-show, something which an isolated order of priests devoted themselves to for a few hundred years, something which did not make much difference to the successes and failures of the European countries in realizing the hopes formulated by the Enlightenment. (Rorty 1985: 171)[5]

Rorty does indeed direct our attention back to some of the other questions raised by the debate about post-modernity. The deconstructionists' attack on reason, and Habermas's defence of it, is one thing, and by no means a small one. For many post-modernists it is what defines the current condition of contemporary societies. But there are also the kinds of concerns exemplified by the writings of Jencks, Jameson, Harvey and others. These point to the economic, social and political changes affecting the contemporary world: such matters as globalization, the rise of the culture industries, new forms of localism, new social movements. How does post-modernity appear in the light of these claims? And what might be the prospects, not for 'a postmodernist form of intellectual life', in which 'the sublime' floats free from social ties, but 'a postmodernist form of social life, in which society as a whole asserts itself without bothering to ground itself' (Rorty 1985: 175)?

Post-modernity: Ideology and Reality

Jameson points to a vexing problem with theories of post-modernity:

> As an ideology which is also a a reality, the 'postmodern' cannot be disproved insofar as its fundamental feature is the radical separation of all the levels and voices whose recombination in their totality alone could disprove it. (Jameson 1992: 376)

Jameson is referring to the way that contemporary social reality is, as he sees it, marked by heterogeneity, 'difference' and fragmentation. It represents the break-up of the order associated not just with the 'organic totality' of pre-industrial societies but also that of classic modern societies of the western type. Reality now is compartmentalized, classified in multiple and overlapping yet separate ways. It is organized 'a little like those networks of political cells whose members have only met their immediate opposite numbers'. The concept of the postmodern itself reflects this cellular reality. It is made up of distinct and overlapping features which cannot be aggregated or integrated, unlike more traditional concepts such as feudalism or capitalism or even 'the modern'. Post-modernity is expressed in the language of 'discourses' and 'voices' rather than of falsifiable propositions. It remains as frustratingly disparate as the reality it purports to mirror and describe (Jameson 1992: 364–76; cf. Bauman 1992: xxiv).

There is also the further problem that, as a number of critics have pointed out, post-modernity does not offer itself as a theory to be tested and assessed in the usual fashion. In a peculiar way, post-modernity has to be assessed not from the detached viewpoint of the external observer but from within, from inside its own discourse. We can choose to ignore postmodern theory; but if we examine it we rapidly come to see that we are dealing with a way of analysing and describing that is so enmeshed with the reality it engages that it is virtually impossible to separate and compare the two. The point is that we are, as Jameson says, to a good extent *within* the culture of postmodernism' and cannot just turn our backs on it (1992: 62). Postmodern architects and urbanists deliberately and self-consciously go out and build postmodernist buildings and postmodernist cities. Postmodern artists and writers create an artistic culture of postmodernism that then becomes an environment for other artists and writers to work within (and against). Postmodern critics write books about post-modernity that become the culture of large parts of the academy, forcing its members to confront it and to some extent to work within it. Post-modernity, as Ihab Hassan has said, is partly about the 'will to power', a bid to establish new theories and concepts in order to 'open for its proponents a space in language.' The critical culture of post-modernity creates such new spaces and opportunities. The debates about it become the proof of its existence. They establish a new reality that then becomes the contentious centre of struggles for cultural power and control. 'The battle of the books is also an ontic battle against death' (Hassan 1985: 120; see also Connor 1989: 10–20; Kermode 1989: 144).

So there is an inescapable degree of 'reflexivity' or self-knowing in post-modernity that is inherent in its condition, and in the discussions about it. That means that there must be a certain rhetorical hyperbole in the question we posed in the last chapter, is post-modernity *true*? The question cannot be answered literally. Post-modernity is true to the extent that it is all around us. The culture industries, which have become central to many western societies, have made it true by their indefatigable creation of an image-saturated environment. Hyperreality – the copy of which the original has been lost – is the world we all inhabit for at least part of the time. The 'ecstasy of communication', in the world of the Internet, is only too manifestly an experience many of us enjoy or suffer in our working as well as our leisure lives. Culture is no longer simply an adjunct to the serious business of getting a living but has in good part become that business. Large numbers of people work in the culture industries and in their spare time also consume its products.

More remarkably, the culture industries have themselves been preoccupied to an extraordinary degree with spreading the vocabulary, imagery and emotional tones of post-modernity. This inevitably heightens the element of reflexivity in the phenomenon. Postmodern intellectuals and artists regularly grace the television screens in late night discussion programmes. Many popular talk shows and comedy programmes have an unmistakeably post-modernist irony and quizzicality about them. Our whole sense of politics and of political efficacy is affected by the constant stream of irreverence and ridicule directed at figures of authority and hallowed national institutions. One result of this promotion of postmodernist culture is that the answer to the question, is post-modernity true, has partly to be couched in terms created by that very culture.

This could be one way of dealing with the similar question, how far is post-modernity an ideology? Ideologies do not always – perhaps not very often in fact – stand 'outside' the reality they supposedly reflect, typically in distorted form. The base-superstructure imagery of Marxism is what leads us to expect this relationship. More commonly the ideology is to be found in the practices and discourses of everyday life. It is a lived existence, and has a palpable feel of common-sense reality about it. To that extent it is internal to the reality whose workings and principles it may nevertheless conceal in some crucial way.

Post-modernity does at least have this much existence. If it is to be thought ideological, it is at least partly in this sense. The characteristic modes and expressions of post-modernity have become familiar aspects of the reality of many people in western societies. Looking around them, people can see post-modernity in the streets, just as, at the turn of the century, the people of Paris and Berlin could see modernity in the streets. When you talk to people about their experiences and expectations, and attempt to account for them in the postmodern terms of fragmentation, 'incoherence', and the loss of certain stabilities and doctrinal beliefs, they seem instantly to recognize the diagnosis.

But this still leaves open the question of how far post-modernity is an ideology in the more general sense. It may be real, in the sense that it is familiarly lived. But does its account of the world mask deeper changes? Is it ideological in the sense that it is the carrier of an economic or political system that is not, or not properly, describable in its terms? What does post-modernity represent?

It is noteworthy that Jameson, for instance, despite his warning about the difficulties of treating postmodernism as a testable theory, again and again reverts to the idea that it is the 'cultural logic of late capitalism'. A similar view is to be found in writers such as Lash, Urry and Harvey. The sense must be that, even if we cannot (or cannot easily) distinguish postmodern culture from post-modern society, we should be able to understand the phenomenon of post-modernity through an analysis of the current condition of capitalism. That, in its turn, should lead us to examine precisely the areas that Rorty alerts us to, the economic, social and political life of the late twentieth-century world. Whether or not we can formally 'test' postmodern theory, in other words (what kind of social theory *can* we test?), we should be able to assess its plausibility at least to some degree by considering the claims it makes about that very palpable reality.

Some of this we have already done under the headings of the information society and post-Fordism. Post-modernity, being a highly comprehensive view of the world, takes in as we have seen many of the things included in those theories. So, we have shown the continuities between past and present in the information economy. We have questioned the idea of a new principle or direction necessarily brought in by the information technology revolution. This is not the whole story of the information society, as we have tried to show in the present chapter. Moreover post-modernity concentrates – in the writings of Baudrillard and others – more on the perceptual and expressive effects of information technology than on its economic impact. But, in so far as the postmodern idea depends on a view of the radicalizing changes brought to the economy and society by the new information technology, the verdict must so far be 'not proven'. Our perceptions of reality, and some aspects of our social behaviour, may have undergone significant changes. But the information society, in its full-blooded claim to be a new social order, certainly warrants the label 'ideological' in the current state of things. To that extent too it contributes an ideological component to the idea of post-modernity.

The evidence from the post-Fordist debate works less obviously against post-modernity. It has been possible to argue persuasively that much of 'flexible specialization' represents little more than a change of strategy by capitalists in a changing environment. The 'renaissance of craftwork' looked for hopefully by Piore and Sabel seems so far a mirage. But the post-Fordist insistence on the changing character of ideologies and alliances, and on the decline of class politics, seems well-founded, as we have noted in this chapter. This chimes in well with the central postmodern claim of the 'death of metanarratives'. It also highlights the post-modern theme of the importance of the new social movements, as compared with older agencies such as trade unions and political parties. In raising questions of ecology and of human rights, the new social movements aspire towards the universal. They stress what is common to humankind. At another level though the new social movements are about 'the politics of difference' so strongly featured in postmodernist writing. They stress plural and multiple identities, what divides us by gender, sexuality, ethnicity, locality. As against the universality and generality of ecology and the global environment, they draw our attention to the particularities of group, place, community and history.

The new social movements are an example of a more general feature of post-modernity: the interaction, or tension, between the global and the local. Here too much is made of the connection with the operations of contemporary capitalism. Post-modernity on this view precisely reflects the globalization of capital, the central feature of 'late capitalism'. Its concern with the particularities of place, locality, 'heritage' and history are all of a piece with global capitalism's renewal of the importance of place. This does not contradict but on the contrary complements capitalism's tendency to compress and unify space in its global phase. The creation of an abstract, homogeneous, global space sets up a contrary impulse towards localization, differentiation and diversity. As Harvey puts it:

> . . . the more unified the space, the more important the qualities of the fragmentations become for social identity and action. The free flow of capital across the surface of the globe . . . places strong emphasis upon the particular qualities of the spaces to which that capital might be attracted. The shrinkage of space that brings diverse communities across the globe into competition with each other implies localized competitive strategies and a heightened sense of awareness of what makes a place special and gives it a competitive advantage. This kind of reaction looks much more strongly to the identification of place, the building and signalling of its unique qualities in an increasingly homogeneous but fragmented world. (Harvey 1989: 271)

Harvey does not deny that there are positive features in this recovery of place. Neglected communities have a spur to regenerate themselves, and to reconstruct identities that may have languished. There is also a greater potentiality for political action.

Working-class groups, and other 'oppositional' groups such as women and ethnic and colonized minorities, are best able to organize on a local basis. Municipal socialism, and the defence of working-class communities, are achievements at the local level that have rarely been matched by comparable successes at the national (let alone international) level. But these victories also reveal the weakness of localism. Groups 'relatively empowered to organize in place' are 'disempowered when it comes to organizing over space.' 'In clinging, often of necessity, to a place-bound identity . . . such oppositional movements become a part of the very fragmentation which a mobile capitalism and flexible accumulation can feed upon' (Harvey 1989: 303).

This is, for Harvey, the important point to insist upon. The rehabilitation of place rides upon forces that lie outside the control and often also the comprehension of place-bound actors. 'Flexible accumulation typically exploits a wide range of seemingly contingent geographical circumstances, and reconstitutes them as structured internal elements of its own encompassing logic' (Harvey 1989: 294). The postmodernist celebration of place and local identities ignores this crucial factor. It sees and applauds decentralization and diversity as expressions of local autonomy. It misses the hidden forces behind the apparently free play of local self-assertion. The 'Third Italy' certainly exploited its peculiar local traditions of craftmanship and communal co-operation; but its success, in Harvey's eyes, turned critically on the fact of the demand for customized goods in the fiercely competitive world economy. Other cities and regions – Los Angeles, South Wales, Taiwan – have made themselves attractive to international capital by heightening certain local features: a particular range of skills, an anti-union culture, a tradition of paternalistic labour management. What matters is not the unique features of local identities but the way these mesh with the requirements of an increasingly mobile capital (cf. also Massey 1992; Lash and Urry 1994: 303–4).

This kind of argument can be deployed against a wide range of post-modern phenomena. Post-modern particularism, pluralism and eclecticism exist, but they are ideological expressions of 'the underlying systemic unity, the imperatives which create the diversity itself while at the same time imposing a deeper and more global homogeneity' (Wood 1990: 79). The pattern, whether of place or product, is similar: globalization linked to localism and diversification. Globalization, following the familiar logic of capitalist development, looks for 'economies of scale'. These favour standardization and homogeneity – the 'global product'. We have the global marketing of McDonald's and Mickey Mouse, *Dallas* and Disneyland, Hilton and Holiday Inn (the American provenance is of course significant). Global media conglomerates such as Rupert Murdoch's News Corporation or the Sony Corporation of Japan diffuse the relevant tastes and attitudes across the world. 'Global cities' such as London, New York and Tokyo are the nodal points and controlling centres of the world-wide flow of images, information, and standardized goods and services.

So far, so familiar. Globalization simply carries the tendencies of earlier forms of capitalism to greater lengths, commensurate with the greater scale of operation. There is nothing here to surprise Marx or Weber – or, for that matter, Henry Ford. Weber's concept of 'rationalization' would adequately cover most of these developments. It would also explain why the routinization and standardization of the 'world product' should increasingly be found in many other spheres – not only production, but also leisure, culture, education, religion and politics. This is a case partly of imitation, partly of determination. What has been called 'the McDonaldization of society' nicely points to the exemplary role of one of the most successful contemporary practitioners of Weberian rationalization (Ritzer 1993). Marxists are more likely to stress the 'commodification of society', the extension of capitalist rationality and the profit motive into ever more areas of social and personal life, and into ever more regions of the globe (Braverman 1974: 271–83; Sklair 1991).

But most Marxist critics of post-modernity do not stop at this familiar point of the analysis. They note that globalization introduces features that carry the appearance of novelty – features that are seized upon by others as the evidence for post-modernity. Universalization and standardization are only one face of globalization. The other is particularization and diversity. In addition to the economies of scale, there are 'economies of scope'. Capitalism in its global, post-Fordist, phase needs to diversify and individualize its products. Cities and regions too have to stress their differences. They have to accentuate their peculiarities of identity and history – their 'heritage' – in order to make themselves attractive not simply to international capital but to world tourism. The result in both cases has been an efflorescence of diversity and particularity. In all industrial societies there is now a remarkable range of specialized and often exotic goods and services: ethnic and regional cuisines, 'folk' art, 'Third World' music, 'traditional' clothes and furniture, new and revived forms of medicine and health products. Similarly there is (or appears to be) a renaissance of small country towns and villages, and a regeneration of old industrial areas, often as tourist regions ('Catherine Cookson country' in the north-east of England, 'Wild West' towns in the old mining areas of America).

What the Marxist critics of post-modernity want to emphasize is the surface appearance of all this, and the deeper logic underlying it. Localism is tied to globalism, and particularity to the requirements of the more developed, post-Fordist, phase of capitalism. The Sony Corporation revealingly speaks of 'global localization' as its current operational strategy; and Theodore Levitt, one of the leading analysts of the new corporate philosophy, argues that the 'world product' is not just about standardization but equally about what he calls the 'cosmopolitanization of speciality'. This accepts, in the celebrated expression of the advertising firm Saatchi and Saatchi, that there are more social differences between mid-town Manhattan and the Bronx than between mid-town Manhattan and the 7th *arrondissement* of Paris. The world market, that is, is socially differentiated, and products have to be specifically designed and aimed at particular segments. But the focus is still the global strategy. Across the world there are like-minded consumers occupying comparable niches in their respective societies. Equally the products aimed at them can be 'cosmopolitan', however marked by specificity of cultural origin. The world is ransacked for all the variety it produces by way of locality and ethnicity – African music, Aboriginal art, Indian rugs, Thai cuisine, and so on. 'De-territorialized', uprooted from their specific contexts – just as, in terms of place, the 'local' is no longer the concretely or authentically local but an element in the global-local nexus – these become the 'cosmopolitan specialities' aimed at particular market segments, especially those in the affluent northern hemisphere. The strategy combines homogeneity with heterogeneity. There are the standardized principles of global marketing, and the differentiated products of global consumption (Robins 1991; Amin and Thrift 1993; see also Featherstone 1990).

Hence the complaint of critics that the more diversity there appears to be, the more it is accompanied by uniformity. Firms such as the Body Shop, Benetton and Laura Ashley may strive to produce different, non-standard, goods, but global marketing means that 'Benetton or Laura Ashley products [end up] in almost every serially produced shopping mall in the advanced capitalist world' (Harvey 1989: 296). The irony is that, in city after city, the up-scale 'post-modern' Laura Ashley shop is likely to find itself cheek-by-jowl with the distinctly 'modern' McDonald eatery, selling the most standardized of 'world products'. The conjunction suggests similar purposes and processes at work.

There is likewise the charge that however post-modern the design of cities, the forms of capitalist growth will ensure that the same designs are repeated mechanically across the nation. There arises what Boyer calls a system of 'serial monotony . . . producing from already known patterns or molds places almost identical in ambience from city to city: New York's South Street Seaport, Boston's Quincy Market, Baltimore's Harbor Place' (in Harvey 1989: 295). Postmodernism may indeed become the new 'international style ' in architecture, repeating the universality and uniformity that were charged against modernism. Postmodernist architects speak the language of 'difference', and the 'hybrid', 'complex', and 'double-coded' character of their work ought to testify to a new sense of rootedness or locality. But, suggests Steve Connor,

> when hybridization itself becomes universal, regional specificity becomes simply a style which can be transmitted across the globe as rapidly as a photocopy of the latest glossy architectural manifesto. Paradoxically, the sign of the success of the anti-universalist language and style of architectural postmodernism is that one can find it *everywhere*, from London, to New York, to Tokyo and Delhi . . . The new language of difference . . . is not a splitting apart of the modernist dream of universality, but a morbid intensification of it. (Connor 1989: 80)

Lyotard, the celebrated but quirky post-modernist, has himself been scathing about the kind of postmodernism that celebrates eclecticism. 'Eclecticism,' says Lyotard, 'is the degro zero of contemporary general culture: one listens to reggae, watches a western, eats McDonald's food for lunch and local cuisine for dinnner, wears Paris perfume in Tokyo and "retro" clothes in Hong Kong: knowledge is a matter for TV games' (Lyotard 1984b: 76). This 'pot-pourri of internationalism', as Harvey calls it, can easily be equated, as it is for Marxists such as Ellen Wood, with 'the ultimate "commodity fetishism", the triumph of "consumer society"' (Harvey 1989: 87; Wood 1990: 78). Post-modernity is, ever more firmly, set within the contours of an evolving capitalism. Harvey's conclusion can be taken as representative of the whole Marxist critique of post-modern theory. There has certainly, he concedes, 'been a sea-change in the surface appearance of capitalism since 1973'. But 'it is not hard to see how the invariant elements and relations that Marx defined as fundamental to any capitalist mode of production still shine through, and in many instances with an even greater luminosity than before, all the surface froth and evanescence' of post-modernity (Harvey 1989: 187–9; see also 121, 343–4; and cf. Callinicos 1989: 121–71).

Allowing for the hyperbole, this is as clear as anyone could ask for. Moreover, there is no point in denying its very real force. The merest survey of developments in the world over the past quarter of a century would quickly show up the extraordinary vitality of capitalism in this period. Its reach has widened to include the whole globe. It can lay fair claim to having toppled the communist regimes of eastern Europe, and to be transforming those that remain elsewhere. It has penetrated more deeply than ever before into the life of western society, touching areas of politics, culture and welfare previously reserved to the public, non-commercial, realm. Education, broadcasting and the arts have felt its influence, along with the health, welfare, police and prison services. Even the government's own bureaucratic agencies have in some cases been thrown open to the market. In the most personal and intimate areas of individual life, too, it has found fresh fields to conquer. Consumerism has entered into bodily and sexual concerns; advertising has sought to make us aware of new anxieties of identity and personal security, and to assure us that there are goods and services to satisfy our every need and to assuage our every fear. In every space of the 'life-world' capitalism has found the material for new forms of commodification and consumerism.

So it is not difficult to see why many theorists feel that the driving force of contemporary change remains capitalism, in however transformed a shape. Post-modernity can easily be made to appear no more than the consumerist gloss on the surface, a mere change of style. Capitalism, we are repeatedly reminded, does not stand still. It is constantly disturbing settled practices and beliefs. The new forms of work, the increasing centrality of culture and information, the changing balance between the public and private spheres, are all expressions of this dynamism. The inner logic of the changes remains capital accumulation and the ever-increasing extensions of the market. Post-modernity is the ideological reflex of this latest phase of capitalism's inventiveness.

This is a familiar kind of analysis, and it runs familiar dangers. The 'capitalist imperative' has been applied to cultural movements as far apart as the Renaissance and Romanticism, and to intellectual developments from Hobbes to Hegel to Hobhouse. Earlier it was applied to modernism as it now is to post-modernism. The objection is the same in most of these cases: not that the analysis is necessarily wrong, but that it is couched at too high a level of generality and abstraction. 'Capitalism' is being made to do too much work. The world is indeed still capitalist, and post-modernity exists in that world. But how far should the post-modern condition be explained by the mechanics of capitalist development? If 'post-modern capitalism' is different from earlier forms of capitalism should not the emphasis lie on the first term as much as the second? How much autonomy exists in the social and cultural spheres? There lurks here, as of old, the scent of an excessive degree of determinism and reductionism.

Several writers have drawn attention to the fact that we can usefully distinguish two main varieties of post-modernity or post-modernism. There is a 'postmodernism of reaction' and a 'postmodernism of resistance' (Foster 1983: xii); there is a 'mainstream' postmodernism and an 'oppositional' postmodernism (Lash 1990: 37). There is, that is, in the first place a postmodernism that seems to fit rather snugly with the requirements of late capitalism. It celebrates mass culture, consumerism and commercialism. It is robustly populist in its attitude to 'high' or elitist culture. It gives amused assent to the T-shirt slogan, 'I shop, therefore I am'. It is a philosophy that seems to fit the life-style and interests of many of the new 'post-industrial' middle classes in the media, advertising, higher education and finance.

On the other hand, there is a postmodernism that seems to stand against the currents of capitalist culture. Postmodernist thought lies behind many of the social movements that have based themselves on the claims of gender, ethnicity and locality. It has aided those seeking to establish an identity – personal or collective – against the rising tide of capitalist homogenization. It has opposed the standardization of place and milieu. It has sought to establish a sense of home in an increasingly abstract, global, homogeneous space (Robins 1991: 39–40; Amin and Thrift 1993: 412–13).

Globalization itself does not only mean standardization and dependency. It can also bring a new cosmopolitanism and global consciousness. Post-modern thought stands against all ethnocentrism, all privileging of one history or one geographical segment of the globe. It opposes not just 'orientalism' but Islamic fundamentalism and all other species of dogmatism and exclusivity. While one aspect of it may encourage the particularity of a potentially fanatical nationalism or regionalism, another aspect forces the recognition that any one nationalism or localism must accept the equal right of all other nationalisms and localisms to flourish. It has been in the best tradition of western thought since the Enlightenment to attempt to transcend place and particular historical experiences. Post-modernity in one way reacts against Enlightenment universalism but in another it promotes Enlightenment cosmopolitanism (Heller and Feher 1988: 2; Lash and Urry 1994: 308–9).

The point is a simple one, and can be put as follows. To eat at McDonald's is not necessarily to be McDonaldized. The 'world product' is consumed and received in different ways, according to different local and national contexts and cultures. Muscovites eating at Moscow's McDonald's are just as likely to make it a part of their existing culture as to be turned into east European Americans. It has been too readily assumed that globalization flows only in one direction. There is evidently power there, but that power has to be expressed in particular places with their own resources of culture. Place matters, not only as the local site of multinational operations, and not only, as in some radical views, as the defensible space of a particular history and experience of locality (an attitude that can lead to reactionary attempts to freeze history at a particular point). Particular places can be the source of local mobilizations attempting to get the best out of the interaction of local and global forces. The identity of place, and of the people associated with it, is not fixed; it is a variable thing, depending on a particular mix of local and non-local forces and circumstances (the phenomenon of 'gentrification' illustrates this well). Place generates fierce loyalties, and while these can always turn exclusive and xenophobic they can also provide the resources for creating a new sense of home and a new negotiation of identity (Massey 1992: 9–13; see also Appadurai 1990; Smart 1994; Samuel 1995).

The issue of capitalism and post-modernity remains a central – perhaps the central – question of contemporary social theory. Is what is happening fundamentally a new departure, or is it simply another twist of the capitalist tale? Some of the most impressive accounts of the contemporary world have made the transformations of capitalism the lynch-pin of their analyses. Writers such as Ernest Mandel and David Harvey have made genuinely illuminating contributions to our understanding of the changes in the world about us. What is especially impressive is that they have not, unlike many Marxists, treated capitalism as some more or less timeless entity but have explored the epochal developments within it. Capitalism for them is the starting point, not the end, of the analysis.

At the same time they have been close observers of the political, cultural, social and spatial changes that have accompanied these transformations of capitalism. It is in this way that they have addressed the question of post-modernity. In the final analysis they remain convinced that the categories of Marxism are the best and most effective tools for understanding the phenomena that others have regarded as post-modern. But at their best – as in the writing of Jameson and Harvey – they have given due weight to the new importance of culture and communications, to the renewed sense of place, and to the creative role of the new social movements.

Capitalism, it is clear, has not reached its limits, whatever socialists may have hoped and striven for. The fall of communist states in eastern Europe, and the waning appeal of socialism in the world as a whole, has given capitalism not just new ideological vigour but also fresh territories to invade. There is still much work in front of it, and not many obstacles to its progress. The old division of the world into Three Worlds is now obsolete. There is only One World, the world of global capitalism. It would be foolish for any social analyst to ignore this overwhelming fact of our contemporary condition, however much he or she may wish it otherwise.

But capitalism is a large, abstract category. How capitalism works, what its effects are, vary enormously in different places and at different times. Post-modernity may be capitalist, but it is capitalism with a new face, one that shows many peculiar and unexpected features. The investigation of this novelty is an important matter in its own right. In the end, the question of whether or not post-modernity is the ideology of (late) capitalism may not be very important – or, perhaps better put, it may be more a matter of emphasis or of the interest of the investigator. 'Post-modern capitalism' shows sufficient distinctiveness to warrant an analysis that respects the radical changes of form at all levels – cultural and political as well as economic – that modern society has undergone in the last third of the twentieth century. If this leads some to conclude that we live in a new world, a post-modern world, they cannot be held guilty of either blindness or naivety. The contemporary world may not be simply or only post-modern; but post-modernity is now a significant, perhaps central, feature of its life, and an important way of thinking about it.

Coda: The Return of Grand Narratives?

Zygmunt Bauman has said that

> the collapse of communism was the final nail in the coffin of the modern ambitions which drew the horizon of European (or Europe-influenced) history of the last two centuries. That collapse ushered us into an as-yet-unexplored world: a world without a collective utopia, without a conscious alternative to itself. (Bauman 1992: xxv)

This echoes Vaclav Havel's remark – quoted as an epigraph to the present chapter – that the fall of communism means that modernity has reached 'a final crisis'. Both Bauman and Havel appear to be saying that, since communism represented modernity's highest ambition, its failure must amount to a question mark over the whole modern project. At the same time, nothing has been put in its place. The world now lacks an overarching vision, a sense of a goal towards which it is striving. It is a world without utopias, without alternatives. It is a world that simply functions (or does not function), like a machine.

This is a post-modernist view indeed. It also seems close to the position of those who, in the wake of the 1989 revolutions in eastern Europe, have pronounced 'the end of history'. What Francis Fukuyama, the best-known exponent of this view, means by this is that, with the defeat of Marxism and communism, all ideological conflict in the world has now been exhausted. History for him, as for Hegel, is the story of the conflict of competing visions of civilization and social order. This is what gives history its forward, progressive, movement. There is now no more such conflict and therefore no more ' history' (although there will still be many events). History has completed its work; all that is left is the idle ticking-over of its engine. What lies ahead for us is merely 'the perpetual caretaking of the museum of human history' (Fukuyama 1989: 18; see also 1992).

But in one crucial sense what Fukuyama and others like him were saying was quite the opposite of Bauman and Havel. For Fukuyama the end of history does not mean that all alternatives are exhausted but that one alternative has won. The defeat of communism has not left the world without visions. It has left one in lonely and unchallenged eminence. Communism has been defeated by capitalism. More concretely, it has been defeated by the liberal-democratic forms of market society. This has been the secret of history since the Renaissance: the evolution and gradual world-wide spread of liberal market society, and the vanquishing of all its rivals (Fukuyama 1992: xii–xiv, 39–51).

Thus, far from modernity being 'in crisis', as Havel suggests, it is for Fukuyama thoroughly vindicated. The victory of liberal market society is the victory of the modern principle (though Fukuyama himself does not see this as the cause for unalloyed rejoicing). This was the premise of the 'modernization theory' of the 1950s in the west. Fukuyama notes that this theory was criticized for its 'ethnocentrism', its apparent elevation of 'the western European and North American development experience to the level of universal truth'. The charge was not simply that there were different paths to modernity than those followed by western nations, but that modernity itself was a western, ethnocentric concept (Fukuyama 1992: 68–9).

Now, says Fukuyama, things seem very different. In the 1990s 'modernization theory looks much more persuasive . . . than it did fifteen or twenty years earlier . . . While there are a variety of routes that countries can take to get to the end of history, there are few versions of modernity other than the capitalist liberal-democratic one that look like they are going concerns' (Fukuyama 1992: 133).

This is a position that can be contested, and has been, in a vigorous debate that has been going on ever since Fukuyama's work first appeared (see, for example, Anderson 1994; Burns 1994). But the more significant thing from our point of view is its general bearing on theories of post-modernity. Theories of post-modernity, like those of post-Fordism and the information society, were developed largely before the events of 1989 and the collapse of communism in eastern Europe. They were elaborated, that is, before the changes that many have come to regard as the most significant historical development of the twentieth century (Hobsbawm 1994; Tiryakian 1994: 132). Does this affect their validity? How much of a challenge does it pose?

In one sense, not much. These theories can actually be said to have anticipated the major developments of the later 1980s. This is partly because things were already happening that were having an influence on the thinking behind these theories. The 'global democratic revolution' was already under way, in the 1970s and 1980s, when most of the theories were being worked out. Socialist parties in the west were already on the defensive, and mostly out of office. In the Soviet Union Gorbachev's policies of *glasnost* and *perestroika*, the harbingers of the 1989 revolutions and the break-up of the Soviet Union, were in full flood. These developments could all easily be accommodated in the idea of the 'end of grand narratives', especially as concerned the grand narrative of Marxism. They showed the affinity between the ideas of post-modernity and the rejection of all dogmatic and authoritarian systems of belief and practice. Even the events of 1989 themselves are not an immediate problem. There is widespread agreement that a significant contribution to them was the information and communication revolution that is central to the idea of the information society (Boden 1992). There is also a specifically post-modernist interpretation of 1989: the rejection of grand narratives, of course, but also the attraction of western consumerism, and the choice, diversity and individualism that were thought to go with it (Bauman 1992: 166–71).

What is problematic for our theories therefore is not the general fact of the failure of communism. That is easily enough squared with postmodernist and related ideas. The real challenge comes from the content of the 1989 revolutions. For this seems to hark back to some of the fundamental themes of classic modernity. Jürgen Habermas has in fact called the revolution of 1989 a 'revolution of recuperation' or retrieval (*nachholende Revolution*). The societies of Central and eastern Europe, he argues, were not attempting anything new but were trying to get back onto the track of modernity from which they had been de-railed by the communist experiment. Their model was quite clearly the constitutional democracy and developed capitalism of the west. Habermas dismisses the idea that the revolution was a postmodernist revolt against reason, or against 'grand narratives' generally. The only grand narrative that the revolutions of 1989 rejected was that of Marxism. In other respects they turned decisively to the grand narratives of western liberalism. The 1989 revolutions were cast in the same mould, and embodied the same aspirations, as the classic bourgeois revolutions of the west. 'The revolutionary collapse of bureaucratic socialism seems . . . to indicate that modernity is extending its borders – the spirit of the West is catching up with the East not simply as a technological civilization, but also as a democratic tradition' (Habermas 1991b: 30; cf. Müller 1992).

The 're-birth of history', or the return to the 'mainstream' of western development, may be an insufficient account of the 1989 revolutions (Kumar 1992, 1995b). But it is undeniably a central theme. One consequence, as both Fukuyama and Habermas in their different ways suggest, is a rehabilitation of the grand narratives of modernity. The 1989 revolutions are modernizing revolutions. They strengthen the modern principle in the world by bringing in, or bringing back, a whole series of societies that had strayed from the modernizing path. They give a renewed vitality to the classic ideas and institutions of modernity.[6] Reason has been refurbished, capitalism, constitutionalism and democracy given fresh lustre. There has even been the revival, from the early days of civic republicanism, of such concepts as citizenship and civil society. Moreover all this has been happening not just in the former communist societies of eastern Europe, but in a gathering revolution of democratization and modernization throughout the world (see, for example, Rustow 1990; Pye 1990).

These developments have not escaped the notice of the critics of post-modernity. For them they are a triumphant vindication of both modernity and modernizing theory. Far from modernity giving way to post-modernity,the principle of modernity is now stronger and more unchallenged than ever before. It expresses the goal of practically every society in the world today. We are seeing not the death of grand narratives but the rebirth of the narratives of modernity on a grand scale. As Jeffrey Alexander puts it:

> Because the recent revivals of market and democracy have occurred on a world-wide scale, and because they are categorically abstract and generalizing ideas, universalism has once again become a viable source for social theory. Notions of commonality and institutional convergence have re-emerged, and with them the possibilities for intellectuals to provide meaning in a utopian way. It seems, in fact, that we are witnessing the birth of a fourth postwar version of mythopeic social thought. 'Neo-modernism' . . . will serve as a rough-and-ready characterization of this phase of postmodernization theory until a term appears that represents the new spirit of the times in a more imaginative way. (Alexander 1994: 184–5; cf. Tiryakian 1991)

At the same time Alexander warns against any simple and uncritical revival of modernization theory. Modernity cannot and should not be identified merely with its western forms, whether as means or ends. They are not necessarily the best, and certainly not the final, expressions of modernity. Modernization, as the example of Japan best shows, is now a global process which will finds its own forms, suitable to the time and place in which it is promoted – just as world religions such as Christianity and Islam have adapted themselves to the particular culture and circumstances of their local environments. 'Neo-modernism' will, to an extent, take on some of the characteristics of post-modern theory. Its universalism will be qualified by a relativism that acknowledges the particularities of time and place. Generally neo-modern theories 'must be pushed to maintain a decentered, self-conscious reflexivity about their ideological dimensions even while they continue in their efforts to create a new explanatory scientific theory . . . In this sense, "neo-" must incorporate the linguistic turn associated with "post-"modern theory, even while it challenges its ideological and more broadly theoretical thrust' (Alexander 1994: 192).

No thoughtful post-modernist should have any great quarrel with that. It keeps the debate open, which is the main thing. In any case, whether we call ourselves neo-modernists or post-modernists; whether we think we live in post-modernity or, as

Giddens and Beck would have it, in 'late' or 'radicalized' modernity, the important thing is to recognize the novelty of our times. As the twentieth century draws to a close we have seen things happen that might have appeared miraculous as little as twenty years ago (and indeed look miraculous even now). Changes in southern and eastern Europe, in South Africa and South America, in parts of southern Asia and the Pacific, have broken patterns of tyranny that many had never thought to see go in their lifetime. The 'balance of terror' held by the two nuclear superpowers has gone. These are the happy, the hopeful things. With them have come more ominous changes. A world dominated by two superpowers, with the enforced stalemate this entailed, has given way to a world in which there is now only one. This, apart from the dangerous monopoly of power that it confers, has created new anxieties and insecurities. It has unleashed new or suppressed demons of separatism and nationalism, new ethnic and racial conflicts. Bloody civil wars have returned to areas, such as Central Asia and the Balkans, from which they have long been absent. New inequalities and new resentments have arisen among populations no longer protected by the paternalist state. The victory of market ideologies virtually throughout the world carries the potential for intense social conflicts and perhaps renewed authoritarian rule. To many observers, what has taken the place of the old world is not a new harmonious system of liberal states but a new 'world disorder' (cf. Jowitt 1992; Huntington 1993).

The theories we have been considering in this book have mostly focused on western societies. But the west is more than ever before joined to the rest of the world. In large measure, for good or ill, it controls a good deal of that world. It is fair to say that the varieties of post-industrial theory that we have examined are fully aware of this. Whether describing the world-wide grid of communication and information, or the post-Fordist reorganization of the capitalist economy, or the waning of some of the cardinal assumptions of modernity, they have drawn attention both to the global character of these alleged developments and to the centrality of the west in their direction and diffusion. To that extent they provide a mirror by which we can consider some of the most significant changes in the world today.

It has not been the main aim of this book to consider the validity of these theories in detail. That would have taken a much longer book. The intention rather has been to explore the theories, to give as clear as possible an account and to raise critical questions concerning them. But the issue of validity can never be left out entirely – not, that is, unless one wants to engage in a rather pointless exercise.

I hope I have shown that these theories do speak to our current condition. Like all theories they are one-sided and exaggerated. That is why they are useful and stimulating. No doubt they leave out much that needs to be considered. Arising as they do out of the recent experiences of western societies, they may carry too much the marks of their origins in particular cultures and even particular classes. The changes of the present decade, and their still uncertain outcomes, may also throw a different light on these theories in the years to come. Nevertheless, what seems to me remarkable is how much of the present state of the world they manage to capture. We do live in a world saturated with information and communication. The nature of work and industrial organization is truly changing with unnerving speed. Modern societies have indeed reached a point where, even if they have not given up on modernity, many of its classic attitudes and assumptions have become seriously questionable.

There is finally another aspect to these theories that is also highly appealing. They are ambitious in their scope, sensitive to historical change, and unwilling to be limited by the boundaries of academic disciplines. At a time when powerful professional and political forces are encouraging the social sciences to become ever more narrowly technical, these are all features to be welcomed. Post-industrial theory seeks, almost by definition, to break with the classic inheritance of nineteenth-century sociology, at least so far as concerns the content of ideas. But it continues the spirit of that tradition, and deserves our attention and respect even if only for that.

Notes

Chapter 1: Introduction

1 Cf. Paul Blumberg: 'Much to the dismay of the post-industrialists, the clock of history seems to be turning counterclockwise' (1980: 217).

2 It is remarkable how frequently, when once you have expounded the postmodernist idea to them, people see postmodernism all about them, with a more or less excited sense of illumination (or of disenchantment).

3 It is true that such theories of a 'new (phase of) society' are a recurrent feature of modern societies. The first wave came in the 1890s and 1900s, and was associated largely with imperialism and the rise of oligopolies – but also with the cultural movement of 'modernism'. There was a second wave in the 1930s, associated mainly with theories of 'organized capitalism', but also with 'the mass society', 'the leisure society', etc.

   The third wave, of the 1970s and 1980s, is not necessarily any more privileged in its grasp on the present and the future. But it occurs within an objective system – the global economy of capitalism – whose current functioning is creating greater upheavals and more widespread disturbances than at any previous time in its history. This at least gives the present crop of theories a special significance, and a certain initial plausibility.

4 The best-known statement is by Francis Fukuyama (1992). Fukuyama is clear that by 'the end of history' he means the end of ideological competition in the world – a fact symbolized for him by the collapse of communism in eastern Europe between 1989 and 1991. But there have also been other, more metaphysical, declarations of the end of history. For a discussion, see Kumar (1993). Certainly, the events in eastern Europe have given added impetus to 'the sense of an ending'

– though not, it seems, to the sense of a new beginning. See further chapter 6, below.

Chapter 2: The Information Society

1   For the history of the computer, and generally of information technology, see Braun and MacDonald 1978; Forester 1980: 3–62; 1985, 1987; Jones 1980: 9–52; King 1982; Ide 1982; Metcalfe 1986; Saxby 1990.

2   It appears that the idea of the information society was first systematically developed by Japanese scholars in the late 1960s. See the report of the Tokyo symposium of 1968 in Yujiro (1970). See also Morris-Suzuki (1988: 7). Japanese thinkers have remained among the most active proponents of the idea – see, for example, Masuda 1981; Kishida 1994.

3   In his later writing, Fritz Machlup questions Porat's distinction of a primary and secondary information sector, and argues for 'the knowledge industries' as an inseparable 'admixture' of the two. But he agrees with Porat's overall reckoning of the total information economy of the US as 46 per cent of GNP in 1967, as compared with his own calculation of 29 per cent in 1958. This 'seems well in line with the relative growth rates which I calculated for the production of knowledge and of other goods and services' (Machlup 1980: 237, n. 4; and generally, 232–40).

4   But cf. Soete 1987: 190, who offers a figure for the UK of 41 per cent for 1981. For Japan, using Porat's classification, Morris-Suzuki gives a figure of 33 per cent for 1982 (1988: 128). Findings for OECD countries generally suggest that an average of 35 per cent of workers are engaged in information activities (Arriaga 1985: 280). There is not much one can do with these discrepancies except note them, and agree that whether one takes the lower figure (roughly 40 per cent) or the higher (roughly 60 per cent) it amounts to a very large number of information workers.

5   For other Japanese visions of computopia, see Morris-Suzuki 1988: 6–24. The utopianizing of the Information Society is rampant in the literature – see, in addition to those mentioned here, Martin 1978; Simon 1980; Garrett and Wright 1980; Williams 1982; Forester 1985; Sussman 1989; Rheingold 1994. For the more euphoric claims of politicians and information technology merchants, see Robins and Webster 1988: 7–24; see also Raulet 1991. The father of this strand of 'technetronic' utopianism is Marshall McLuhan. Electric technology was for him the means whereby the primal organic wholeness of humanity would be restored. See especially McLuhan 1967.

6   This conclusion finds strong support in the extensive literature: see, for example, for the UK, Gill 1985: 37–60; for the US, Blumberg 1980: 37–45; Murolo 1987; for Japan, Morris-Suzuki 1988: 116–24. Production workers in the high-tech computer industry may derive

some glamour from their association with the new technology, but the reality of their working lives often echoes that of the earlier factory system. As Everett Rogers and Judith Larsen put it for the US:

> Silicon Valley means low-wage, dead-end jobs, unskilled, tedious work, and exposure to some of the most dangerous occupational health hazards in all of American industry. (Quoted in Roszak 1988: 42)

7   This is perhaps too one-sided a view. The question of how much, and how many, jobs are being de-skilled remains a hotly contested one. For a more cautious view, see Bryn Jones 1982; Gill 1985: 63–87; Lane 1988; Appelbaum and Albin 1989; Kuhn 1989. For an upbeat assessment, concluding that the general trend is towards rising levels of skill in both office and factory, see Block 1990: 85–112. See also Morris-Suzuki 1988: 107–24, who distinguishes between re-skilling in the factory and de-skilling in the office.

   Many of these writers suggest that gender is the key factor: jobs held largely by males are less likely to be de-skilled than jobs held largely by females. See, for example, Murolo 1987; and for a general discussion of 'IT and Women', see Webster and Robins 1986: 155–81. The whole question of what is or is not a 'skilled' job is in any case, Jane Jensen (1989) argues, gender-related.

   In an interesting contribution, Shoshana Zuboff suggests that information technology can de-skill or re-skill depending on how it is viewed, especially by management. IT, she argues, 'informates' as well as 'automates'. In the former case, but not the latter, IT 'produces a voice that symbolically renders events, objects and processes so that they become visible, knowable and shareable in a new way'. This is the difference between IT and the older machine technology.

> As long as the technology is treated narrowly in its automating func-tion, it perpetuates the logic of the industrial machine that, over the course of this century, has made it possible to rationalize work while decreasing the dependence on human skills. However, when the technology also informates the processes to which it is applied, it increases the explicit information content of tasks and sets into motion a series of dynamics that will ultimately reconfigure the nature of work and the social relationships that organize productive activity. (Zuboff 1988: 10)

See also Baran (1988), who also argues that 'social choice' is the key to whether information technology re-skills or de-skills and degrades work.

   It is obvious that the differential rate of application of information technology in different industries (and different societies) makes it very difficult to make general statements about de-skilling/re-skilling at the moment. The argument as presented in the text relates more to a pressure which is consistent with managerial objectives of greater productivity, efficiency and control – that is, precisely, to a certain kind of 'social choice'. One might expect this to lead, as in the past, to a greater fragmentation and standardization of work. As Paul Thompson says: 'Deskilling remains the major *tendential* presence, within the development of the capitalist labour process' (1989: 118, and, generally, 89–121, 214–18; see also Child 1988).

Finally, in considering the relation between Taylorism and the computerization of work, it is relevant to note Norbert Wiener's explicit reference to the importance of F. W. Taylor's ideas to him in the development of 'computing machines':

> The notion of programming in the factory had already become familiar through the work of Taylor and the Gilbreths on time study, and was ready to be transferred to the machine. This offered considerable difficulty of detail, but no great difficulty of principle. I was thus convinced as far back as 1940 that the automatic factory was on the horizon . . . The consequent development of automatization . . . has convinced me that I was right in my judgement and that this development would be one of the great factors in conditioning the social and technical life of the age to come, the keynote of the second industrial revolution. (Wiener 1968: 131)

8   For the US, see Rothschild 1981: 12–13; 1988: 46; Walker 1985: 45; Castells 1989: 186–8; Soja 1989: 186–7; Sayer and Walker 1992. Alain Lipietz speaks of the American economy as undergoing 'third-worldization': 'A huge number of "collective servants", such as parking-lot attendants, golf-course caddies or fast-food employees, throw into sharp relief the image of the US as the "Brazil of the 1980s"' (1989: 40–1). For a similar picture of the nature of employment growth in Britain in the 1970s and 1980s, see Leadbeater and Lloyd 1987: 31; Pollert 1988a: 288; Walby 1989; Lovering 1990: 12.

9   There is a fundamental ambiguity in the use of the concept of information among information society theorists. They are very fond of quoting some well-known lines from T. S. Eliot's choruses from *The Rock* (1934):

> Where is the wisdom we have lost in knowledge?
> Where is the knowledge we have lost in information?
> (See, for example, Bell 1980a: 500; Machlup 1980: 58)

What is striking though is how incurious they are in following up the implications of these lines. They seem to be quoted merely to show a certain sophisticated knowingness. Machlup discusses the distinction between 'information' and 'knowledge' only to hold that 'all information, in the sense of contents conveyed, is knowledge' (although he accepts that 'not all knowledge may properly be called information') (Machlup 1980: 58). Bell uses 'information' and 'knowledge' more or less synonymously and interchangeably, though he argues that he is not giving an 'absolute' definition of knowledge, only an 'instrumental' definition, namely, what kinds of knowledge could be measured, stored readily, retrieved and used within an instrument that could be designed for that purpose. I do believe . . . that judgemental knowledge and evaluative knowledge cannot be ordered in the form that some computer scientists believe. (See the exchange between Bell and Joseph Weizenbaum in Forester 1980: 550–74)

It does seem to be the case that most theorists of the information society assume that the sheer increase in the volume and availability of information is by itself transforming society. They go on at length about the increase in computer power, the extraordinary capacity of fibre optic cable, the growth in the number of VCRs and computers per household, etc. They seem far less concerned about the purposes to which all this information technology is put. For a good discussion of this question, see Roszak 1988, *passim.*

Mark Poster, in a related criticism of Bell and the information theorists, notes their tendency to treat information either as an economic commodity, on a par with other commodities, or as uniform 'bits' of information, as with cyberneticians. Most serious is their 'repression of language', their incuriosity about language itself, the very stuff of information.

> Even though they give priority to phenomena like knowledge, informa-tion, and communication they do not treat these phenomena as linguistic issues and they give no heed to the linguistic quality of their own discourses.

They thereby do not see what is, or might be, truly new about a society characterized by a 'mode of information', in which the main feature is 'the transformations of language' (Poster 1990: 26, 29).

Chapter 3: Fordism and Post-Fordism

1 For the 'Third Italy' generally, see in addition to the sources cited in the text Becattini 1978; Sabel 1984: 220–31; Brusco 1986; Goodman et al. 1989; Pyke et al. 1990.
2 For the general critique, see Regalia et al. 1978: 103; Sassoon 1986: 74–75; Murray 1987, 1988; Sayer 1989; Amin 1991. For comments on this, see Berger and Piore 1980: 28–33; Sabel 1984: 158–67; 1989.
3 'The attempt made by Ford, with the aid of a body of inspectors, to intervene in the private lives of his employees and to control how they spent their wages and how they lived is an indication of these tendencies' (Gramsci 1971: 304).
4 As a further example, cf. Robin Murray: 'In spite of the fact that basic needs are still unmet, the high street does offer a new variety and creativity in consumption which the left's puritan tradition should also address' (1989a: 44).
5 The language of inter-left strife can be very colourful. 'New Times is a fraud, a counterfeit, a humbug. It palms off Thatcherite values as socialist, shores up the Thatcherite market with the pretended

politics of choice, fits out the Thatcherite individual with progressive consumerism, makes consumption itself the stuff of politics'
(Sivanandam 1990: 1). 'The core worker produces designer goods
for the core New-Timer citizen' (Pollert 1991b: 30). 'The post-
Fordist utopia, which combines the apparently antithetical vision of
self-realisation through insatiable consumption, and self-realisation
through creative labour, may make sense to contemporary academics . . . but this kind of Yuppy vision can hardly be expected to have
a wider appeal' (Clarke 1990b: 149). New Times's post-Fordism 'is
little more than pop sociology . . . *Marxism Today's* analysis comes
close to celebrating Thatcherism' (Hirst and Zeitlin 1991: 11–12).

6 For the approach of the Regulation School, see Aglietta 1979, 1982;
Lipietz 1982, 1987, 1989, 1992; Boyer 1990. It was this group of
writers that was mainly responsible for popularizing the concept
of Fordism in the 1980s. A thorough review and criticism of this
School is Brenner and Glick 1991; see also Amsden 1990; Hirst and
Zeitlin 1991: 17–22. For a parallel American approach, which focuses
on the 'social structure of accumulation', and contains a broadly
similar analysis of the current crisis to the French Regulationists,
see Gordon 1988. Harvey also broadly accepts the Regulationist
framework: 1989: 121–4; see also Castells 1989: 21–8. Piore and Sabel
employ certain parts of the Regulationists' analysis, for instance the
idea of a 'regulation crisis' in America in the 1890s and 1930s
(1984: 5). At the same time they appear to *endorse* something like
the strategy of 'world Fordism' (1984: 279). On 'neo-Fordism' see
also Wood, 1989b: 20–8. Wood comments (p. 27) that 'neo-Fordism
need not be seen as a transitional state or a pathological response
to an assumed crisis of Fordism', but rather 'a major aspect of the
strategies of some core firms in the economy'. Harvey also notes that
neo-Fordist strategies of 'flexible accumulation' do not imply that
capitalism is becoming more 'disorganized': rather it is 'becoming
ever more highly organized *through* dispersal, geographical mobility,
and flexible responses in labour markets, labour processes, and
consumer markets . . . ' (1989: 159; see also 179ff).

7 For a brief account of Henry Ford's thought and achievement, see
Beynon 1973: ch. 1; Sabel 1984: 32–4; Harvey 1989: 125–40. And cf.
Harvey's comment:

> Fordist modernity is far from homogeneous. There is much here that is
> about relative fixity and performance – fixed capital in mass production,
> stable, standardized, and homogeneous markets, a fixed configuration
> of political-economic influence and power, easily identifiable authority
> and meta-theories, secure grounding in materiality and technical-scientific
> rationality, and the like. But all of this is ranged around a social and
> economic project of Becoming, of growth and transformation of social
> relations, of auratic art and originality, of renewal and avant-gardism.
> (1989: 339)

Sabel makes clear his equation of Fordism and Taylorism:
'Taylorism presupposes Fordism and Fordism implies Taylorism'

(1984: 236, n. 5). Other accounts deny the link: see Williams et al. 1992. On the general features of the 'new man' of Fordism, see Gramsci 1971; see also Clarke 1990b. Aldous Huxley's *Brave New World* (1932), whose inhabitants worship 'our Ford', is essentially a satire on Fordism.

8 Charles Sabel has interpreted this development optimistically: the branch plants of the big firms, like independent small firms, will nurture the growth of industrial districts:

> The activities of the giant corporations would more closely resemble and actually blend into the activity of the industrial districts. An engine plant which participates in the design of the engine and depends on highly specialised local suppliers to produce it is both part of a multinational car firm *and* an independent industrial district. (1989: 40)

As Amin and Robins comment, 'Sabel offers no explanation of why the new type of branch plant or division should establish its linkages in the area of location' (1990: 202).

In a wide-ranging discussion and critique, Hirst and Zeitlin have defended Sabel and, like him, argued that despite initial appearances the theory of flexible specialization does not privilege small firms on the 'Third Italy' model. It is equally compatible with restructuring in large firms. There is, as it were, a 'convergence' of two strategies: a 'building up' of small firms to form and cement industrial districts, and a 'building down' of large firms to create 'semi-autonomous sub-units that may cooperate one with another or with other firms in an industrial district' (1991: 45). More radically, they are concerned to separate flexible specialization, as a new and hopeful 'technological paradigm', from the more general theory of post-Fordism associated with the New Times theorists, Lash and Urry, and the Regulation school. For Hirst and Zeitlin the evidence for post-Fordism is scanty at best, and the theory in any case conceptually flawed. Flexible specialization on the other hand is empirically based and more theoretically sophisticated (1991: 2–22, 24–8).

While this more cautious and limited approach may be more realistic, it is also less interesting and less stimulating. Whatever the weaknesses of post-Fordist theory, by its very range it raises important and challenging questions about contemporary developments. As a framework for discussion it is infinitely more 'heuristic' than the narrow flexible specialization theory that Hirst and Zeitlin seek to defend.

9 The 'world car model' refers to the strategy of the major car producers according to which cars are designed in a small number of firms in only one or two centres, usually in the advanced industrial countries, and parts are manufactured and assembled in the regions of lower labour costs, usually in the newly industrializing countries. Ford's Escort and GM's Cavalier are the best-known examples of this strategy. The division of labour implied in this organization of production is directly opposed to that envisaged in post-Fordist

scenarios. See Wood 1989b: 13–14, 23–4. For the comparable case of the 'world steer' in the food industry, see Sklair 1991: 115.

10 'It could be the case that students of society are confronted with a paradigm shift, in the sense of Thomas Kuhn, except that the anomalous instances, the elements that resist the old frameworks, have not yet reached a critical mass or do not yet constitute a large enough corpus to convince observers that traditional positions need to be abandoned in favour of new ones' (Poster 1990: 21).

Chapter 4: Modernity and Post-Modernity (I)

1 Tilo Schabert points out that this is true even of the very earliest contrast between antiquity and modernity, in the writings of Theodoric the Great's historiographer, the Roman scholar and monk Cassiodorus (485–580).

> Cassiodorus called his contemporaries the 'Moderns' [*moderni*] because he believed that it was their task to reacquire by their own efforts [following the fall of the Western Roman Empire] the knowledge and culture of the 'Ancients' [*antiqui*], the Roman *antiquitas*, and render it fruitful again for their epoch. Accordingly, Cassiodorus' distinction was in no way intended to promote, after the fall of Rome and the emergence of the new Germanic kingdoms, a replacement of the culture of antiquity by a 'new' one. On the contrary, Cassiodorus saw his contemporaries as the heirs and renewers of the old culture, so to speak the 'new ancients'. His concept of 'modernity' referred therefore not to any break in the cultural tradition of antiquity, but explicitly to its uninterrupted continuity. (Schabert 1985: 1)

There was indeed a tendency among some of the earliest Christian fathers, such as Origen, Eusebius and Gregory of Nyssa, to protest vigorously against the historical cyclism of pagan thought, and to draw the strongest possible contrast between this and the Christian view of history as directional, purposeful and even progressive.. Later, when antiquity was more thoroughly rehabilitated, a favourite compromise – found for instance in Otto of Freising's *History of the Two Cities* (1146) – was to see the shape of profane history as cyclical, and that of sacred history as meaningful progression (Manuel 1965: 10–13, 32–5; see also Mommsen 1951; Momigliano 1977: 107–26; Gurevich 1985: 124).

2 Schabert notes that the idea that it is we, not the 'ancients, who are older and therefore wiser, already occurs in Giordano Bruno's *La cena de le ceneri* (1584), and that Jean Bodin in his *Methodus ad facilem historiarum cognitionem* (1566) also expresses an almost Baconian confidence in the superior knowledge of the modern over the ancient world. But he accepts that it was not until the end of the seventeenth century, in the *querelle*, that the moderns really won out over the ancients. Schabert (1985: 3–4; cf. Kolakowski 1990: 7).

3 One way of expressing the new concept of modernity was to

distinguish the 'Modern' period, which begins in the sixteenth
century with the Renaissance, the Reformation, and the discovery
of the New World, from the 'contemporary' or 'most recent' period,
the time of the Enlightenment and the French Revolution, when the
seeds sown by the Modern age finally came to fruition. With this we
have reached, as Hegel put it, 'the last stage in History, our world,
our own time' (Hegel 1956: 442; see also Koselleck 1985: 231–66;
Habermas 1987: 5–7).

4   'That the History of the World, with all the changing scenes which its
annals present, is this process of development and the realization of
Spirit – this is the true *Theodicaea*, the justification of God in History'
(Hegel 1956: 457).

5   On the contradictions in culture and society at the end of the
nineteenth century, cf. the following passage from Robert Musil's
epic novel, *The Man Without Qualities*:

> Out of the oil-smooth spirit of the last two decades of the nineteenth
> century, suddenly, throughout Europe, there rose a kindling fever.
> Nobody knew exactly what was on the way; nobody was able to
> say whether it was to be a new art, a New Man, a new morality
> or perhaps a re-shuffling of society. So everyone made of it what he
> liked. But people were standing up on all sides to fight against the
> old way of life . . . Talents developed that had previously been choked
> or had taken no part at all in public life. They were as different from
> each other as anything well could be, and the contradictions in their aims
> were unsurpassable. The Superman was adored, and the Subman was
> adored; health and the sun were worshipped; people were enthusiastic
> hero-worshippers and enthusiastic adherents of the social creed of the
> Man in the Street; one had faith and was sceptical, one was naturalistic
> and precious, robust and morbid; one dreamed of ancient castles and
> shady avenues, autumnal gardens, glassy ponds, jewels, hashish, disease
> and demonism, but also of prairies, vast horizons, forges and rolling mills,
> naked wrestlers, the uprisings of the slaves of toil, man and woman in the
> primeval Garden, and the destruction of society. Admittedly these were
> contradictions and very different battle-cries, but they all breathed the
> same breath of life. If that epoch had been analysed, some such nonsense
> would have come out as a square circle supposed to be made of wooden
> iron; but in reality all this had blended into shimmering significance.
> This illusion, which found its embodiment in the magical date of the
> turn of the century, was so powerful that it made some hurl themselves
> enthusiastically upon the new, as yet untrodden century, while others
> were having a last fling in the old one, as in a house that one is moving
> out of anyway, without either one or the other party feeling that there
> was much difference between the two attitudes. (Musil 1979: 59)

6   The link is provided by Morris's insistence that 'art' and 'craft' are
not separate activities, that 'use' and 'beauty' should go together,
and that the artist cannot hold himself apart but must become fully
involved in the design of the modern world. This, together with
the attention paid to materials, and the concern with the design of
the whole work, was what appealed to modernist designers and

architects, even though they did not accept Morris's rejection of industrial materials and industrial technology. See Pevsner (1975: 19–39).

7   Cf. Charles Jencks: 'Whereas Modernism in architecture has furthered the ideology of industrialization and progress, Modernism in most other fields has either fought these trends or lamented them' (1989: 28).

8   The contradictory character of Modernism has led some commentators to dismiss it altogether as a useful category of cultural history. For Perry Anderson this judgement can be made to implicate post-modernism as well.

> Modernism as a notion is the emptiest of all cultural categories. Unlike the terms Gothic, Renaissance, Baroque, Mannerist, Romantic or Neo-Classical, it designates no describable object in its own right at all: it is completely lacking in positive content. In fact . . . what is concealed beneath the label is a wide variety of very diverse – indeed incompatible – aesthetic practices: symbolism, constructivism, expressionism, surrealism. These, which do spell out specific programmes, were unified *post hoc* in a portmanteau concept whose only referent is the blank passage of time itself. There is no other aesthetic marker so vacant or vitiated. For what once was modern is soon obsolete. The futility of the term, and its attendant ideology, can be seen all too clearly from current attempts to cling to its wreckage and yet swim with the tide still further beyond it, in the coinage of 'post-modernism': one void chasing another, in a serial regression of self-congratulatory chronology. (Anderson 1984: 112–13)

Chapter 5: Modernity and Post-Modernity (II)

1   On the overlap between post-modernism and post-industrialism, cf. Fred Block, who says of post-modernism that 'although originating in the analysis of art, it has been broadened to characterize all of social life, and it now competes directly with the concept of post-industrialism . . . It would seem that the choice of the label *postmodern* or *postindustrial* to describe the intellectual project of constructing [a postmodern] social theory is arbitrary.' The arbitrariness of the choice is made even clearer in Block's definition of postindustrialism, which is more abstract than Bell's and puts him very close to some postmodernists: '"Postindustrial society" is the historical period that begins when the concept of industrial society ceases to provide an adequate account of actual social development. This definition is meant to locate the key change as occurring at the level of ideas and understanding – that is, our loss of a persuasive master concept for making sense of our own society' (Block 1990: 4, 11).

Fredric Jameson also notes that though postmodernism is generally considered a break in cultural styles, 'the break in question [should not] be thought of as a purely cultural affair: indeed, theories of the postmodern . . . bear a strong family resemblance to all those more ambitious sociological generalizations which, at much the same time, bring us the news of the arrival and inauguration of a whole new type of society, most famously baptized 'postindustrial society' (Daniel Bell) but often also designated consumer society, media society, information society, electronic society or high tech, and the like' (Jameson 1992: 3).

On the links between postmodernism and post-Fordism, see Lash and Urry (1987: 300–13), who see both in the context of 'disorganized capitalism'. See also the 'New Times' theorists who, within a generally post-Fordist perspective, include a concern with postmodernist themes of identity and consumption (Hall and Jacques 1989a: 137–72).

The most comprehensive view of post-modernity is taken by David Harvey, who includes in his account of the concept almost all the features associated with the information society and post-Fordism (Harvey 1989: *passim*, especially 159–60, 340–1). A similarly broad view is taken, though more cursorily, by Jencks (1989: 43–56).

2 In an essay of 1924, 'Mr Bennet and Mrs Brown', Virginia Woolf wrote: 'In or about December 1910, human character changed . . . All human relations have shifted . . . and when human relations change there is at the same time a change in religion, conduct, politics and literature.' D. H. Lawrence wrote in *Kangaroo* (1923) that 'it was in 1915 the old world ended.'

3 Cf. Calinescu: 'Metaphorically speaking, it was architecture that took the issues of postmodernism out of the clouds and down to earth to the realm of the visible' (Calinescu 1987: 281). Linda Hutcheon also considers architecture 'the best model for a poetics of postmodernism' (Hutcheon 1988: 22). See also Jameson 1992: 2.

4 In a later, more euphoric, account Hassan uses Bakhtin's concept of 'carnivalisation' to cover a good deal of what he means by postmodernism. Carnivalisation 'riotously embraces indeterminacy, fragmentation, decanonisation, selflessness, irony, hybridisation' – the principal defining elements of postmodernism. 'But the term also conveys the comic or absurdist ethos of postmodernism . . . Carnivalisation further means "polyphony", the centrifugal power of language, the "gay relativity" of things, perspectivism and performance, participation in the wild disorder of life, the immanence of laughter. Indeed, what Bakhtin calls novel or carnival – that is, anti-system – might stand for postmodernism itself, or at least for its ludic and subversive elements that promise renewal' (Hassan 1992: 198).

One might say that, as is especially clear in Hassan, many proponents of postmodernism have simply given a positive valuation to the tendencies towards anarchy and indeterminacy that Toynbee had earlier identified, in a negative, pessimistic vein, in his concept of the post-Modern. For the history of the concept of the post-modern, going back to its first uses in the 1870s, see Rose 1991: 3–20, 171–5; Smart 1992: 141–82; Huyssen 1992; Lyon 1994: 4–18.

5 Literary critics tend on the whole to be rather vague on the connection between postmodern culture and social change. Ihab Hassan, for instance, argues that 'the culture of postmodernism' derives from 'larger dispositions in society', but his listing of these dispositions is disappointingly thin and unspecific: 'a rising standard of living in the West, the disruption of institutional values, freed desires, liberation movements of every kind, schism and secession around the globe, terrorism rampant' (Hassan 1985: 126).

6 An intriguing and entertaining variation on the idea of the predominantly economic determinants of postmodernist culture is Charles Newman's view that postmodernism is a response to the inflation that has become a systematic feature of western economies in the last quarter of this century. See Newman 1985. For Eagleton, postmodernist culture is a debased form of modernism, one which complacently accepts 'the dissolution of art into the prevailing forms of commodity production' (Eagleton 1985: 60).

7 'What "late" generally conveys is . . . the sense that something has changed, that things are different, that we have gone through a transformation of the lifeworld which is somehow decisive but incomparable with the older convulsions of modernization and industrialization, less perceptible and dramatic, somehow, but more permanent precisely because more thoroughgoing and all-pervasive' (Jameson 1992: xxi).

8 Cf. Steven Connor on Lyotard, Baudrillard and Jameson: 'For all these writers, postmodernity may be defined as those plural conditions in which the social and the cultural become indistinguishable' (Connor 1989: 61).

Andreas Huyssen provides another example of the rather reluctant admission of the impossibility of keeping the categories of culture and society separate. He wishes to see postmodernism as 'a slowly emerging cultural transformation in Western societies, a change in sensibility . . . ' But, he says, 'I don't want to be misunderstood as claiming that there is a wholesale paradigm shift of the cultural, social and economic orders' (Huyssen 1992: 42). Nevertheless before he has finished his discussion of postmodernism he has clearly moved from the cultural to the political and social, even if not so far as to announce the coming of a new type of society. He agrees with Habermas as well as 'neo-conservatives' like Bell that 'postmodernism is not so much a question of style as it is a question of politics and culture at large.' He notes the importance of the women's movement, the ecology movement, and movements among minorities such as blacks and gays, in providing both the impetus to, and a good deal of the substance of, postmodernist culture in its more recent phase. And he concludes: 'it is easy to see that a postmodernist culture emerging from these political, social and cultural constellations will have to be a postmodernism of resistance', even if it can no longer share in the universalist hopes of emancipation of Enlightenment modernity (Huyssen 1992: 53–4,

59, 68–9). Once more an account that purports to stay within the realm of the cultural is forced by the logic of its own analysis to move outwards to politics and society.

9 Cf. Jeffrey Alexander, who argues that we cannot understand the appeal of postmodernism simply by considering its 'middle range' models of change in culture and society. 'These discussions have become significant only because they are taken to exemplify broad new trends of history, social structure, and moral life. Indeed, it is by intertwining the levels of structure and process, micro and macro, with strong assertions about the past, present, and future of contemporary life that postmodernism has formed a broad and inclusive general theory of society . . . ' (Alexander 1994: 179).

10 For these characteristics of post-modernity, variously linked to theories of post-industrialism, post-Fordism, the information society, 'disorganized' or 'late' capitalism, see Lash and Urry 1987: 5–16, 285–300; 1994: 279–313; Harvey 1989: 293–6, 302–3, 338–42; Hassan 1985: 125–7; Jencks 1989: 43–52; 1992: 33–5; Soja 1989: 157–89; Huyssen 1992: 68–9; Crook et al. 1992: 32–41, 220–3.

11 There has been considerable discussion of the urban styles and forms of post-modernity, especially with reference to American cities. In addition to Soja, see Cook 1988; Zukin 1991, 1992; Davis 1992; Lash and Urry 1994: 193–222; Brain 1995.

12 The literature on poststructuralism and deconstructionism is enormous. For clear and helpful summaries of some of the main concepts, see Selden 1985: 72–105 and Abrams 1985, both of which also contain good bibliographies.

13 Cf. Hassan: 'God, King, Father, Reason, History, Humanism have all come and gone their way, though their power may still flare up in some circles of faith. We have killed our gods – in spite or lucidity, I hardly know – yet we remain ourselves creatures of will, desire, hope, belief. And now we have nothing – nothing that is not partial, provisional, self-created – upon which to found our discourse' (Hassan 1992: 203).

14 In view of the importance of 'paralogical' thinking in much postmodern theory it should perhaps be pointed out that the medical definition of 'paralogia' is 'illogical or incoherent speech, as in delirium or schizophrenia' (*OED*).

15 The term 'post-industrial' has of course also been used in other ways as well – for instance, by Guild Socialists such as Arthur Penty in the early part of this century. For him it meant 'the break-up of Industrialism' and the *return* to something more approaching 'Medievalism', in the spirit of William Morris. See Rose 1991: 21–4.

16 Many of the publications of the *Theory, Culture and Society* (UK) group fall into this category, as do several of the contributors to the journal *Telos* (US). Cf. also Soja who, despite his reservations, speaks of post-modernity as 'a possibly epochal transition in both critical thought and material life' (1989: 5).

17 Cf. Jameson: 'Rigorously conducted, an inquiry into this or that

feature of the postmodern will end up telling us little of value about postmodernism itself, but against its own will and quite unintentionally a great deal about the modern proper, and perhaps the converse will also turn out to be true . . . ' (Jameson 1992: 66).

Umberto Eco similarly suggests that we do not treat post-modernism as a historical period but as 'a metahistorical category'. 'I believe that postmodernism is not a trend to be chronologically defined, but, rather, an ideal category or, better still, a *Kunstwollen*, a way of operating. We could say that every period has its own postmodernism, just as every period would have its own mannerism . . . ' Eco (1992: 73). There is an echo here of Lyotard's view of postmodernism as a recurring stage within the modern.

18 Bauman says that with the advent of postmodernity, 'no new and improved order has emerged . . . from beneath the debris of the old and unwanted one. Postmodernity . . . does not seek to substitute one truth for another, one standard of beauty for another, one life ideal for another . . . It braces itself for a life without truths, standards and ideals' (1992: ix). This is consistent with the view of postmodernity as a perspective on modernity, 'modernity conscious of its true nature'. But elsewhere Bauman is more convinced that we can indeed talk of a new postmodern society taking the place of the old society. This is largely owing to the fact that 'in present-day society, consumer conduct (consumer freedom geared to the consumer market) moves steadily into the position of, simultaneously, the cognitive and moral focus of life, the integrative bond of society, and the focus of systemic management. In other words, it moves into the selfsame position which in the past – during the "modern" phase of capitalist society – was occupied by work in the form of wage labour. This means that in our time individuals are engaged (morally by society, functionally by the social system) first and foremost as consumers rather than as producers.' It is this that allows us to see postmodernity not just as a deviation from modernity, nor a disease of it, nor even a protest against it, but rather as 'an aspect of a fully-fledged, viable social system which has come to replace the "classical" modern, capitalist society and thus needs to be theorized according to its own logic' (Bauman 1992: 49, 52).

There need not be any real incompatibility between these two positions. The 'absences' and 'errors' of modernity, as seen through the lens of postmodernity, can from a different point of view look like the lineaments of a new society in the making – one that incorporates these suppressed features and insights as its working principles. But there is undoubtedly a difference of emphasis – one largely critical, the other more constructive – between the two positions. For the elements of the more constructive 'sociology of postmodernity' that is now required, see Bauman (1992: 48–53, 189–96).

19 One of the objections Giddens makes to the idea of post-modernity as a new stage is that this would violate one of its own premises: 'To speak of post-modernity as superseding modernity appears to invoke

that very thing which is declared (now) to be impossible: giving some coherence to history and pinpointing our place in it' (Giddens 1990: 47; see also Kellner 1988: 250).

There is a good discussion of this predicament in Crook et al. 1992: 231–6. These authors take the view that the way out is not to speak of post-modernity but of 'postmodernization'. This is a process whereby modernity is overreaching itself, imploding by the hyperextension of its principle of differentiation, so that many features of what others call post-modernity are beginning to show themselves ('hyper-differentiation' is beginning to look like post-modern 'de-differentiation', in the economy, polity and culture). But we are not yet certain of the ultimate direction of change; we have not yet achieved the condition of post-modernity. So we can still use the categories of 'modern' social theory for analyzing many of the transitional developments ('postmodernization'). See Crook et al. 1992: 1–2, 36–41, 220–39.

20 For various listings of 'prepostmodernists', postmodernists *avant la lettre*, see Hassan 1985: 119, 122; Calinescu 1987: 297, 357; Turner 1989: 212–15; 1990b: 8–9; Eco 1992: 73–4; Barth 1992: 142–3; Jameson 1992: 4, 302–3. It would be wrong to say that such lists are entirely idiosyncratic, though there are some striking differences and disagreements. But a 'canon' (or 'de-canon') of postmodernist writers and thinkers does seem to be emerging.

21 Cf. Kermode: 'Postmodernism is another of those period descriptions that help you to take a view of the past suitable to whatever it is you want to do. It ceases to be attached to a particular historical moment. Instead of coming after Modernism it can be regarded as coeval with it, or even as preceding it' (Kermode 1989: 132).

Chapter 6: Millennial Themes

1 It has to be said that there have been some brave and stimulating efforts to take on the full range of changes from the personal to the global levels – see, for example, Beck 1992, Giddens 1990, 1991, 1992, and Beck et al. 1994. There is now also a considerable literature on 'globalization': see, for example, Featherstone 1990, Sklair 1991 and Robertson 1992.

2 The breakdown of spatial boundaries by the electronic media has led some such as Joshua Meyrowitz to see the information society as reconstituting not just the subject but also society along free-floating lines, as with the nomadic societies of the past.

> Many of the features of our 'information age' make us resemble the most primitive of social and political forms: the hunting and gathering society. As nomadic peoples, hunters and gatherers have no loyal relationship to territory. They, too, have little 'sense of place'; specific activities are not totally fixed to specific physical settings. The lack of boundaries both in hunting and gathering and in electronic societies leads to many striking parallels. Of all known societal types before our own, hunting

and gathering societies have tended to be the most egalitarian in terms of the roles of males and females, children and adults, and leaders and followers. The difficulty of maintaining many 'separate places', or distinct social spheres, tends to involve everyone in everyone else's business. (Meyrowitz 1986: 315)

3   He had even conceived the idea of a 'World Brain', an amalgamation and storehouse of all the available knowledge in the world, that remarkably anticipates the claims made on behalf of the Internet. *The Open Conspiracy* was published in 1928, *The World Brain* in 1938, but both drew upon ideas Wells had elaborated before the First World War.

4   That some people, such as Anthony Giddens and Ulrich Beck, choose to do this rethinking under the label of 'late' or 'radicalized' or 'reflexive' modernity, rather than 'post-modernity', does not of course affect the main point. It rather confirms it. It shows that these thinkers too agree with the postmodernists that some new term or concept might be necessary to reflect the changes in modernity. See Giddens 1990; Beck 1992; Beck et al. 1994.

5   It is rather extraordinary, as Rorty indicates, that so much of the debate on modernity and post-modernity should have turned on the thought of a group of German thinkers – from Kant to Nietzsche – whose reflective activity took place in a country at that time barely touched by the currents of modernization. Early nineteenth-century Germany, by comparison with Britain, France or Belgium, was one of the least modern societies in Europe. Hence the strength there, as Karl Mannheim noted, of a vigorous school of conservative thought. It was Britain and France, homes of the Industrial and Political Revolutions, that were the standard-bearers of modernity. It was their thinkers, from Smith to Mill and Saint-Simon to Comte, who took the measure of the momentous economic and social changes set in train by the dual revolution. Of the German thinkers, it was Marx alone who broke with the speculative tradition of reflection on modernity; and as is well known it took the stimulus of his friend, Friedrich Engels, with his experience of Manchester life, to turn him towards the detailed exploration of capitalist industrialism – the exemplary case of which he took to be England.

6   Cf. Berman: '1989 was not only a great year, but a great *modernist* year. First, because millions of people learned their history was not over, that they had the capacity to make their own history . . . Second, because in the midst of their motions, those men and women identified with each other: even in different languages and idioms, even thousands of miles apart, they saw how their stories were one story, how they were all trying to make the modern world their own' (Berman 1992: 55).

References

Abercrombie, N., Hill, S. and Turner, B. S. 1986: *Sovereign Individuals of Capitalism*. London: Allen and Unwin.

Abrams, M. H. 1985: *A Glossary of Literary Terms*, sixth edition. Fort Worth, TX: Harcourt Brace Jovanovich.

Adas, M. 1994: 'Between Triumphalism and Apocalypse: The Great Transformation and the Global Predicament at Two Fin de Siècles'. Paper given at the conference, 'At the End of the Century: Looking Back to the Future', Library of Congress, Washington D.C., November 3–5.

Agnew, J. A. and Duncan, J. S. (eds) 1989: *The Power of Place*. Boston: Unwin Hyman.

Aglietta, M. 1979: *A Theory of Capitalist Regulation: The U.S. Experience*. London: Verso.

Aglietta, M. 1982: 'World Capitalism in the Eighties'. *New Left Review*, 136: 5–41.

Alexander, J. 1994: 'Modern, Anti, Post, and Neo: How Social Theories Have Tried to Understand the "New World" of "Our Time"'. *Zeitschrift für Soziologie*, 23 (3): 165–97.

Amin, A. 1989: 'A Model of the Small Firm in Italy'. In Goodman et al. 1989: 111–22.

—— 1991: 'Flexible Specialization and Small Firms in Italy: Myths and Realities'. In Pollert 1991a: 119–37.

—— 1994: 'The Difficult Transition from Informal Economy to Marshallian Industrial District'. *Area*, 26 (1): 13–24.

Amin, A. and Robins, K. 1990: 'Industrial Districts and Regional Development: Limits and Possibilities'. In Pyke et al. 1990: 185–219.

Amin, A. and Thrift, N. 1993: 'Globalization, Institutional Thickness and Local Prospects.' *Revue d'Economie Régionale et Urbaine*, 3: 406–27.

Amsden, A. 1990: 'Third World Industrialization: "Global Fordism" or a New Model?' *New Left Review*, 182: 5–31.

Anderson, P. 1984: 'Modernity and Revolution'. *New Left Review*, 144: 96–113.

—— 1994: *The Ends of History*. London: Verso.

Appadurai, A. 1990: 'Disjuncture and Difference in the Global Cultural Economy'. In Featherstone 1990: 295–310.

Appelbaum, E. and Albin, P. 1989: 'Computer Rationalization and the Transformation of Work: Lessons from the Insurance Industry'. In Wood 1989a: 247–65.

Ariès, P. 1973: *Centuries of Childhood*. Harmondsworth: Penguin Books.

Arnold, M. 1970: 'On the Modern Element in Literature' [1857]. In P. J. Keating (ed.), *Matthew Arnold: Selected Prose*. Harmondsworth: Penguin Books, 57–75.

Arriaga, P. 1985: 'Toward a Critique of the Information Economy'. *Media, Culture and Society*, 7: 271–96.

Ashley, D. 1990: 'Habermas and the Completion of the "Project of Modernity"'. In Turner 1990a: 88–107.

Bacon, F. 1860: *The Physical and Metaphysical Works of Lord Bacon*, ed. J. Devey. London: Henry Bohn.

Bacon, F. 1906: *Essays*. London: Blackie and Son.

Baker, K. 1982: *Towards an Information Economy*. London: Department of Trade and Industry.

Bamford, J. 1987: 'The Family, Agriculture and the Community in Italian Small Firm Development'. Paper presented to the Acton Society Conference, 'Small Firms in Italy', Fiesole, 14–16 April.

Baran, B. 1988: 'Office Automation and Women's Work: The Technological Transformation of the Insurance Industry'. In Pahl 1988: 684–706.

Barker, J. 1981: 'Technological Change and Quick Obsolescence of Qualifications.' Paper presented to the FAST seminar, 'Attitudes to Work', Marseilles, 23–26 November.

Barnaby, F. 1982: 'Microelectronics in War'. In Friedrichs and Schaff 1982: 243–72.

Barron, I. and Curnow, R. 1979: *The Future with Microelectronics: Forecasting the Effects of Information Technology*. London: Frances Pinter.

Barth, J. 1992. 'The Literature of Replenishment: Postmodernist Fiction'. In Jencks 1992a: 172–80.

Baudelaire, C. 1981: *Selected Writings on Art and Artists*, trans. P. E. Charvet. Cambridge: Cambridge University Press.

Baudrillard, J. 1983: 'The Ecstasy of Communication'. In Foster 1983: 126–34.

—— 1987a: 'Modernity'. *Canadian Journal of Political and Social Theory*, 11 (3): 63–72.

—— 1987b: *Forget Foucault* and *Forget Baudrillard: An Interview with Sylvère Lotringer*. New York: Semiotext(e).

—— 1988a: *Selected Writings*, ed. M. Poster. Cambridge: Polity Press.

—— 1988b: 'Simulacra and Simulations'. In Baudrillard 1988a: 166–84.

—— 1989: *America*. London: Verso.

Bauman, Z. 1987: *Legislators and Interpreters: On Modernity, Post-Modernity and Intellectuals*. Cambridge: Polity Press.

—— 1992: *Intimations of Postmodernity*. London and New York: Routledge.

Becattini, G. 1978: 'The Development of Light Industry in Tuscany: An Interpretation'. *Economic Notes*, 2/3: 107–23.

—— 1990: 'The Marshallian Industrial District as a Socio-Economic Notion'. In Pye et al. 1990: 37–51.

Beck, U. 1992: *Risk Society: Towards a New Modernity*, trans. M. Ritter. London: Sage Publications.

Beck, U., Giddens, A. and Lash, S. 1994: *Reflexive Modernization: Politics, Tradition and Aesthetics in the Modern Social Order*. Cambridge: Polity Press.

Becker, C. L. 1932: *The Heavenly City of the Eighteenth-Century Philosophers*. New Haven: Yale University Press.

Bell, D. 1973: *The Coming of Post-Industrial Society*. New York: Basic Books.

—— 1976: *The Cultural Contradictions of Capitalism*. London: Heinemann.

—— 1980a: 'The Social Framework of the Information Society'. In Forester 1980: 500–49.

—— 1980b: 'Teletext and Technology'. In *Sociological Journeys: Essays 1960–1980*, London: Heinemann, 34–65.

—— 1980c: 'Beyond Modernism, Beyond Self.' In *Sociological Journeys: Essays 1960–1980*, London: Heinemann, 275–302.

—— 1987: 'The world and the United States in 2013'. *Daedalus*, 116: 1–31.

Bellah, R., Madsen, R., Sullivan, W., Swidler, A. and Tipton, S. 1985: *Habits of the Heart*. Berkeley, CA: University of California Press.

Bellandi, M. 1989a: 'The Role of Small Firms in the Development of Italian Manufacturing Industry'. In Goodman et al. 1989: 31–68.

Bellandi, M. 1989b: 'The Industrial District in Marshall'. In Goodman et al. 1989: 136–52.

Benedetti, F. de, 1979: 'The Impact of Electronic Technology in the Office'. *Financial Times* Conference: *Tomorrow in World Electronics*, March 21–22. London: Financial Times.

Beniger, J. R. 1986: *The Control Revolution: Technological and Economic Origins of the Information Society*. Cambridge, MA and London: Harvard University Press.

Berger, S. and Piore, M. J. 1980: *Dualism and Discontinuity in Industrial Societies*. Cambridge: Cambridge University Press.

Berman, M. 1983: *All That Is Solid Melts Into Air: The Experience of Modernity*. London: Verso.

Berman, M. 1992: 'Why Modernism still Matters'. In Lash and Friedman 1992: 33–58.

Bernstein, R. J. (ed.) 1985: *Habermas and Modernity*. Cambridge: Polity Press.

Beynon, H. 1973: *Working for Ford*. Harmondsworth: Penguin Books.

Biddiss, M. D. 1977: *The Age of the Masses: Ideas and Society in Europe Since 1870*. Harmondsworth: Penguin Books.

Bjorn-Anderson, N., Earl, M., Holst, O. and Mumford, E. (eds) 1982:

Information Society: For Richer, For Poorer. Amsterdam: North-Holland Publishing Company.

Block, F. 1990: *Postindustrial Possibilities: A Critique of Economic Discourse*. Berkeley, CA: University of California Press.

Blumberg, P. 1980: *Inequality in An Age of Decline*. New York: Oxford University Press.

Boden, D. 1992: 'Reinventing the Global Village: Communication and the Revolutions of 1989'. In A. Giddens (ed.), *Human Societies: A Reader*, Cambridge: Polity Press, 327–31.

Boden, M. 1980: 'The Social Implications of Intelligent Machines'. In Forester 1980: 439–52.

Boyer, R. 1990: *The Regulation School: A Critical Introduction*. New York: Columbia University Press.

Bradbury, M. and McFarlane, J. (eds) 1976: *Modernism: 1890–1930*. London: Penguin Books.

Brain, D. 1995: 'From Public Housing to Private Communities'. In J. Weintraub and K. Kumar (eds), *Public and Private in Thought and Practice*, Chicago: University of Chicago Press.

Braun, E. and MacDonald, S. 1978: *Revolution in Miniature: The History and Impact of Semiconductor Electronics*. Cambridge: Cambridge University Press.

Braverman, H. 1974: *Labor and Monopoly Capital: The Degradation of Work in the Twentieth Century*. New York and London: Monthly Review Press.

Brenner, R. and Glick, M. 1991: 'The Regulation Approach: Theory and History'. *New Left Review*, 188: 45–119.

Brunt, R. 1989: 'The Politics of Identity'. In Hall and Jacques 1989a: 150–9.

Brusco, S. 1982: 'The Emilian Model: Productive Decentralisation and Social Integration.' *Cambridge Journal of Economics*, 6: 167–84.

Brusco, S. 1986: 'Small Firms and Industrial districts: the experience of Italy'. In D. Keeble and E. Wever (eds), *New Firms and Regional Development in Europe*, London: Croom Helm, 184–202.

Brusco, S. 1989: 'A Policy for Industrial Districts'. In Goodman et al. 1989: 259–69.

Brzezinski, Z. 1971: *Between Two Ages: America's Role in the Technetronic Era*. New York: Viking Press.

Bullock, A. 1976: 'The Double Image'. In Bradbury and McFarlane 1976: 58–70.

Bürger, P. 1992: 'The Decline of Modernism'. In *The Decline of Modernism*, trans. N. Walker, Cambridge: Polity Press, 32–47.

Burns, T. (ed.) 1992: *After History? Francis Fukuyama and His Critics*. London: Eurospan.

Bury, J. B. 1955: *The Idea of Progress: An Inquiry into Its Origin and Growth*. New York: Dover Publications.

Calinescu, M. 1987: *Five Faces of Modernity*. Durham, NC: Duke University Press.

Callinicos, A. 1989: *Against Postmodernism: A Marxist Critique*. Cambridge: Polity Press.

Carnoy, M., Castells, M., Cohen, S. and Cardoso, F. H. 1993: *The World Economy in the Information Age*. London: Macmillan.

Carter, E., Donald, J. and Squires, J. (eds) 1993: *Space and Place: Theories of Identity and Location*. London: Lawrence and Wishart.

Castells, M. 1989: *The Informational City: Information Technology, Economic Restructuring and the Urban-Regional Process*. Oxford: Basil Blackwell.

Child, J. 1988: 'Managerial Strategies, New Technology and the Labour Process'. In Pahl 1988: 229–57.

Clark, T. J. 1973: *The Absolute Bourgeois: Artists and Politics in France 1848–1851*. London: Thames and Hudson.

Clark, T. J. 1982: 'Clement Greenberg's Theory of Art.' *Critical Inquiry*, 9 (1), 139–56.

Clarke, S. 1990a: 'The Crisis of Fordism or the Crisis of Social Democracy?' *Telos*, 83, 71–98.

Clarke, S. 1990b: 'New Utopias for Old: Fordist Dreams and Post-Fordist Fantasies'. *Capital and Class*, 42, 131–55.

Coleman, A. 1985: *Utopia on Trial: Vision and Reality in Planned Housing*. London: Hilary Shipman.

Collingwood, R. G. 1961: *The Idea of History*. Oxford: Oxford University Press.

Connor, S. 1989: *Postmodernist Culture: An Introduction to Theories of the Contemporary*. Oxford: Basil Blackwell.

Cook, P. 1988: 'Modernity, Postmodernity and the City.' *Theory, Culture and Society*, 5: 475–92.

Cooley, M. 1981: *Architect or Bee? The Human/Technology Relationship*. Slough: Langley Technical Services.

—— 1982: 'Computers, Politics and Unemployment'. In Sieghart 1982: 72–97.

Crompton, R. and Reid, S. 1983: 'The Deskilling of Clerical Work.' In S. Wood (ed.), *The Degradation of Work? Skill, Deskilling and the Labour Process*, London: Hutchinson, 163–78.

Crook, S., Pakulski, J. and Waters, M. 1992: *Postmodernization: Change in Advanced Society*. London: Sage Publications.

Davis, M. 1992: *City of Quartz: Excavating the Future in Los Angeles*. London: Vintage.

Derrida, J. 1994: *Specters of Marx*. London and New York: Routledge.

Descartes, R. 1968: *Discourse on Method and the Meditations*, trans. F. E. Sutcliffe. London: Penguin Books.

Dore, R. 1987: *Flexible Rigidities: Industrial Policy and Structural Adjustment in the Japanese Economy, 1970–1980*. London: Athlone Press.

Douglas, S. and Guback, T. 1984: 'Production and Technology in the Communication/Information Revolution'. *Media, Culture and Society*, 6, 233–45.

Drucker, P. 1969: *The Age of Discontinuity*. London: Heinemann.

Eagleton, T. 1985: 'Capitalism, Modernism and Revolution'. *New Left Review*, 152, 60–73.

Eco, U. 1987: *Travels in Hyperreality*, trans. W. Weaver. London: Picador.

—— 1992: 'Postscript to *The Name of the Rose*'. In Jencks 1992a: 73–5.

Edwards, R. 1979: *Contested Terrain: The Transformation of the Workplace in the Twentieth Century*. London: Heinemann.

Evans, J. 1982: 'The Worker and the Workplace'. In Friedrichs and Schaff 1982: 157–87.

Featherstone, M. (ed.) 1990: *Global Culture: Nationalism, Globalization and Modernity*. London: Sage Publications.

Ferguson, M. (ed.) 1986: *New Communication Technologies and the Public Interest*. London and Beverly Hills, CA: Sage Publications.

Ferkiss, V. 1979: 'Post-Industrial Society: Theory, Ideology, Myth'. *Political Science Reviewer*, 9, 61–102.

Fiedler, L. 1971: *The Collected Essays of Leslie Fiedler*, vol. 2. New York: Stein and Day.

Foden, G. 1994: 'Trawling in Cyberspace'. *Times Literary Supplement*, 13 May, 11.

Forester, T. (ed.) 1980: *The Microelectronics Revolution*. Oxford: Basil Blackwell.

—— (ed.) 1985: *The Information Technology Revolution*. Oxford: Basil Blackwell.

—— 1987: *High-Tech Society: The Story of the Information Technology Revolution*. Oxford: Basil Blackwell.

—— 1988: 'The Myth of the Electronic Cottage'. *Futures*, 20 (3), 227–40.

Foster, H. (ed.) 1983: *The Anti-Aesthetic: Essays on Postmodern Culture*. Port Townsend, Washington: Bay Press.

Foucault, M. 1970: *The Order of Things: An Archaeology of the Human Sciences*. London: Tavistock Publications.

Freeman, C. 1987: 'Information Technology and Change in the Techo-Economic Paradigm.' In Freeman and Soete 1987: 49–69.

Freeman, C. and Soete, L. (eds) 1987: *Technical Change and Full Employment*. Oxford: Basil Blackwell.

Friedrichs, G. 1982: 'Microelectronics and Macroeconomics'. In Friedrichs and Schaff 1982: 189–211.

Friedrichs, G. and Schaff, A. (eds) 1982: *Microelectronics and Society: For Better or For Worse*. Oxford: Pergamon Press.

Frisby, D. 1985: *Fragments of Modernity: Theories of Modernity in the Work of Simmel, Kracauer and Benjamin*. Cambridge: Polity Press.

Fukuyama, F. 1989: 'The End of History?' *The National Interest*, 16, 3–18.

—— 1992: *The End of History and the Last Man*. London: Penguin Books.

Garrett, J. and Wright, G. 1980: 'Micro is Beautiful'. In Forester 1980: 488–96.

Geertz, C. 1983: *Local Knowledge: Futher Essays in Interpretive Anthropology*. New York: Basic Books.

Gellner, E. 1988: *Plough, Sword and Book: The Structure of Human History*. London: Collins Harvill.

Gellner, E. 1992: *Postmodernism, Reason and Religion*. London: Routledge.

Gershuny, J. I. 1978: *After Industrial Society? The Emerging Self-Service Economy*. London: Macmillan.

Gershuny, J. I. and Miles, I. 1983: *The New Service Economy: The Transformation of Employment in Industrial Societies*. London: Frances Pinter.

Gibbins, J. R. (ed.) 1989: *Contemporary Political Culture: Politics in a Postmodern Age*. London: Sage Publications.

Gibson, W. 1984: *Neuromancer*. New York: Ace Books.

Giddens, A. 1990: *The Consequences of Modernity*. Cambridge: Polity Press.

—— 1991: *Modernity and Self-Identity*. Cambridge: Polity Press.

—— 1992: *The Transformation of Intimacy*. Cambridge: Polity Press.

Gill, C. 1985: *Work, Unemployment and the New Technology*. Cambridge: Polity Press.

Goldthorpe, J. 1982: 'On the Service Class, its Formation and Future'. In A. Giddens and G. Mackenzie (eds), *Social Class and the Division of Labour*, Cambridge: Cambridge University Press, 162–85.

Goodman, E. 1989: 'The Political Economy of the Small Firm in Italy'. In Goodman et al. 1989: 1–30.

Goodman, E., Bamford, J. and Saynor, P. (eds) 1989: *Small Firms and Industrial Districts in Italy*. London: Routledge.

Gordon, D. M. 1988: 'The Global Economy: New Edifice or Crumbling Foundations?' *New Left Review*, 168, 24–64.

Gorz, A. 1982: *Farewell to the Working Class: An Essay on Post-Industrial Socialism*, trans. M. Sonenscher. London: Pluto Press.

Gorz, A. 1989: *Critique of Economic Reason*. London: Verso.

Greenberg, C. 1980: *The Notion of 'Post-Modern'*. Sydney: Bloxham and Chambers.

—— 1993: 'Avant-Garde Attitudes: New Art in the Sixties' [1969]. In J. O'Brian (ed.), *Clement Greenberg: The Collected Essays and Criticism*, vol. 4, Chicago and London: University of Chicago Press, 292–303.

Gramsci, A. 1971: 'Americanism and Fordism'. In Q. Hoare and G. Nowell-Smith (eds), *Selections from the Prison Notebooks of Antonio Gramsci*, London: Lawrence and Wishart, 277–318.

Griffin, D. R. (ed.) 1988: *The Re-enchantment of Science: Postmodern Proposals*. Albany: State University of New York Press.

Gurevich, A. J. 1985: *Categories of Medieval Culture*, translated by G. L. Campbell. London: Routledge and Kegan Paul.

Guy, K. 1987: 'The UK Tertiary Sector'. In Freeman and Soete 1987: 169–88.

Habermas, J. 1981: 'Modernity versus Postmodernity'. *New German Critique*, 22, 3–14.

—— 1987: *The Philosophical Discourse of Modernity: Twelve Lectures*, trans. F. Lawrence. Cambridge: Polity Press.

—— 1991a: *The Structural Transformation of the Public Sphere*, trans. T. Burger and F. Lawrence. Cambridge, MA: MIT Press.

—— 1991b: 'What Does Socialism Mean Today? The Revolutions of Recuperation and the Need for New Thinking'. In R. Blackburn (ed.), *After the Fall: The Failure of Communism and the Future of Socialism*, London: Verso, 25–46.

—— 1992: 'Further Reflections on the Public Sphere'. In C. Calhoun (ed.), *Habermas and the Public Sphere*, Cambridge, MA: MIT Press, 421–57.

Hakim, C. 1988: 'Homeworking in Britain'. In Pahl 1988: 609–32.

Hall, P. 1988: *Cities of Tomorrow: An Intellectual History of Urban Planning and Design in the Twentieth Century*. Oxford: Basil Blackwell.

Hall, S. and Jacques, M. (eds) 1989a: *New Times: The Changing Face of Politics in the 1990s*. London: Lawrence and Wishart.

—— 1989b: 'Introduction'. In Hall and Jacques 1989a: 11–20.

Hamelink, C. J. 1986: 'Is There Life after the Information Society?' In M. Traber (ed.), *The Myth of the Information Revolution: Social and Ethical Implications of Communication Technology*, London and Beverly Hills, CA: Sage Publications, 7–20.

Harvey, D. 1989: *The Condition of Postmodernity: An Inquiry into the Origins of Cultural Change*. Oxford: Basil Blackwell.

Hassan, I. 1985: 'The Culture of Postmodernism'. *Theory, Culture and Society*, 2 (3), 119–31.

—— 1987: *The Postmodern Turn: Essays in Postmodern Theory and Culture*. Columbus, Ohio: Ohio State University Press.

—— 1992: 'Pluralism in Postmodern Perspective'. In Jencks 1992a: 40–72.

Havel, V. 1992: 'The End of the Modern Era'. *New York Times*, March 1, 15.

Hebdige, D. 1988: *Hiding in the Light: On Images and Things*. London and New York: Routledge.

Hegel, G. F. W. 1956: *The Philosophy of History*, trans. J. Sibree. New York: Dover Publications.

—— 1971: 'The Positivity of the Christian Religion' [1795–1800]. In *Early Theological Writings: G. F. W. Hegel*, trans. T. M. Knox, Philadelphia: University of Pennsylvania Press, 67–181.

Heim, M. 1994: *The Metaphysics of Virtual Reality*. Oxford: Oxford University Press.

Heller, A. 1990: *Can Modernity Survive?* Cambridge: Polity Press.

Heller, A. and Feher, F. 1988: *The Postmodern Political Condition*. Cambridge: Polity Press.

Henderson, H. 1978: *Creating Alternatives Futures*. New York: Berkeley Publishing Corporation.

Hepworth, M. E. 1989: *Geography of the Information Revolution*. London: Belhaven Press.

Hines, C. and Searle, G. 1979: *Automatic Unemployment*. London: Earth Resources Research.

Hirsch, F. 1977: *Social Limits to Growth*. London: Routledge and Kegan Paul.

Hirst, P. and Zeitlin, J. 1991: 'Flexible Specialization versus Post-Fordism: Theory, Evidence and Policy Implications.' *Economy and Society*, 20 (1), 1–56.

Hitchcock, H. R. 1968: *Architecture: Nineteenth and Twentieth Centuries*, third edition. Harmondsworth: Penguin Books.

226 *References*

Hobsbawm, E. J. 1987: *The Age of Empire 1875–1914*. London: Weidenfeld and Nicolson.
—— 1994: *Age of Extremes: The Short 20th Century*. London: Michael Joseph.
Howe, I. 1970: 'Mass society and Post-Modern Fiction' [1959]. In I. Howe (ed.), *The Decline of the New*, New York: Harcourt, Brace and World, 190–207.
Hughes, H. S. 1958: *Consciousness and Society: The Reorientation of European Social Thought 1890–1930*. New York: Vintage Books.
Huntington, S. P. 1993: 'The Clash of Civilizations?' *Foreign Affairs*, 72 (Summer): 22–49.
Hutcheon, L. 1988: *A Poetics of Postmodernism: History, Theory, Fiction*. London and New York: Routledge.
Huyssen, A. 1992: 'Mapping the Postmodern'. In Jencks 1992a: 40–72.
Hyman, A. 1980: *The Coming of the Chip*. London: New English Library.
Hyman, R. 1991: '*Plus ça change*? The Theory of Production and the Production of Theory'. In Pollert 1991a: 259–83.
Ide, T. R. 1982: 'The [New] Technology'. In Friedrichs and Schaff 1982: 37–88.
Jacobs, J. 1965: *The Death and Life of Great American Cities*. Harmondsworth: Penguin Books.
Jameson, F. 1992: *Postmodernism, or, The Cultural Logic of Late Capitalism*. London: Verso.
Jay, M. 1993: 'Apocalypse and the Inability to Mourn'. In *Force-Fields: Between Intellectual History and Cultural Criticism*, London: Routledge, 84–98.
Jencks, C. 1977: *The Language of Post-Modern Architecture*, first edition. London: Academy Editions.
—— 1989: *What is Post-Modernism?*, third edition. London: Academy Editions.
—— (ed.) 1992a: *The Post-Modern Reader*. London: Academy Editions.
—— 1992b: 'The Post-Modern Agenda'. In Jencks 1992a: 10–39.
—— 1992c: 'The Post-Avant-Garde'. In Jencks 1992a: 215–24.
Jenkins, C. and Sherman, B. 1979: *The Collapse of Work*. London: Eyre Methuen.
Jensen, J. 1989: 'The Talents of Women, the Skills of Men: Flexible Specialization and Women'. In Wood 1989a: 141–55.
Jessop, B., Bonnett, K., Bromley, S. and Ling, T. 1987: 'Popular Capitalism, Flexible Accumulation and Left Strategy'. *New Left Review*, 165, 104–22.
Jones, Barry 1982: *Sleepers, Wake! Technology and the Future of Work*. Brighton: Wheatsheaf.
Jones, Bryn 1982: 'Destruction or Redistribution of Engineering Skills? The Case of Numerical Control'. In S. Wood (ed.), *The Degradation of Work?*, London: Hutchinson, 179–200.
Jones, R. F. 1961: *Ancients and Moderns: A Study of the Rise of the Scientific Movement in Seventeenth Century England*, second edition. Berkeley, CA: University of California Press.

Jones, T. (ed.) 1980: *Microelectronics and Society*. Milton Keynes: Open University Press.

Jowitt, K. 1992: *New World Disorder: The Leninist Extinction*. Berkeley, CA: University of California Press.

Jussawalla, M. 1985: 'Constraints on Economic Analysis of Transborder Data Flows'. *Media, Culture and Society*, 7, 297–312.

Kellner, D. 1988: 'Postmodernism and Social Theory'. *Theory, Culture and Society*, 5: 239–69.

Kermode, F. 1961: *Romantic Image*. London: Routledge and Kegan Paul.

—— 1968a: 'Modernisms'. In *Continuities*, London: Routledge and Kegan Paul, 1–32.

—— 1968b: *The Sense of An Ending: Studies in the Theory of Fiction*. London: Oxford University Press.

—— 1989: *History and Value*. Oxford: Clarendon Press.

King, A. 1982: 'A New Industrial Revolution or Just Another Technology?' In Friedrichs and Schaff 1982: 1–36.

Kishida, J. 1994: 'The Technology of Global Management'. Paper given at the conference, 'At the End of the Century: Looking Back at the Future', Library of Congress, Washington D.C., November 3–5.

Klibansky, R. 1936: 'Standing on the Shoulders of Giants'. *Isis*, 26, 147–9.

Kolakowski, L. 1990: 'Modernity on Endless Trial'. In *Modernity on Endless Trial*, Chicago and London: University of Chicago Press, 3–13.

Koselleck, R. 1985: *Futures Past: On the Semantics of Historical Time*, trans. K. Tribe. Cambridge, MA: MIT Press.

Kraft, P. 1987: 'Computers and the Automation of Work'. In Kraut 1987: 89–105.

Kraut, R. E. (ed.) 1987: *Technology and the Transformation of White-Collar Work*. Hillside, NJ: Lawrence Erlbaum Associates.

Kuhn, S. 1989: 'The Limits to Industrialization: Computer Software Development in a Large Commercial Bank'. In Wood 1989a: 266–78.

Kumar, K. (ed.) 1971: *Revolution: The Theory and Practice of a European Idea*. London: Weidenfeld and Nicolson.

—— 1978: *Prophecy and Progress: The Sociology of Industrial and Post-Industrial Society*. Harmondsworth: Penguin Books.

—— 1988a: *The Rise of Modern Society: Aspects of the Social and Political Development of the West*. Oxford: Basil Blackwell.

—— 1988b: 'The Limits and Capacities of Industrial Capitalism'. In Kumar 1988a: 100–28.

—— 1988c: 'The Rise of Modern Society'. In Kumar 1988a: 3–35.

—— 1988d: 'Twentieth Century Revolutions in Historical Perspective'. In Kumar 1988a: 169–205.

—— 1992: 'The Revolutions of 1989: Socialism, Capitalism and Democracy'. *Theory and Society*, 21, 309–56.

—— 1993: 'The End of Utopia? The End of Socialism? The End of History?' In K. Kumar and S. Bann (eds), *Utopias and the Millennium*, London: Reaktion Books, 63–80.

—— 1995a: 'Apocalypse, Millennium and Utopia Today'. In M. Bull (ed.), *Apocalypse Theory*, Oxford: Basil Blackwell.

—— 1995b: 'The 1989 Revolutions and the Idea of Revolution'. In R. Kilminster and I. Varcoe (eds), *Culture, Modernity and Revolution*, London: Routledge.

—— 1995c: 'Home: The Nature of Private Life at the End of the Twentieth Century.' In J. Weintraub and K. Kumar (eds), *Private and Public in Thought and Practice*, Chicago: University of Chicago Press.

Laclau, E. and Mouffe, C. 1985: *Hegemony and Socialist Strategy*. London: Verso.

Lane, C. 1988: 'New Technology and Clerical Work'. In D. Gallie (ed.), *Employment in Britain*, Oxford: Basil Blackwell, 67–101.

Lash, S. 1990: *Sociology of Postmodernism*. London and New York: Routledge.

Lash, S. and Friedman, J. (eds) 1992: *Modernity and Identity*. Oxford:Basil Blackwell.

Lash, S. and Urry, J. 1987: *The End of Organized Capitalism*. Cambridge: Polity Press.

Lash, S. and Urry, J. 1994: *Economies of Signs and Space*. London: Sage Publications.

Leadbeater, C. 1989: 'Power to the Person'. In Hall and Jacques 1989a: 137–49.

Leadbeater, C. and Lloyd, J. 1987: *In Search of Work*. Harmondsworth: Penguin Books.

Le Goff, J. 1982: *Time, Work and Culture in the Middle Ages*, translated by A. Goldhammer. Chicago: University of Chicago Press.

Levin, H. 1966: 'What was Modernism?' In *Refractions: Essays in Comparative Literature*, New York: Oxford University Press, 271–95.

Lipietz, A. 1982: 'Towards Global Fordism?' *New Left Review*, 132, 33–47.

—— 1987: *Miracles and Mirages: The Crisis of Global Fordism*. London: Verso.

—— 1989: 'The Debt Problem, European Integration, and the New Phase of the World Crisis'. *New Left Review*, 178, 37–50.

—— 1992: *Towards a New Economic Order: Postfordism, Ecology and Democracy*. Cambridge: Polity Press.

Littler, C. R. 1978: 'Understanding Taylorism'. *British Journal of Sociology*, 29, 185–202.

Littler, C. R. 1982: *The Development of the Labour Process in Capitalist Societies*. London: Heinemann.

Lovering, J. 1990: 'A Perfunctory Sort of Post-Fordism: Economic Restructuring and Labour Market Segmentation in Britain in the 1980s'. *Work, Employment and Society*, May Special Issue, 9–28.

Löwith, K. 1949: *Meaning in History*. Chicago: University of Chicago Press.

Lyon, D. 1988: *The Information Society: Issues and Illusions*. Cambridge: Polity Press.

Lyon, D. 1994: *Postmodernity*. Buckingham: Open University Press.

Lyotard, J-F. 1984a: *The Postmodern Condition: A Report on Knowledge*, trans. G. Bennington and B. Massumi. Manchester: Manchester University Press.

—— 1984b: 'Answering the Question: What is Postmodernism?' Trans. R. Durand. In Lyotard 1984a: 71–82.

Machlup, F. 1962: *The Production and Distribution of Knowledge in the United States*. Princeton: Princeton University Press.

Machlup, F. 1980: *Knowledge: Its Creation, Distribution, and Economic Significance*, vol. 1: *Knowledge and Knowledge Production*. Princeton: Princeton University Press.

Mandel, E. 1978: *Late Capitalism*. London: Verso.

Manifesto For New Times 1989: Special Issue, *Marxism Today*, June.

Manuel, F. E. 1965: *Shapes of Philosophical History*. Stanford CA: Stanford University Press.

Marien, M. 1985: 'Some Questions for the Information Society'. In Forester 1985: 648–60.

Marin, L. 1984: 'Utopic Degeneration: Disneyland'. In *Utopics: The Semiological Play of Textual Spaces*, trans. by R. A. Vollrath, Atlantic Highlands, NJ: Humanities Press International, 239–57.

Martin, J. 1978: *The Wired Society*. Englewood Cliffs, NJ: Prentice-Hall.

Marquand, D. 1988: *The Unprincipled Society*. London: Fontana.

Massey, D. 1992: 'A Place Called Home?' *New Formations*, 17, 3–15.

Masuda, Y. 1981: *The Information Society as Post-Industrial Society*. Bethesda, MD: World Futures Society.

—— 1985: 'Computopia'. In Forester 1985: 620–34.

Masur, G. 1966: *Prophets of Yesterday: Studies in European Culture, 1880–1914*. New York: Harper and Row.

McFarlane, J. 1976: 'The Mind of Modernism'. In Bradbury and McFarlane 1976: 71–93.

McLuhan, M. 1967: *Understanding Media: The Extensions of Man*. London: Sphere Books.

Meegan, R. 1988: 'A Crisis of Mass Production?' In J. Allen and D. Massey (eds), *The Economy in Question*, London: Sage Publications, 136–83.

Merritt, G. 1982: *World Out of Work*. London: Collins.

Metcalfe, S. 1986: 'Information and Some Economics of the Information Revolution'. In Ferguson 1986: 37–51.

Meyrowitz, J. 1986: *No Sense of Place: The Impact of Electronic Media on Social Behavior*. Oxford: Oxford University Press.

Miles, I. 1988a: *Home Informatics: Information Technology and the Transformation of Everyday Life*. London: Pinter Publications.

Miles, I. 1988b: 'The Electronic Cottage: Myth or Near-Myth? *Futures*, 20 (4), 355–66.

Miles, I. and Gershuny, J. 1986: 'The Social Economics of Information Technology'. In Ferguson 1986: 18–36.

Mingione, E. 1991: *Fragmented Societies: A Sociology of Economic Life Beyond the Market Paradigm*. Oxford: Basil Blackwell.

Momigliano, A. 1977: *Essays in Ancient and Modern Historiography*. Oxford: Basil Blackwell.

Mommsen, T. E. 1942: 'Petrarch's Conception of the "Dark Ages"'. *Speculum*, 17, 226–42.

Mommsen, T. E. 1951: 'St.Augustine and the Christian Idea of Progress: The Background of the City of God'. *Journal of the History of Ideas*, 12, 346–74.

Morris-Suzuki, T. 1984: 'Robots and Capitalism'. *New Left Review*, 147, 109–21.

—— 1986: 'Capitalism in the Computer Age'. *New Left Review*, 160, 81–91.

—— 1988: *Beyond Computopia: Information, Automation and Democracy in Japan*. London and New York: Kegan Paul International.

Mort, F. 1989: 'The Politics of Consumption'. In Hall and Jacques 1989a: 160–72.

Mouffe, C. 1993: *The Return of the Political*. London and New York: Verso.

Mulgan, G. J. 1991: *Communication and Control: Networks and the New Economies of Communication*. Cambridge: Polity Press.

Mulgan, G. J. 1994: *Politics in an Unpolitical Age*. Cambridge: Polity Press.

Müller, K. 1992: '"Modernising" Eastern Europe: Theoretical Problems and Political Dilemmas'. *European Journal of Sociology*, 33, 109–50.

Murolo, P. 1987: 'White-Collar Women and the Rationalization of Clerical Work'. In Kraut 1987: 47–65.

Murray, F. 1987: 'Flexible Specialisation in the "Third Italy"'. *Capital and Class*, 33, 84–95.

—— 1988: 'The Decentralization of Production – the Decline of the Mass-Collective Worker?' In Pahl 1988: 258–78.

Murray, R. 1989a: 'Fordism and Post-Fordism'. In Hall and Jacques 1989a: 38–53.

—— 1989b: 'Benetton Britain: The Economic Order'. In Hall and Jacques 1989a: 54–64.

Musil, R. 1979: *The Man Without Qualities*, vol. 1 [1930], trans. E. Wilkins and E. Kaiser. London: Picador.

Naisbitt, J. 1984: *Megatrends: Ten New Directions Transforming Our Lives*. New York: Warner Books.

Naisbitt, J. and Aburdene, P. 1990: *Megatrends 2000*. London: Sidgwick and Jackson.

Nash, J. M. 1974: *Cubism, Futurism and Constructivism*. London: Thames and Hudson.

Nederveen Pieterse, J. (ed.) 1992: *Emancipations, Modern and Post-Modern*. London: Sage Publications.

Newman, C. 1985: *The Post-Modern Aura: The Act of Fiction in an Age of Inflation*. Evanstown: Northwestern University Press.

Newman, R. and Newman, J. 1985: 'Information Work: the new divorce?' *British Journal of Sociology*, 36, 497–515.

Nisbet, R. A. 1970: *Social Change and History: Aspects of the Western Theory of Development*. New York: Oxford University Press.

Noble, D. F. 1979: 'Social Choice in Machine Design: the Case of

Automatically Controlled Machine Tools'. In A. Zimbalist (ed.), *Case Studies in the Labor Process*, New York: Monthly Review Press, 39–63.

Noble, D. F. 1986: *Forces of Production: A Social History of Industrial Automation*. New York: Oxford University Press.

Nora, S. and Minc, A. 1980: *The Computerisation of Society: A Report to the President of France*. Cambridge MA: MIT Press.

Norris, C. 1991: *What's Wrong With Postmodernism? Critical Theory and the Ends of Philosophy*. Brighton: Harvester Wheatsheaf.

Nowotny, H. 1982: 'The Information Society: Its Impact on the Home, Local Community and Marginal Groups'. In Bjorn-Anderson et al. 1982: 97–113.

Offe, C. 1985: *Disorganized Capitalism: Comtemporary Transformations of Work and Politics*. Cambridge: Polity Press.

Pahl, R. E. (ed.) 1988: *On Work: Historical, Comparative and Theoretical Approaches*. Oxford: Basil Blackwell.

Pangle, T. L. 1992: *The Ennobling of Democracy: The Challenge of the Postmodern Age*. Baltimore and London: The Johns Hopkins University Press.

Patel, P. and Soete, L. 1987: 'Technological Trends and Employment in the UK Manufacturing Sectors'. In Freeman and Soete 1987: 122–68.

Perez, C. 1985: 'Microelectronics, Long Waves and World Structural Change: New Perspectives for Developing Countries'. *World Development*, 13, 441–63.

Pevsner, N. 1975: *Pioneers of Modern Design: From William Morris to Walter Gropius*. London: Penguin Books.

Piore, M. J. 1990: 'Work, Labour and Action: Work Experience in a System of Flexible Production'. In Pyke et al. 1990: 52–74.

Piore, M. J. and Sabel, C. F. 1984: *The Second Industrial Divide: Possibilities for Prosperity*. New York: Basic Books.

Plato 1977: *Timaeus and Critias*, trans. D. Lee. Harmondsworth: Penguin Books.

Plumb, J. H. 1973: *The Death of the Past*. Harmondsworth: Penguin Books.

Pollert, A. 1988a: 'The "Flexible Firm": Fixation or Fact?' *Work, Employment and Society*, 2 (3), 281–316.

—— 1988b: 'Dismantling Flexibility'. *Capital and Class*, 34, 42–75.

—— (ed.) 1991a: *Farewell to Flexibility*? Oxford: Basil Blackwell.

—— 1991b: 'The Orthodoxy of Flexibility'. In Pollert 1991a: 3–31.

Popcorn, F. 1992: *The Popcorn Report*. New York: Harper Collins.

Porat, M. 1977: *The Information Economy: Definition and Measurement*. Washington D.C.: US Department of Commerce.

Portoghesi, P. 1992: 'What is the Post-Modern?' In Jencks 1992a: 208–14.

Poster, M. 1990: *The Mode of Information: Poststructuralism and Social Context*. Cambridge: Polity Press.

Putnam, R. 1994: *Bowling Alone: Democracy at the End of the Twentieth Century*. Princeton: Princeton University Press.

Pye, L. 1990: 'Political Science and the Crisis of Authoritarianism'. *American Political Science Review*, 84, 5–19.

Pyke, F., Becattini, G. and Sengenberger, W. (eds) 1990: *Industrial Districts and Inter-Firm Cooperation in Italy*. Geneva: International Institute for Labour studies.

Rabinow, P. 1986: 'Representations are Social Facts: Modernity andPost-Modernity in Anthropology'. In J. Clifford and G. E. Marcus (eds), *Writing Culture: The Poetics and Politics of Ethnography*, Berkeley CA: University of California Press, 234–61.

Rada, J. F. 1982: 'A Third World Perspective'. In Friedrichs and Schaff 1982: 213–42.

Raulet, G. 1991: 'The New Utopia: Communication Technologies'. *Telos*, 81, 39–58.

Regalia, I., Regini, M. and Reyneri, E. 1978: 'Labour Conflicts and Industrial Relations in Italy.' In C. Crouch and A. Pizzorno (eds), *The Resurgence of Class Conflict in Western Europe Since 1968*, vol. 1, London: Macmillan, 101–58.

Rey, G. 1989: 'Small Firms: Profile and Analysis, 1981–85'. In Goodman et al. 1989: 69–110.

Rheingold, H. 1994: *The Virtual Community: Finding Connection in a Computerised World*. London: Secker and Warburg.

Ritzer, G. 1993: *The McDonaldization of Society*. Thousand Oaks, CA: Pine Forge Press.

Robertson, R. 1992: *Globalization: Social Theory and Global Culture*. London: Sage Publications.

Robins, K. 1989: 'Global Times'. *Marxism Today*, December, 20–7.

Robins, K. 1991: 'Tradition and Translation: National Culture in its Global Context'. In J. Corner and S. Harvey (eds), *Enterprise and Heritage: Crosscurrents of National Culture*, London and New York: Routledge, 21–44.

Robins, K. 1994: *Cyberspace and the World We Live In*. Newcastle-upon-Tyne: Centre for Urban and Regional Development Studies, University of Newcastle.

Robins, K. and Webster, F. 1987: 'Information as Capital: A Critique of Daniel Bell'. In J. D. Slack and F. Fejes (eds), *The Ideology of the Information Age*, Norwood, NJ: Ablex Publishing Corporation, 95–117.

Robins, K. and Webster, F. 1988: 'Athens Without Slaves . . . Or Slaves Without Athens? The Neurosis of Technology'. *Science as Culture*, 3, 7–53.

Robins, K. and Webster, F. 1989: *The Technical Fix: Education, Computers and Industry*. London: Macmillan.

Rorty, R. 1985: 'Habermas and Lyotard on Postmodernity'. In Bernstein 1985: 161–75.

—— 1992: 'Cosmopolitanism without Emancipation: a Response to Lyotard'. In Lash and Friedman 1992: 59–71.

Rose, M. A. 1991: *The Post-Modern and the Post-Industrial: A Critical Analysis*. Cambridge: Cambridge University Press.

Rosenberg, H. 1970: *The Tradition of the New*. London: Paladin.

Rosenbrock et al. [sic.] 1985: 'A New Industrial Revolution?' In Forester 1985: 635–47.

Ross, G. 1974: 'The Second Coming of Daniel Bell'. In R. Miliband and J. Saville (eds), *The Socialist Register 1974*, London: Merlin Press, 331–48.

Roszak, T. 1988: *The Cult of Information: The Folklore of Computers and the True Art of Thinking*. London: Paladin.

Rothschild, E. 1981: 'Reagan and the Real America'. *New York Review of Books*, February 5, 12–18.

Rothschild, E. 1988: 'The Real Reagan Economy'. *New York Review of Books*, June 30, 46–53.

Rustin, M. 1989: 'The Politics of Post-Fordism: or, The Trouble with "New Times"'. *New Left Review*, 175, 54–77.

Rustow, D. A. 1990: 'Democracy: A Global Revolution?' *Foreign Affairs*, 69, 75–91.

Sabel, C. F. 1984: *Work and Politics: The Division of Labor in Industry*. Cambridge: Cambridge University Press.

—— 1989: 'Flexible Specialisation and the Re-emergence of Regional Economies'. In P. Hirst and J. Zeitlin (eds), *Reversing Industrial Decline? Industrial Structure and Policy in Britain and her Competitors*. Oxford: Berg, 17–71.

Sabel, C. F. and Zeitlin, J. 1985: 'Historical Alternatives to Mass Production: Politics, Markets and Technology in Nineteenth-Century Industrialization'. *Past and Present*, 108, 133–76.

Samuel, R. 1977: 'Workshop of the World: Steam Power and Hand Technology in Mid-Victorian Britain'. *History Workshop Journal*, 3, 6–72.

Samuel, R. 1995: *Theatres of Memory, vol. I: Past and Present in Contemporary Culture*. London and New York: Verso.

Sassen, S. 1991: *The Global City: New York, London, Tokyo*. Princeton: Princeton University Press.

Sasson, D. 1986: *Contemporary Italy: Politics, Economy and Society since 1945*. London and New York: Longman.

Saunders, P. 1990: *A Nation of Home Owners*. London: Unwin Hyman.

Sayer, A. 1989: 'Postfordism in Question'. *International Journal of Urban and Regional Research*, 13 (4), 666–95.

Sayer, A. and Walker, R. 1992: *The New Social Economy: Reworking the Division of Labour*. Cambridge, MA: Blackwell Publishers.

Sayer, D. 1991: *Capitalism and Modernity: An Excursus on Marx and Weber*. London: Routledge.

Saxby, S. 1990: *The Age of Information: The Past Development and Future Significance of Computing and Communications*. Basingstoke and London: Macmillan.

Schabert, T. 1985: 'A Culture of Dissent'. In A. Moulakis (ed.), *The Promise of History*. New York: Doubleday, 1–12.

Schiller, H. I. 1985: 'Strengths and Weaknesses of the New International Information Empire'. In P. Lee (ed.), *Communication For All*, New York: Orbis, 3–23.

Schwartz, H. 1990: *Century's End: A Cultural history of the Fin-de-Siècle from the 900s to the 1990s*. New York: Doubleday.

Scully, V., Jr. 1961: *Modern Architecture*. London: Prentice-Hall International.

Selden, R. 1985: *A Reader's Guide to Contemporary Literary Theory*. Brighton: Harvester Press.

Sforzi, F. 1990: 'The Quantitative Importance of Marshallian Industrial Districts in the Italian Economy'. In Pyke et al. 1990: 75–107.

Short, R. 1976: 'Dada and Surrealism'. In Bradbury and McFarlane: 292–308.

Sieghart, P. (ed.) 1982: *Microchips with Everything: The Consequences of Information Technology*. London: ICA/Comedia.

Simon, H. A. 1980: 'What Computers Mean for Man and Society'. In Forester 1989: 419–33.

Singelmann, J. 1978: 'The Sectoral Transformation of the Labor Force in Seven Industrialized Countries, 1920–1970'. *American Journal of Sociology*, 83, 1224–34.

Sivanandam, A. 1990: 'All That Melts Into Air Is Solid: The Hokum of New Times.' *Race and Class*, 31, 1–31.

Sklair, L. 1991: *Sociology of the Global System*. Hemel Hempstead: Harvester Wheatsheaf.

Slack, J. D. 1984: 'The Information Revolution as Ideology'. *Media, Culture and Society*, 6, 247–56.

Slater, P. *The Pursuit of Loneliness: American Culture at the Breaking Point*, revised edition. Boston: Beacon Press.

Smart, B. 1992: *Modern Conditions, Postmodern Controversies*. London and New York: Routledge.

—— 1993: *Postmodernity*. London and New York: Routledge.

—— 1994: 'Sociology, Globalisation and Postmodernity'. *International Sociology*, 9 (2), 149–59.

Smith, C. 1991: 'From 1960s Automation to Flexible Specialization: a *déja vu* of Technological Panaceas'. In Pollert 1991a: 138–57.

Social Research 1989. 'The French Revolution and the Birth of Modernity'. Special Issue, 56 (1).

Social Trends 1990: London: HMSO.

Soete, L. 1987: 'The Newly Emerging Information Technology Sector'. In Freeman and Soete 1987: 189–220.

Soja, E. W. 1989: *Postmodern Geographies: The Reassertion of Space in Critical Social Theory*. London: Verso.

Stehr, N. and Böhme, G. 1986: *The Knowledge Society*. Dordrecht: D. Reidel.

Stone, L. 1991: 'History and Post-Modernism'. *Past and Present*, 131, 217–18.

Stonier, T. 1983: *The Wealth of Information: A Profile of the Post-Industrial Economy*. London: Thames Methuen.

Stretton, H. 1976: *Capitalism, Socialism and the Environment*. Cambridge: Cambridge University Press.

Sussman, L. 1989: 'The Information Revolution: Human Ideas and Electrical Impulses'. *Encounter*, 73. 60–5.

Thompson, P. 1989: *The Nature of Work*, second edition. London: Macmillan.

Tiryakian, E. A. 1991: 'Modernisation: Exhumetur in Pace (Rethinking Macrosociology in the 1990s)'. *International Sociology*, 6 (2), 165–80.
—— 1994: 'The New Worlds and Sociology'. *International Sociology*, 9 (2), 131–48.
Tocqueville, A. de, 1988: *Democracy in America* [1835–40], ed. J. P. Mayer, trans. G. Lawrence. New York: Harper and Row.
Toffler, A. 1970: *Future Shock*. New York: Random House.
Toffler, A. 1981: *The Third Wave*. New York: Bantam Books.
Toynbee, A. 1948: *Civilization on Trial*. London: Oxford University Press.
Toynbee, A. 1954: *A Study of History*, vols 7–10. London: Oxford University Press.
Triglia, C. 1989: 'Small-Firm Development and Political Subcultures in Italy'. In Goodman et al. 1989: 174–97.
—— 1990: 'Work and Politics in the Third Italy'. In Pyke et al. 1990: 160–84.
Traber, M. 1986: 'Introduction'. In M. Traber (ed.), *The Myth of the Information Revolution*, London and Beverly Hills, CA: Sage Publications, 1–6.
Trilling, L. 1967: 'On the Teaching of Modern Literature'. In *Beyond Culture: Essays on Literature and Learning*, Harmondsworth: Penguin Books, 19–41.
Turner, B. S. 1989: 'From Postindustrial Society to Postmodern Politics: the Political Sociology of Daniel Bell'. In Gibbins 1989: 199–217.
—— (ed.) 1990a: *Theories of Modernity and Postmodernity*. London: Sage.
—— 1990b: 'Periodization and Politics in the Postmodern'. In Turner 1990a: 1–13.
Tuveson, E. L. 1964: *Millennium and Utopia: A Study in the Background of the Idea of Progress*. New York: Harper Torchbooks.
Vonnegut, K. 1969: *Player Piano*. St. Albans: Panther Books.
Walby, S. 1989: 'Flexibility and the Changing Sexual Division of Labour'. In Wood 1989a: 127–40.
Walker, R. A. 1985: 'Is There a Service Economy? The Changing Capitalist Division of Labor'. *Science and Society*, 49, 42–83.
Wallerstein, I. 1974: *The Modern World System: Capitalist Agriculture and the Origins of the European World-Economy in the Sixteenth Century*. New York: Academic Press.
Webster, F. 1986: 'The Politics of the New Technology'. In R. Miliband, J. Saville, M. Liebman and J. Panitch (eds), *The Socialist Register 1985/86*, London: Merlin Press, 385–413.
Webster, F. and Robins, K. 1986: *Information Technology: A Luddite Analysis*. Norwood, NJ: Ablex Publishing Corporation.
—— 1989: 'Plan and Control: Towards a Cultural History of the Information society.' *Theory and Society*, 18, 323–51.
Weeks, J. 1989: 'Value for Many'. *Marxism Today*, December, 30–5.
Weintraub, J. and Kumar, K. (eds) 1995: *Private and Public in Thought and Practice*. Chicago: University of Chicago Press.
Weizenbaum, J. 1976: *Computer Power and Human Reason: From Judgment to Calculation*. San Francisco: W. H. Freeman.

Wellmer, A. 1991: *The Persistence of Modernity: Essays on Aesthetics, Ethics and Postmodernism*, trans. D. Midgley. Cambridge: Polity Press.

Wiener, N. 1968: *The Human Use of Human Beings: Cybernetics and Society* [1954]. London: Sphere Books.

Wilde, O. 1975: 'The Critic as Artist' [1891]. In *Oscar Wilde: Plays, Prose Writings, and Poems*, London: Dent, 3–65.

Williams, F. 1982: *The Communications Revolution*. Beverly Hills, CA: Sage Publications.

Williams, R. 1963: *Culture and Society 1780–1950*. Harmondsworth: Penguin Books.

Williams, K., Cutler, T., Williams, J. and Haslam, C. 1987: 'The End of Mass Production?' *Economy and Society*, 16 (3), 405–39.

Williams, K., Haslam, C. and Williams, J. 1992: 'Ford versus "Fordism": The Beginning of Mass Production?' *Work, Employment and Society*, 6 (4), 517–55.

Wollen, P. 1993: *Raiding the Icebox: Reflections on Twentieth-Century Culture*. London: Verso.

Wood, E. M. 1990: 'The Uses and Abuses of "Civil Society"'. In R. Miliband and L. Panitch (eds), *The Socialist Register 1990*, London: Merlin Press, 60–84.

Wood, S. (ed.) 1989a: *The Transformation of Work? Skill, Flexibility and the Labour Process*. London: Unwin Hyman.

Wood, S. 1989b: 'The Transformation of Work?' In Wood 1989a: 1–43.

Yujiro, H. (ed.) 1970: *Perspectives on Postindustrial Society*. Tokyo: University of Tokyo Press.

Zuboff, S. 1988: *In the Age of the Smart Machine: The Future of Work and Power*. Oxford: Heinemann Professional Publishing.

Zukin, S. 1991: *Landscapes of Power: From Detroit to Disney World*. Berkeley and Los Angeles: University of California Press.

Zukin, S. 1992: 'Postmodern Urban Landscapes: Mapping Culture and Power'. In Lash and Friedman 1992: 221–47.

Index